Nancy Brachey's
GUIDE TO
Piedmont
Gardening

The Charlotte Observer

by Nancy Brachey

edited by Sandy Hill

© 2001 *The Charlotte Observer*

Publisher: Joseph J. Bannon Jr.

Managing Editor: Michelle Summers

Design and production: Fabi W. Preslar, SPARK Enterprises

Cover photo: Jeff Siner, *The Charlotte Observer*

Art assistance: Jo Miller and George Breisacher, *The Charlotte Observer*

Proofreader: David Hamburg

ISBN: 1-57167-490X

Library of Congress Catalog Card Number: 00-107772

Printed in the United States

Bannon Multimedia Group

http://www.BMGpub.com

Nancy Brachey's
GUIDE TO
Piedmont
Gardening

The Charlotte Observer

by Nancy Brachey

edited by Sandy Hill

Contents

Contents

Introduction

WELCOME TO PIEDMONT GARDENING

Between the mountains and the coastal plain of the Southeastern

United States lies a region that was made for gardening, gardening all year.

It is the Piedmont, a place of mild, evergreen winters; pink, yellow

and purple springs; hot, green summers; and long, mellow autumns.

Within this region awaits a huge range of opportunities to specialize

– perhaps yours will be roses or rhododendrons – or generalize with

a huge array of bulbs, perennials, shrubs and trees.

And despite the sometimes difficult clay soil, the erratic summer

rainfall and the hot blaze of the Southern sun, the potential for

success is huge. There is no reason not to have something in

bloom every day of the year and a fine, varied crop of

vegetables over three seasons.

For nearly 25 years, I've been privileged to write about the gardens and gardeners of this outstanding region for *The Charlotte Observer*. Every day, I learn something new about plants and practices and techniques. And perhaps the most important thing I've learned is that, as a region, ours stands second to none for year-round beauty and the terrific variety of plants that prosper here.

Others may come home from southern England and declare, "Aren't the gardens fabulous." Yes, indeed, they are. And so are ours; they're just not as old, as mature. But they are coming along, and it has been wonderful to watch and write about the increasing diversity of plants chosen by gardeners for their homes, their business property, even the medians and planters of city streets and interstate highways.

Gardeners want something for every season, from the surprising snowdrops of January through the amazing range of flowering shrubs and perennials of spring and summer to the last berries and blooms of late autumn. That's why we've organized this book – drawn largely from articles, illustrations and photographs published in *The Charlotte Observer* – on a month-by-month basis.

I've learned from the Piedmont's gardeners. They've asked questions, expressed hopes, recounted their successes and failures and shared their knowledge. These nonprofessional – I can hardly call them "amateur" – gardeners have taught me a lot and kept me up to the minute on what people really want and need in their home landscapes.

The pros – university professors, county agents, garden directors, industry representatives – have also been generous in sharing their accumulated knowledge of everything from insects and diseases to better ways to handle such mundane yet important tasks as watering and pruning.

A third set of people, my editors over the years at *The Charlotte Observer,* have taught me much about writing and particularly the value of explanatory journalism that is clear and easy-to-read and that moves swiftly to the heart of the story. Sandy Hill, my editor for many years, has been a trusted and valued guide on this road, patient with my idiosyncrasies, skillful in developing a story idea and editing it to a high standard. Besides the duties of daily journalism at *The Charlotte Observer,* she has taken on the editing of this book, and it would not be here without her effort and editing talent.

I hope this book helps to make you a better gardener and your garden more beautiful every day of the year.

Why not? This is the southeastern Piedmont.

Nancy Brachey

January

WINTER WOES

Holiday bills and tax forms slide into mail boxes

with unnerving speed. The sky looks gloomy; the air feels cold.

Even the poinsettia, so perky just two weeks ago,

is looking like it feels the January blues.

Yet, gardening, which has been off the schedules

of many people since Thanksgiving, suddenly stirs our

interest again. Oh, we know ice and snow might

still befall us. But the days are getting longer and

spring is getting closer.

PLAN A BETTER GARDEN IN THE COMING YEAR

It's the start of a new year. This year, make resolutions you can keep, ones that will make you a better gardener. Consider these.

- **I resolve to get rid of the plants I hate** (or that cover windows, create a mess, are never healthy). For many homeowners, taking ax to plant is difficult. After all, it's a living thing. Someone, somewhere may like it. Who knows, it may even recover. Forget all that; if you have a plant that is driving you nuts for any reason, deal with it. Cut it back, if possible, to clear windows. Cut it out, if that's what's needed. (I am thinking of the continuing debacle of leaf fungus on red-tips.) And feel no guilt about this. Then add a new plant – one that's beautiful, healthy and the right size – to take the place of the departed one.

- **I shall buy no plant without a spot to put it**. This can be difficult, even for a gardener with a well-defined landscape plan. My driveway regularly gets covered in potted shrubs and perennials, even trees, because the temptation to shop and buy is too hard to resist. I see a new camellia and must have it; multiply that weekend after weekend and the driveway disappears under pots while I move stuff to make room for the new plants. This year, stick to your plan.

- **I'll make the garden bloom every day of the year.** This takes planning, but is not a hard task here. Even under a January snow, snowdrops can glisten and the early winter crocuses pop out merrily. Gardeners have come a long way from the day when color erupted for a month or so in spring, then disappeared under a blanket of green the rest of the year. A combination of annuals, bulbs, perennials, shrubs and ornamental trees will do the job. Start by jotting down the months of the year, and noting which plants you have already that give special interest (including autumn berries and winter bark and silhouettes) in each month. When you shop and plant this year, make filling the gaps a priority.

- **I'll choose plants for beauty and ease of care**, not because they are cheap or free. Nothing challenges the gardener's resolve to stick to a plan like the prospect of plants on sale at irresistible prices or – even more difficult – handed to you free because

other people are thinning out their plant zoo. If you're developing a garden or have cleared space already, it's a great thing. If the plants are trouble-free, it's another great thing. Just be sure what you're getting is worth the time it will take to plant and the space it will require. Remember that, while it hurts, it is not fatal to take things out.

- **I shall keep records**. Do you look at plants you bought and wonder "What is that thing?" Write it down because the tag that came with the plant can easily fade or disappear. Better still, draw a little map of your property and put wiggly circles in spots where you plant shrubs and trees. Write each plant's name, botanical or common, on the circle. With perennials and bulbs, make a list of names with the approximate dates of bloom and their general location (front row of square flower bed in front yard, for example).

- **I'll reject distractions and get stuff done.** List the five most important, permanent things you want to accomplish in the garden (which could include patio or deck building, irrigation installation, construction of raised beds) and focus on them.

Winter

5 EASY HOUSEPLANTS ANYONE CAN GROW

New houseplants will herald the transition into a new year with their fresh foliage and blooms. But not difficult houseplants. You want ones that are tame and easy to manage. Many will fill the bill, but some do better than others. Here are five favorites whose easy care and lovely appearance make them worth a prime spot in the house. I think they're also better looking and more interesting than other tropical houseplants grown for the ease of culture, such as heart-leaf philodendron, sansevieria and schefflera. Yet these plants and others like them need some care. Given time and space on the windowsill, even small ones will grow into dramatic, valuable plants.

• **Golden pothos.** Green leaves splashed with yellow create a lively look, and the plant is just as easy to grow as the less dynamic philodendron. Give it curtain-filtered sunlight and typical household temperature and humidity. By nature a vine, golden pothos also makes a lovely trailer for mantelpiece, desk or a hanging basket. To slow down its yen to sprawl and thus get a bushier plant, pinch the tips occasionally. Shiny leaves are natural, so give it a shower or damp wipe occasionally to remove dust.

• **Grape ivy.** Another vine that you can encourage to grow into a compact shape, grape ivy has dark green foliage that resembles – naturally – grape leaves. Very attractive and adaptable to the low light of house life, grape ivy goes slightly dormant in the winter, so water it less then and withhold fertilizer. The deep green foliage has a more formal appearance than the kicky green and yellow of pothos, making it well suited for living or dining room.

• **Prayer plant.** This plant has interest in two dimensions. Not only does it fold its leaves at dark in a prayer-like fashion, but the leaves also have intricate patterns of green, brown and red. Direct sun, especially in the summer, may harm leaves. Over the winter, allow the soil to dry out before watering, and hold the fertilizer until growth begins in spring. Occasionally, you may see a bloom, but the interesting foliage is the reason to own this plant.

• **Peace lily.** When not in bloom, the peace lily is just another dark green tropical plant. But when the flowers rise – as they do reliably – the peace lily has new status. The white flowers look a lot like calla lilies and are definitely worth bragging about, even though they are very easy to get. However, the peace lily prospers in high humidity, so mist it regularly and keep it away from the heat of floor registers and bright, direct sunshine.

• **Chinese evergreen.** Slow-growing and adaptable, aglaonema is a plant for the floor rather than the table since it can reach 3 feet. While high humidity is beneficial to growth, normal household light, temperature and humidity also suit it. Leaves of the most interesting plants are marked with silver, gray or a lighter shade of green. Do not overwater this plant in any season. Keep it barely moist through the year and fertilize occasionally.

You might also try a dramatic dracaena, a no-fuss aspidistra or even a blooming chrysanthemum with flowers so pink, purple or yellow, you will see spring.

Peace lily

TRY THESE HOUSEPLANTS FOR DIM, DARK LOCATIONS

Of all the perplexing problems that face the house-plant gardener, the most vexing are dim locations. You want a pretty plant to brighten those dark corners of north-facing rooms, dim halls, windowless stairways and bathrooms. But these are environmental challenges that only a few plants – mostly natives of the jungle floor – are up to meeting. Most of the good houseplants, especially the flowering ones, demand some rays of sunlight to keep them fat and happy and blooming.

So what do you grow in the dim and the dark? Some of the choices are dull. Others are the wrong shape or size for the spot. For example, the upright sansevieria, better known as the snake plant or mother-in-law's tongue, is a good selection for dim spots only if you can stand the sight of it. Its wavy verticality possesses some architectural style, but the color is such a deep and deadly green that it tends to fade into oblivion when surrounded by other plants. Still, it will grow just fine in very low light and hang around for years, even if you forget to water it for ages.

Philodendron is another possibility, and it's traditional for bathrooms, although the typical heart-shaped philodendron leaf is not much of a stimulant in the early-morning light. Other types of philodendron with variegated leaves make better choices. And like sansevieria, this is a plant that will survive the forgetful gardener.

Like the so-called snake plant, another good plant for the dim and the dark bears an unfortunate descriptive name. This is the cast-iron plant or aspidistra, which tells you something about its rugged constitution. It was a fixture of dark, poorly heated front halls and parlors in Victorian England town houses. But aspidistra is a better-looking and more interesting plant than either sansevieria or philodendron. It makes a large but low plant suitable for a big pot or basket in your darkest corner. The leaves are broad and deep forest green. It needs practically no care, although dusting the leaves occasionally is a good idea.

The Chinese evergreen, aglaonema, is perhaps the best of the lot. It would be worth having even if it were temperamental, which it isn't. It's mild and mellow unless you overwater it, which I did once, and then it dies without a whimper. Some are gray with dark green edges, others have waxy, dark green foliage.

Other possibilities include the bird's nest fern, parlor palm, spathiphyllum and dieffenbachia. However, none of these are plants you can neglect.

Philodendron

Winter

CURE THE WINTER DOLDRUMS WITH A TROPICAL TONIC

Who doesn't look at winter's leafless trees and bare flowerbeds and let the mind wander to the tropics, that exotic wonderland of warmth, bloom and lively color? If we can't go there, we can at least bring it to our desktops and coffee tables. There we can have an array of winter-blooming plants. Brimming with rich shades of hot pink, brick red and sunshine yellow, they bring the feel and look of the tropics.

Take kalanchoe. Native to the island of Madagascar, off the southeastern coast of Africa, it shows up routinely in Piedmont garden centers, flower shops and groceries each winter, bearing colorful red, yellow, pink or orange blooms. Or consider calceolaria, better known as the pocketbook plant for its distinctive pouch-shaped red, yellow or orange blooms. It originates in Central and South America, but grabs our attention here in January.

An array of these wonderful plants can find a home on your desktops. Some will be with you a long time.

Others, because of their finicky requirements of temperature, light and water, may be transient residents. One of my first tropical houseplants, decades ago, was an aphelandra, which is often called the zebra plant because of the distinctive white stripes on its deep green, almost black, foliage. It dropped dead overnight when I overwatered it in the winter. 'Twas a painful lesson.

But some of you may rise to the challenge and take pride in knowing exactly when the begonia or zebra plant needs watering, or just the right temperature to keep the kalanchoe or streptocarpus flourishing.

These are not expensive plants. If they give you pleasure for a month or so, that's a fair price. Perhaps the only thing these plants, with all their tropical flair, lack is a sense of the sea and the salty air we associate with the tropics. For that, you'll have to travel farther than the nearest garden center.

Zebra plant

Some will be with you a long time. Others, because of their finicky requirements of temperature, light and water, may be transient residents.

Winter

5 GOOD CHOICES FOR
YOUR DESKTOP IN WINTER

- **Zebra plant.** Indoor gardeners enjoy the zebra plant for its striped foliage and long-lasting blooms. Keep it warm. Most of the year it requires evenly moist soil, but not in winter. Let the soil dry out between waterings and use lukewarm water, not cold tap water. Keep it in the light, but away from direct sun all year.

- **Pocketbook plant.** Keep it cool and give it good light, but not direct sun. Like paperwhites and cyclamen, the pocketbook plant does better in chilly rooms. If you can keep the plant at least part of the time in temperatures in the high 50s or low 60s, it will last longer. And keep this one watered. Don't let the soil dry out.

- **Streptocarpus.** This elegant plant has trumpet-shaped pink, white, purple, red or blue flowers above oval leaves. It requires bright light or diffused sunlight indoors, even moisture and moderate air temperatures no higher than 70 degrees in the daytime and a bit cooler at night.

- **Kalanchoe.** Notable for its bright winter flowers and thick, scalloped leaves, the kalanchoe prospers in bright light. It requires warm air much of the year, but cooler temperatures in the 60s or high 50s during the winter. In the summer, let the soil dry out between waterings, and keep the plant rather dry in the winter. It's very difficult to get it to bloom again. So enjoy, and then pitch it.

- **Rieger begonia.** Spectacular in bloom, these hybrid begonias of cheerful colors belong to a family of plants hailing from tropical Asia, Africa and the Americas. The plants need bright light, but not direct sun, and temperatures in the high 60s and low 70s. They are extremely particular about water, and will die from overwatering. Let the soil dry out at least 1 inch before you water; water even less in winter. When watering, direct the water away from the center of the plant.

Kalanchoe

Notable for its bright winter flowers and thick, scalloped leaves, the kalanchoe prospers in bright light.

Winter

MASS APPEAL: GROUP SEVERAL HOUSEPLANTS IN THE SAME POT

Here's the scene: a Dallas fern in one corner, a Chinese evergreen in another; English ivy trails along by itself, and blooming kalanchoe is going solo on the coffee table. Why not put them together? In short, make a bouquet.

Houseplants aren't usually thought of as the stuff of bouquets. Granted, creeping fig isn't a long-stemmed red rose. But various houseplants can be called on to fulfill the functions of tall and stately cut flowers as well as fluffy fillers and winding trailers. Grouped in a large pot, they can create the effect of a bouquet, particularly if you pop in a small flowering plant in bloom.

Here are things to keep in mind when you select and arrange your houseplant bouquet.

- **Choose a variety of colors, shapes and textures.** An arrangement is more interesting and beautiful when sparked by varying shades of green from palest, or nearly white, to deepest, or almost black. Variety of shape also raises interest. Tuck in a heart-leaf philodendron, an arrowhead-shaped syngonium, a lance-shaped dracaena or a ruffle-leaved ficus. Add texture with the corduroy-like leaves of peperomia, the fluffiness of a fern, the white ribbed leaves of fittonia.

- **Add seasonal colors.** Small pots of flowers such as cyclamens, begonias, chrysanthemums or primroses will jazz up a houseplant bouquet temporarily. Do not expect this to be a permanent part of the arrangement; pull it out as the flowers fade and tuck in a new one that is seasonally appropriate.

- **Combine upright, spreading and trailing plants.** Try to follow the same rule that applies when making a bouquet in a container: The height of the arrangement should be 1 1/2 times the height of the pot. But since some vertical plants such as Chinese evergreen, dieffenbachia, aralia or croton grow rapidly, you could start shorter than the rule. Spreading plants such as the prayer plant, holly fern, fittonia,

piggyback plant, spider plant or peperomia will fill out the sides of the bouquet, as will fluffy ferns such as the Dallas fern. Trailers come in many forms, including creeping fig, English ivy, pothos and philodendron.

- **Choose plants that require similar amounts of light and water.** Various cacti combine nicely, but a desert cactus and a moisture-loving maidenhair fern do not make a happy couple. Nor is an aloe, which demands bright light, content in the dim light a Dallas fern enjoys. Check the tag with the plant or ask the staff at the garden center.

- **Arrange your plants so that the pot looks full, like a bouquet or centerpiece**. As plants grow, trim back the leaves or pull a plant out gently and replace it with one the right size. The outgrown plant can grow solo or be the start of another houseplant bouquet.

- **While many plants are well suited for growing indoors**, some do best when they get bright light from a window nearby. Others, which originated in such dark places as the forest floor of the tropics, will grow in dim or fluorescent-lighted interiors that get little natural sunlight.

Plants suited for medium to dim interiors:

Aloe, asparagus sprengeri, cast-iron plant, Chinese evergreen, devil's ivy, dieffenbachia, fittonia, ivy, peperomia, pothos, prayer plant; also, most tropical ferns, including brake, maidenhair, shield and Dallas.

Plants that need bright, indirect light indoors:

Croton, euphorbia, fatshedera, grape ivy, pittosporum, podocarpus, sansevieria, schefflera, umbrella plant, velvet plant.

Winter

What's blooming in January

- ❀ Early camellias
- ❀ Pansies
- ❀ Wintersweet
- ❀ Winter honeysuckle
- ❀ Winter jasmine
- ❀ Mahonia
- ❀ Winter aconites
- ❀ Snowdrops
- ❀ Japanese apricot

HEDGES DO MORE THAN LOOK PRETTY

I like to think of hedges and screens in two ways: friendly and unfriendly. A friendly one has soft leaves, bendable branches and no sharp points. If it could talk, the message would be an inviting "Step right through." An unfriendly one is as much of a deterrent as a fence. It has prickles, briars and thorns. Instead of a sweet invitation, it growls, "Keep out. This means you." Clearly, these plants do more than define property lines, screen views and create privacy.

Barberry makes a classic unfriendly hedge. Its leaves, yellow flowers and red berries combine to create a pretty, even an inviting, picture. But along the stems, nestled among the leaves, are those distinctly uninviting 1-inch thorns and their even more distinct sharp points.

Canada hemlock is a classic friendly hedge. Its evergreen needles are soft, light green; the drooping branches bend easily to let you pass.

Between those extremes are other evergreen plants that, with proper shearing, turn into ideal hedges. Some grow tall enough to make a screen. I think that a hedge or screen should be evergreen. A plant that keeps its leaves fulfills a hedge's mission of creating privacy. A deciduous hedge of quince, forsythia or spirea, beautiful though it is while in bloom and full leaf, offers no screening value all winter, when you may need it most.

Good-neighbor hedges also include the boxwood, Carolina cherry laurel, Japanese holly, nandina, ligus-trum, glossy abelia, cleyera and various kinds of azaleas and rhododendrons. Some, such as the Carolina cherry laurel, hardy anise and the cypress, eventually make screens because they grow 10 feet and taller. They grow reasonably fast, but never as fast as the fleet-of-growth red-tips, which are out of favor due to a fungus that is very hard to control.

Glossy abelia, boxwood and the Japanese holly are better suited for hedges you want to keep low enough to see the street or your neighbor's property. With reasonable pruning, you can keep them short enough to hop, and that's a friendly message in itself.

If you want a loose barrier hedge, consider pyracantha, English, American and Burford Chinese hollies, mahonia and, of course, the barberry.

If your goal is a screen but not a barrier, consider nandina, which grows 4 to 6 feet tall and can be pruned and shaped to grow dense enough to form a hedge, but not so thick that a neighbor or child can't slide through it. Nandina isn't used enough in this fashion. It shows up at the corners of houses, in front of fences and under trees. But it is wonderful as a loose hedge, has no pest problems and benefits from pruning.

A hedge may require a significant investment, but don't be afraid to select smaller plants in 1-gallon containers if you must meet a budget. With patience and a few years, you'll have a dense hedge.

An unfriendly hedge is as much of a deterrent as a fence.

Winter

WINTER HONEYSUCKLE OFFERS FABULOUS FRAGRANCE

The scent of winter honeysuckle drifts across the landscape these days, luring the gardener to the distant corner where it grows anonymously all year. No show-stopper in appearance, not even a nuisance like its notorious vine cousin, winter honeysuckle stands out in January for its breathtaking aroma, sweet and powerful.

And while it is related to the obnoxious Japanese honeysuckle, the rampant vine that wraps itself around young trees, threatening to strangle them, winter honeysuckle causes no problems.

Except for a similar scent, you might not think they are related. Indeed, winter honeysuckle, a native of China brought to Europe in about 1845, is a defined shrub that grows about 6 feet tall; the arching branches spread about the same distance, creating a graceful, round shape.

The foliage is oval and light green. The look is average, so you probably wouldn't plant it in a primo spot.

But it is the bell-shaped white flowers – just 1/2 inch long – and their fabulous fragrance that raise the value of lonicera fragrantissima from merely average to absolutely worthy. Just put it a bit out of the way, in a sunny or shady spot.

I always hesitate to proclaim a plant foolproof, but it's probably safe to say so about this beauty. A dozen or so years ago, a friend had several in her back garden and offered me two. We dug them up with no particular care; I carted them home, planted them and waited to see what happened.

They lived. They grew. They bloomed. I have never seen a pest on them, never sprayed to ward off fungus, never even fertilized them. Once, during a stretch of very wet winter weather, they sat in a pool of cold rainwater until it finally drained. They are fine.

I expect they will outlive me.

Winter honeysuckle stands out in January for its breathtaking aroma, sweet and powerful.

WAKE UP THE WINTER LANDSCAPE WITH SPARKS OF COLOR

Painters, calendar photographers and poets almost invariably paint winter in shades of gray, beige, silver and brown. But winter's palette isn't beige and gray. It can be pink and red camellias, a cloud of pink from the Japanese apricot, scented yellow wintersweet, red holly and orange pyracantha berries, blue flowers on rosemary, white and cinnamon brown tree trunks, and even purple leaves on mahonia. Granted, this isn't April's riot of color, but it's a far cry from the chilly gray and beige scenes that artists link to January.

If you plan well, there won't be a single color missing from your winter landscape. It's not just the blooms that make winter colorful. It's berries, buds and bark, too. The buds of Chinese paperbush, Edgeworthia papyrifera, are fat, white globes that look like they've been dusted with snow. The gently peeling bark of paperbark maple, Acer griseum, is brown, but not any old dull brown. This is cinnamon brown that exudes vitality and verve. The berries of autumn, notably hollies and pyracantha, linger well into winter, creating the brightest spots of all.

The fifth element that will bring color to your winter landscape is, of course, foliage. In the dimmer light of winter, the various shades of green stand out far more clearly. The bluish-greens of conifers look bluer; the chartreuse greens seem brighter, the deepest greens of spruces, blacker. Variegated foliage becomes even more important, its white or yellow markings brightening the scene.

It's not just the blooms that make winter colorful. It's berries, buds and bark, too.

EXPAND YOUR LANDSCAPE'S PALETTE OF COLOR IN FIVE DISTINCT WAYS:

- **Buds.** Daphne and pieris bear buds that are colorful and distinct in the winter. So are the fuzzy buds of pussy willow.

- **Blooms.** Intensely fragrant wintersweet, the spidery blooms of witch hazel, the huge range of camellias, winter jasmine, Japanese apricot (Prunus mume) and early bulbs such as snowdrops, chionodoxa and bunch crocuses lead the list of winter flowers for the Piedmont.

- **Bark**. Peeling or unusually colored bark stands out in winter. The birches, crape myrtles and paperbark maples are notable for this.

- **Berries.** Burford Chinese holly, nandina and pyracantha are not your only choices. Look for winterberry, a deciduous holly, and the little ground cover wintergreen, which bears waxy red berries.

- **Variegated foliage.** White, yellow and other markings on leaves add fresh color and variety to the winter landscape. Variegation is the distinctive characteristic of shrubs such as aucuba and variegated euonymus and thorny elaeagnus. Even monkey grass comes in a beautiful form, with white margins along the leaves.

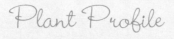

Plant Profile

FICUS ELASTICA

NAME:
Ficus (FY-cuss) elastica may have been the first houseplant you owned. It's been in foyers, dens and offices for generations, but varieties such as Tricolor with pink and cream markings and Variegata with a yellow border and markings give the durable old favorite a new look.

HOME GROUND:
Tropical Asia, where it got the name India-rubber tree.

VITAL STATS:
Broad leaves with a bronze hue emerge from red sheaths at the top of the plant, which can hit your 8-foot ceiling and aim for the attic. Outdoors, in a tropically warm climate, the rubber tree can top out at 100 feet, but don't expect that indoors. The leaves are thick and rubbery, 8 to 12 inches long and 4 to 6 inches wide. They turn a glossy green as they mature.

FAVORITE SPOT:
Set the plant (remember, large ones may be hard to move) in a place with bright, indirect light or sunlight filtered by a curtain.

GROWING TIPS:
Let the soil dry out between waterings; to induce better branching, cut off the tip of a young plant.

FOR THE FUTURE:
When this plant outgrows its place in your house, prune back the plant at the tips, root a new plant or offer the old one to a school, institution or business with high ceilings.

PUT YOUR FIREPLACE ASHES TO GOOD USE

Those wood ashes your fireplace is producing are a source of potash, or potassium, an important element in plant growth.

Indeed, we get the word potash from the original method of getting potassium by leaching the wood ashes and then evaporating the solution in pots.

You can also use wood ashes to make soil less acidic, which is why you should not use them on plants that thrive in acidic soil, such as azaleas, camellias, blueberries, hollies and rhododendrons.

But you can spread ashes in rose beds, flower gardens and vegetable gardens. Wood ashes have been credited with pushing hesitant peonies into bloom. You also can add them in very thin layers to compost bins, helping to reduce the acidity of compost.

Soil in the Piedmont is acidic to some degree. A regular pH test of your flower and vegetable garden soil will tell you how acidic yours is. If it is highly acidic, wood ashes will help make it less acidic and thus more hospitable to most plants. If you regularly put wood ashes in the soil, check the pH every year to make sure you are not overdoing it.

The nutrients in wood ashes are soluble, so don't store the ashes where they will be rained on. Keep your surplus in a dry place, such as your garage or shed.

Wood ashes have been credited with pushing hesitant peonies into bloom.

Winter

WINTER JASMINE:
MORE THAN A FORSYTHIA LOOK-ALIKE

"The forsythia is blooming. The forsythia is blooming." I hear that cry every winter, when a certain yellow flower erupts into bloom. People think it's spring.

Well, it isn't forsythia, and it isn't spring.

The charming shrub that so surprises people is winter jasmine. But don't let the name fool you. This isn't a fragrant Confederate jasmine that got confused and bloomed three months ahead of schedule. Nor is it one of those tropical jasmines that wouldn't have lasted past the first hard freeze in the Piedmont.

This is winter jasmine, botanically named Jasminum nudiflorum. And a bold and brave shrub it is.

That it erupts in a blaze of golden flowers in the dead of winter is remarkable enough, but camellias do that too. Winter jasmine's flowers, however, are more tolerant of freezing weather than are the camellias'. And winter jasmine is one tough plant, adaptable to many environmental situations and easy to grow. All that combines to make a good, all-around shrub.

As more Piedmont gardeners discover the pleasures of winter gardening and look beyond camellias for flowers in January and February, winter jasmine could shed its anonymity and take a richly deserved place in the landscape.

A native of China, ancestral home of so many of America's favorite shrubs, winter jasmine brought a boatload of good features when it arrived in the mid-19th century. Adaptable to a wide range of well-drained soils, this jasmine even performs well in poor soils. It withstands drought to a remarkable degree and should be considered when selecting a group of plants for a space you don't plan to water in dry weather.

It transplants easily and grows about 4 feet tall, spreading 3 to 5 feet. Though it blooms best in full sun, the plant tolerates light shade. I would not plant winter jasmine in full shade since its best feature is the array of yellow flowers in winter; shade will make them less plentiful.

The deep-green shiny foliage is attractive – but not remarkable. The green stems, however, are distinctive and another way to tell winter jasmine from forsythia, which has beige stems. The winter jasmine's stems also are more trailing and horizontal than the forsythia's more vertical and arching style. Winter jasmine's

trailing manner -- I call it a graceful sprawl -- makes it particularly useful to cover banks or cascade over low walls.

One unfortunate thing happens to winter jasmine, though. Instead of letting it grow into a graceful, natural shape, many people prune it into a tight, rigid form. This is against the plant's loose and flowing nature and reduces the amount of flowers. But winter jasmine is not alone in being the victim of this harsh treatment. It happens to forsythia with the same bad results.

Promise me you won't prune your jasmine or your forsythia into round balls, unnatural squares or awful ovals this year. If your winter jasmine – or your forsythia – is in too small a space, move it. Some pruning may be done every few years by thinning out the older stems to encourage new ones to rise from the base of the plant. Cut back the oldest stems to the ground after flowering.

When you combine winter jasmine with other plants with winter interest such as winter daphne, early daffodils, early crocuses and witch hazel, you will have a special place outdoors in the winter.

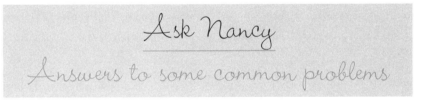

Winter

It's time to...

- Get the last of those spring flower bulbs planted quickly.

- Check out what cool-weather weeds sprouted while you weren't looking in December.

- Prepare for snow. Keep handy a broom to dust powdery snow off boxwoods and other evergreens before it freezes.

- Watch houseplants for hints that foliage is getting paler. It needs more fertilizer.

- Keep long-blooming winter houseplants such as kalanchoe and ornamental peppers in a cool, brightly lit spot.

- Stay calm and unpanicked as the first green tips of daffodil bulbs emerge. They're on schedule.

- Check your trees for broken or cracked limbs after every winter windstorm.

- Either pitch bulbs of paper-white narcissus that have finished blooming or plant them outdoors in a warmish spot near the house, where they should bloom again – eventually.

- Decide where you'll put a new flower or vegetable bed this year so you can work on it as the weather permits. Start by outlining the area with your garden hose.

- Give your houseplants some sparkle by dusting their leaves or by giving them a gentle shower in the tub.

- Cut back your pampas grass to make way for fresh growth from the crown.

- Check the blades on your pruning shears for sharpness. The season to prune boxwoods and hollies is just ahead.

Ask Nancy
Answers to some common problems

WHEN DO I PRUNE SASANQUAS?

The fall-flowering sasanqua is a camellia loved by many gardeners for its white, light pink or rose blooms. Commonly grown in rows as a hedge or as a shrub solo, the sasanqua also makes a dramatic small tree with a broad canopy.

Whatever form your plants take, January and February are good times to prune this fine plant. Simply cut back wayward branches and even up the sides and tops of hedges. But don't try to give it the look of a sheared hedge. The sasanqua looks best loose and informal rather than tightly sheared.

If you want to maintain a loose hedge, trim the plant evenly from top to bottom so that the sides will remain roughly even. Some gentle pruning of the tips of the branches will accomplish this and encourage side growth that will make the plant denser.

Plants can also be trained into tree form. Allow the central leader to form the trunk of the tree, from which side branches will form the horizontal canopy. Clear the trunk of the lower lateral stems. Do this gradually over several winters, especially if the plant is mature. This treatment is best done while the plant is young and you can train it to tree form from the beginning.

Camellia japonica, the winter and spring flowering types, should not be pruned until after bloom. They look best when allowed to grow into their natural, vertical form and can become quite large, formal plants useful as screens in a shady garden.

Ask Nancy
Answers to some common problems

WHAT'S A GOOD SCREEN FOR A SHADY AREA?

First, get the dimensions of the area you want to screen. This will guide your selection and help you figure out how many plants you should buy. Some shrubs grow shorter and wider, others, taller and narrower.

Plan to use evergreens for most of your screen; you could add smaller, deciduous plants such as spirea in a second row on your side of the screen.

Some evergreens that grow at least 5 feet tall (some much higher) but don't spread too wide or can be kept reasonably narrow with pruning are aucuba, Camellia sasanqua, Japanese boxwood, cleyera, nandina and English laurel. An informal mix of these plants could be very attractive and more interesting to look at than a single row of plants that are all the same kind. If you opt for a single species, consider adding a second row of plants such as azaleas and pieris that bear seasonal flowers. Look at these plants and others at a garden center to see what suits your eye and budget. Ask about their mature size and rate of growth and determine how many plants you need. Set the screening plants far enough from any area where people may walk, like a sidewalk, so that they don't eventually grow into that space and have to be cut back.

WHY DID MY PYRACANTHA BERRIES DIE?

If berries die quickly, it could be lack of water. If you have a new transplant, it needs regular water even in the cool of autumn and winter because it is adjusting from the tight confines of a pot to the roominess of soil. Water a transplanted pyracantha at least once a week, if it doesn't rain. In early spring, fertilize the plant very lightly because it is still adjusting. One of the slow-release fertilizers would be good. A year from this spring, fertilize at the normal rate.

Another reason berries die quickly is a fungus called scab, which usually appears first as dark spots on the leaves; the berries later turn black. Many varieties of pyracantha sold today are resistant to this problem. But should yours have it, spray the plant with the fungicide called Daconil when it blooms in the spring, then about three more times at intervals of 10 days or so. The problem is most common in cool, wet springs.

WHY DID MY BOXWOOD LEAVES TURN ORANGE?

Orange, orangish-red and reddish-brown often show up on boxwood leaves during the winter. Cold and wind will cause this discoloration, particularly if a sudden chill follows weeks of warmth in the autumn and early winter. Dry weather may contribute to the problem.

The so-called "winter burn" is usually mild. The leaves feel soft when you touch them. Leaves in the interior of the plant remain soft and green. They look normal. Don't panic; new growth in the spring should restore the plant's appearance nicely.

But if the off-color leaves are drier, almost crispy, those leaves and perhaps the stems (but not the plant) will probably die and have to go. To be sure, wait to prune off the dying foliage until late winter or early spring, just before the plant puts out new growth.

All of this is why people should plant boxwoods in an area protected from winter winds and keep the plants mulched. With mulch, the soil won't dry out or freeze and you should get less cold damage.

A second orange problem is the despicable boxwood leaf miner, which causes yellow-orange or orange blisters on the leaves. The leaves look smaller than healthy ones, may be paler green or almost white and will drop off. Look for the blisters or little tunnels where the larvae feed on the leaf, making it paler.

After spending the winter tunneling around the leaves, the larvae turn into little flies in April (after the plant's new growth comes out) and then lay eggs on the boxwood foliage. That sets up a new generation and more trouble unless you intervene by spraying the plant with Orthene when the flies emerge.

Whether your boxwoods are affected by one or both of these problems, be grateful. You haven't got boxwood root rot, the worst thing there is for boxwoods and usually fatal. To the plant, that is.

February

FICKLE FEBRUARY

You just never know about February. One moment,

the weather is perfectly beautiful, a blue-sky day with dry air

and shirtsleeve temperatures. The next day, it's miserable, all cold,

gloomy and icy, with a chill in the air that makes spring seem as

remote as Mars. Amid the unpredictable temperatures, pansies

bloom, the early daffodils pop up and evergreens glisten

on frosty mornings. The garden is waking up after its

short slumber. You can see it in fattening buds on the

trees and snowdrops rising through the leaf litter.

They tell you winter is leaving town.

PRUNE SHRUBS THE RIGHT WAY – AT THE RIGHT TIME

For best results, prune at the right season. **Now** – the middle of winter – is the time to trim some shrubs, but not others. Their turn comes later. Various evergreen shrubs such as hollies, boxwood, ligustrum, red-tips and cleyera benefit from pruning in mid-to-late winter because it puts the plant in the right shape and size before new growth emerges in early spring. However, evergreens that bloom in the winter or spring, notably camellias, azaleas, rhododendrons, daphne and pieris, must not be pruned until after their flowers fade. Separating the do-now shrubs from the do-later ones is a vexing issue for many gardeners. So are pruning styles. But it's easier if you break them into three basic techniques.

Pruning

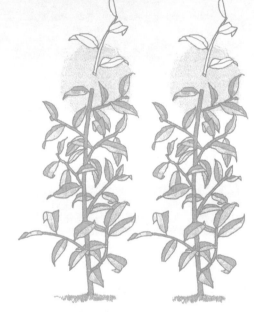

This is the simplest, gentlest method. You look over a plant, observe a wayward stem and trim it back. This is such minimum work that people scarcely think of it as pruning. But cutting back the tip of a branch encourages side branching that will produce a fuller, bushier plant.

Tool: Pruning shears, sometimes called bypass clippers, the kind that have the sharp cutting edge on one handle to pass by the anvil on the other handle. They make sharp, clean cuts.

Technique: Look over the plant carefully to see what branches need tip pruning to keep the plant in its natural shape. Just above a branch, leaf or bud, cut each stem at an angle.

Thinning

This method removes entire, older stems or branches at the point where they branch off from the main trunk or rise from the ground and preserves the natural, floral fountain shape of such plants as forsythia or bridal-wreath spirea. Applied to boxwood plants, it produces a much better looking, fuller plant than does the method called shearing.

This type of pruning is applied often to rejuvenate an older plant, let sunlight into its interior and provide space for new growth to rise from the base of the plant.

Tool: Long-handled loppers or lopping shears have more cutting power than hand pruners because the long handles increase the leverage. Their length also makes it easier to reach the base of large shrubs.

Technique: Reach into the shrub and make a clean, neat cut where it emerges, either at ground level or from a larger branch.

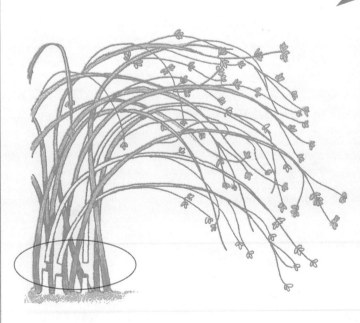

Winter

Shearing

This even-surface pruning requires specific tools to cut the plant evenly across the top or sides. It is often done to create a formal hedge with even sides and tops and sharp edges. It may be used on such hedge plants as Japanese hollies and ligustrum, which have dense foliage. The result will produce an even amount of new growth over the sheared area. Don't trim more than one-third of the plant.

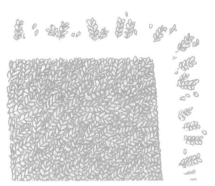

Tool: Use hedge clippers or shears that cut off stretches of foliage at once. For big jobs, powered hedge trimmers are easier.

Technique: Cut back the hedge evenly to the desired height, allowing space for this year's new growth. Then cut back the sides to the desired width, also allowing space for the new growth. Sloping the sides gently to make the top of the hedge slightly narrower than the bottom will allow sunlight to reach the entire plant and should keep it in healthier condition.

FOR BERRIES ON HOLLY, PRUNE WITH CARE

Here's a common problem: You've got hollies. You've got windows. You have to prune to keep the hollies from covering your windows. The result: no pretty berries in winter, unless you know what to do.

In a perfect world, you could prune your hollies to the desired height this month, and they would put out new growth this spring, produce flowers, then bear fruits. This is not a perfect world. Your hollies grew wood last year that is destined to bloom this spring. Those blooms – clusters of fuzzy yellow flowers – will turn into red berries. When you step into this orderly process with pruning shears, things get decidedly out of whack as far as this berry-bearing business. If you cut off last year's growth, it doesn't matter whether you do it before or after flowering – the potential berries are gone.

So what do you do? You could cut the plants well back this spring to give them space for several years of growth before you pruned again. That is likely to produce another berryless winter. A better choice would be to hold the pruning shears and wait for blooming season. Then you can see exactly where the berries will show up. Then do some strategic pruning, leaving as many stems as possible for berries.

GET A HEAD START ON LAWN CARE

The fescue grass stayed green all winter. Surprised you, didn't it?

Thank last fall's fertilizer. Now the lawn needs another dose to carry it through spring. This is not the heavy lifting you did last September when you gave the grass a total overhaul with aeration, seeding, lime and fertilizer. But it is a detail that will give the grass the power it needs to grow vigorously through spring, before sinking into semidormancy during the heat of summer.

Use a slow-release fertilizer formulated for lawns about mid-month, and apply it at the rate directed on the package. If you use a pre-emergent crabgrass product, apply it between late February and mid-March, but not where you're putting grass seeds. It keeps both the crabgrass seeds and the grass seeds from germinating.

Even if your lawn looks good, it may have a few spots that need a boost from seeds. Sow these seeds by early March, digging up the bare spots a couple of inches, sprinkling the seeds and taking care not to step on the young grass once it pops up.

Also popping up are lawn weeds such as chickweed, which flourish in the cool weather of a mild winter. To avoid even more plants, get them out before they set seeds. Chickweed plants are so easy to pull out, I sometimes wonder if they sit on the ground instead of growing in it.

HOW TO TRAIN YOUR PYRACANTHA INTO A WORK OF ART

Pyracantha plants rank among the most popular choices for using a technique – really an art form – to create an espalier. An espalier (es-PAL-yer) is a plant pruned and trained to grow flat, usually against a wall or trellis. The French get credit for the idea and it gained wide acceptance in parts of Europe where people wanted to grow fruit trees in small spaces, such as walled gardens.

While the technique isn't as widespread in the United States, it is still an elegant way to adapt plants to tight spaces. A pyracantha espaliered against a tall brick wall can be quite gorgeous, provided you select a pyracantha variety whose red, orange or orange-red berries live handsomely with your shade of brick.

While many styles of espalier exist, probably the simplest one is a single or double cordon. A single stem rises from the ground to form the trunk of the espalier; for a single cordon, one horizontal line is trained to create a T shape. In a double cordon, a second horizontal line runs parallel with the top line, but about halfway between it and the ground.

Start with a young plant. Pick a plant with a strong, straight central stem to make the vertical trunk. You will have to find a way to brace this against the wall with nails suitable for use in brick or by attaching it to lengths of heavy wire stretched horizontally along the wall and attached, for example, to window frames very securely.

Then look along this stem for two pairs of branch-es – one for the top horizontal line and a second for the one midway up the trunk. One side of each pair will be trained to the right side, and one to the left. These are called "arms." Trim each to the same length and cut away extra lateral growth on the main trunk. Side growth on the arms will produce the flowering and fruiting wood that makes pyracantha plants so pretty and interesting. This year's growth produces next year's beauty.

If the required side shoots aren't present at planting time, tip-prune the top of the main stem to induce some fresh lateral growth next spring from which you can select and begin training the arms early next summer. Young growth is quite flexible, so you may be able to wind it around the horizontal wires. But once pyracantha wood matures, it will be difficult to wind, and you should plan on attaching it with strips of rubber or strong string.

As the arms develop, keep an eye on the new growth to maintain the desired horizontal and vertical lines. Once established, pyracantha is a vigorous grower. Side growth that comes off the arms may have to be cut back slightly in late spring or early summer to keep the shape right. Tip-pruning those shoots slightly should make the growth along the arms bushier during the balance of the growing season.

Wear long sleeves and good gloves to protect yourself from the sharp spines of this plant.

OUT WITH THE BAD SHRUBS, IN WITH THE GOOD

February is a time to think seriously about improving the landscape by removing some shrubs and trees and adding others. This is a prime time for such tasks because the garden's structure – its bare-bones form – is most clearly apparent before the leaves emerge in spring. Come April and May, when the trees are in leaf, the flowers in bloom and the grass at its annual best, it is easy to forget you needed to transplant a small tree to a sunnier space or should have thrown away certain spindly shrubs.

First, take a hard look at your trees and shrubs and decide what you want to get rid of. Some may be over-grown and unattractive, perhaps even rising above the window sills, as my camellias have magically done. Others may be the shade plants that are now in the sun or vice versa; either way, they are not thriving. Some may have taken a serious hit in winter snow or ice storms. Or perhaps you are simply tired of looking at the spirea or vitex planted by someone else and want a more interesting flowering shrub.

Once you've decided to do this, do it. And don't feel guilty for a second. After all, aren't the chief purposes of ornamental trees and shrubs to beautify the home landscape, to provide shade from the hot sum-

Winter

mer sun and give us creative pleasure? Without doing that work, they have no reason for being.

The placement of trees and shrubs, in addition to enhancing the appearance of the house, should help create good views. The dining room window should face serenity, not the heavy-duty action of a basketball goal. A kitchen and den window might well look toward a children's play area. A bedroom window might offer a peek at a colorful flower garden as the perfect way to start the day right.

The view from the outside is just as important. Plants provide efficient and attractive screens that conceal unsightly views. Correctly situated, they make decks and patios more private and enjoyable, especially when a cardinal pauses on a branch within a few feet of your deck chair. What beats a moment like that?

This is a good planting time for trees and deciduous shrubs. Evergreen shrubs may be planted now, which will give them a good chance to settle in before summer arrives. Many of you who aren't familiar with the names of azalea varieties will, however, wait for blooming time so you can choose the plants by color.

Removing old, unattractive plants that you plan to throw away is simple if they aren't too large. You can just cut them off where the main stems or trunk reaches the ground, although some sprouting is likely to occur if the roots are left. If you do not plan to replant in the space, it isn't necessary to dig up the roots. But if you are replanting the area around the foundation of your house, and the old shrubbery was large, it will help to get large sections of the roots out to make space for new ones. This is hard work, and it may be worth hiring a person with a root grinder to get them out.

HOW TO HANDLE ICE AND COLD

When it turns cold suddenly – and blooms are out – what's a gardener to do? Actually, experts say there's not much you can do to ward off cold damage, particularly when there's a stiff wind that lowers the chill factor. Frostbitten blooms are part of the risk Southerners take to enjoy year-round beauty.

When you have advance warning, covering flowers such as daffodils or small, young flowering shrubs with a box could offer some protection. Or you could use a sheet, but the weight could break the stems of daffodils.

Once cold strikes, how much damage a plant will suffer depends on several variables, including wind, location and duration of the hard freeze. Foliage and flower buds on azaleas are almost certainly unaffected by a late-winter freeze. Young plants of hardy vegetable crops such as lettuce and spinach are probably OK, too. But keep an eye on camellia or daffodil blossoms after a freeze. In a day or so, browning edges caused by decaying cells will signal cold damage. If you suspect that's happened, don't wait for them to fade away – pick and enjoy the blooms indoors. The blooms of exotics, or non-natives like the saucer magnolia, are in peril by unexpected cold. On the other hand, native plants such as dogwoods and redbuds remain safe. They've learned not to bloom early.

Ice storms are a bigger problem because the damage they cause tends to be heavier, long-lasting and sometimes expensive to deal with. Here's what you can do.

- Check your trees carefully for branches broken by ice storms recently. Some might be lodged precariously in other limbs. Check the shrubs, too.

- Trim broken limbs cleanly, just outside the branch collar.

- Trim torn fibers sticking out of tree wounds. Try not to damage the bark further.

- Be extremely careful with chain saws. Leave off-the-ground work to the pros.

- Get a certified arborist to evaluate trees that suffered serious damage to their canopy.

- Do not work on trees in contact with or close by power lines. Be selective about hiring someone to work on your trees. Check out references. Ask for proof of insurance. Get several prices.

- Look over your trees and shrubs after the cleanup. Gentle pruning could restore their shape. Give them time to look good again.

Winter

What's blooming in February

❀ Early daffodils	❀ Camellias	❀ Iris reticulata
❀ Quince	❀ Crocuses	❀ Japanese apricot
❀ Pansies	❀ Grape hyacinths	❀ Lenten rose
❀ Star magnolia	❀ Scilla	

FOR A HINT OF SPRING INDOORS, FORCE BLOOMS

Forcing stems of flowering shrubs such as forsythia, pussy willow and quince into early bloom is a favorite trick of many gardeners in winter. You can force these shrubs because their natural bloom time is early spring, which isn't that far away. By now, the plants have had enough of a winter chill to permit them to break dormancy and bloom.

Look for branches of forsythia, quince or pussy willow that have a lot of buds. Select neither the thickest nor the thinnest stems to cut, but those of medium size.

Good blooms do not open magically. Once you select your stems, cut them from the plant slightly longer than you need, say 2 feet or more. Before you cut, consider the overall appearance of the plant. Don't destroy its natural shape. You should be able to remove branches for forcing from a well-developed plant and leave no hint that something has been taken off.

Use your sharpest knife or pruning shears to make a clean, slanted cut that will encourage maximum uptake of water. Then make a sharp vertical cut to split the bottom of the stem for a couple of inches.

Next, bundle all the branches together and submerge them in a large bucket filled with warm water. Keep them there for several hours while the branches absorb water. The water will also soften the bark surrounding the buds, their natural protector from harsh winter weather. It also washes off any stray debris or dirt. Submerging the branches tends to encourage faster opening of buds. Once the buds and branches are clean and soft, they are ready for the next step.

Place the branches loosely in a tall, narrow container such as a vase with several inches of water in the bottom to cover the stem ends. Put the container in a cool room of about 65 to 70 degrees. A 60-degree room is best, but hard to find. The water will evaporate, so keep an eye on the level to make sure it doesn't disappear. Changing it every few days will keep it fresh and avoid the development of bacteria that could clog the stems.

A fresh trim of the stem ends every few days will keep the branches in good condition because it permits them to take up water.

A warm location in a sunny window will encourage faster bloom. A cooler spot will hold back blooms. It takes branches about three to four weeks to unfold in rooms kept about 68 degrees.

Once the buds begin to open, use them as a table-top display or arrange with other flowers.

Forsythia

Winter

BRAVE BLOOMS LIGHT UP THE LANDSCAPE

Japanese apricot trees blooming in February. Lenten roses poking their way through cold, damp leaf litter. A cap of ice on a bright camellia. These brave plants never fail to surprise, even amaze us with their eye-catching blooms in the midst of winter.

   Mostly what's blooming are imports from mild-winter areas of Asia and the eastern Mediterranean that settled down happily in the Piedmont. Many of the trees and shrubs we've embraced, such as quince, Japanese apricot and camellias, tend to flower early in their homelands. That tendency toward early bloom persists when brought to the Piedmont, even though it's still winter here. Here's some of what is in bloom now.

❀ **Camellias** start out as evergreen shrubs. Some eventually become small- to medium-size evergreen trees, possibly 20 feet tall. Camellias are natives of such Asian countries as India, Indonesia, China and Japan. They are loved for their beautiful blossoms, which are mostly white, pink, rose or red and come in many forms: single, double, rose, peony and anemone. Camellia japonica is the popular species for winter blooms in the Piedmont. The large number of named varieties makes this a plant for collectors. Camellias need acid soil that is rich and well drained. Give the plant partial shade for best blooming. Camellia flowers are quite susceptible to frost, which often nips the January bloomers. For insurance, look for the late-winter bloomers.

❀ **Flowering quince**, from China and Japan, is a medium to large shrub, usually about 3 to 8 feet tall, with a brushy, thorny texture that fastidious gardeners may not love. But who wouldn't love the early blooms of the Chaenomeles in delicious shades of peach, salmon, coral and orange, as well as red or white? It's not too picky, but give this plant full sun for the best flowers.

❀ **Japanese apricot** may not stop traffic, but it will slow down the rush to work when you glimpse the pretty white, pink or rose blooms filling leafless branches in mid-winter. People often think this tree is the better-known Yoshino cherry that has simply erupted into bloom four to six weeks early. It has a

botanical name of its own, Prunus mume, and is a medium-size ornamental tree that grows about 20 feet high and wide. Despite its common name, it originated in China and Korea and does not bear apricots.

❀ **Lenten rose** is a perennial, Helleborus orientalis, that people enjoy discovering. The blooms rise at midwinter as greenish white, cream or purplish flowers. This native of northeastern Greece and northern Turkey rises about 18 inches and repopulates itself readily by self-sown seeds. It prefers a moist, shaded environment. A relative from Central Europe, the Christmas rose, Helleborus niger, blooms even earlier.

Camellia japonica

Camellia japonica is the popular species for winter blooms in the Piedmont.

PERENNIAL PLEASURES FOR SUNNY SPOTS

Perennial gardens offer a variety of form, the spectrum of color and something for every season. February is a good time to plan the garden and compile the plant list. Perennials are the hardy flowers whose roots and sometimes leaves last from year to year, sending up new foliage and flowers.

The sunny garden plan described here uses perennials that are easy to grow, reliable in the hot Southern summer, long-lived and widely available in retail garden centers and catalogs. And the colors say summer: golden yellows, sky blues, cheerful pinks. Such easy-care perennials will form the basis of a flower garden you can supplement with spring-flowering bulbs and annuals.

You can, of course, make substitutes. For example, the winsome Sunny Border Blue veronica could grow in place of the Victoria salvia; a rich array of daylilies in appealing shades of yellow, pink or peach could stand in for the reliable Stella d'Oro.

This garden is small for a perennial border, about 3 1/2 by 12 feet, a size big enough for a variety of flowers that will stretch the blooming season, yet small enough for easy tending.

Meet the Plants

❀ **Shasta daisy.** A classic perennial garden favorite, the Shasta daisy adds a fresh, cool effect to the garden. White daisies with yellow centers appear in spring and summer, depending on the variety. If you need a short, compact Shasta, consider Snow Lady, which grows and spreads only about 1 foot tall, or Snowcap, which grows 12 to 18 inches tall. The hot Shasta, though, is Becky, which starts to bloom at midsummer on sturdy, straight stems,

about 3 to 4 feet tall. Alaska is an old favorite. For the longest season of Shasta bloom, plant several kinds and cut off the spent blooms.

❀ **Salvia.** If you like blue flowers, salvias offer a lot of choice, ranging from pale sky blue to boldest indigo such as the ever-popular Victoria. It's a golden age for salvias, with lots of good kinds on the market that are hardy in this area. Even the marginally hardy are worth planting for their dramatic bloom. Some are short, such as May night, an early

Tips For Success

• Start with good soil. Remove the grass and dig the bed deeply, at least 10 inches, getting out any rocks, hard clods or other debris along the way. Enrich the soil with liberal amounts of good topsoil and compost. Fertilizer will not make up for hard, compacted soil.

• Avoid straight lines. The back edge of a rectangular border that is next to a wall, fence or shrubbery may be straight, but the side and front lines should weave gently. This is often accomplished simply by letting the edging plants spill forward slightly. As you place the plants in the interior of the bed, stagger them slightly, or arrange them as points on a triangle. This adds to the informal and natural look.

• Balance the seasons. Don't let your garden's beauty depend on a single month. Even if it peaks in early summer, as many perennial gardens do, plant things that will bloom earlier, such as candytuft, and later, such as rudbeckia. That keeps your garden going and interest alive. A larger garden could have more plants for spring, summer and autumn.

• Add mulch for neatness. In its youth, and each spring before the growing gets going, the garden will show large stretches of earth. Choose a uniform mulch to make the garden look neater and help suppress weeds.

Winter

bloomer (mid-April) that grows 18 inches tall with dark indigo blooms. Others are quite tall, such as Salvia guaranitica, which can hit 6 feet and has deep blue flowers; in between is the long-blooming Indigo Spires, 4 to 5 feet. The variety, beauty and usefulness of the genus may turn you into a salvia hobbyist.

Daylily. Daylilies come in thousands of colors from white to nearly black on plants usually 2 to 3 feet tall, though dwarf and taller varieties exist. Daylilies bloom in late spring to about midsummer, depending on the variety. The golden Stella d'Oro is a classic daylily. Each bloom lasts just a day, but each plant produces many buds on arching stems called scapes. Choose daylilies to suit your budget and taste in color. To stretch the blooming season, plant as many varieties as you have space to grow.

Candytuft. A great edger for flower beds, candytuft bears white flowers in clusters for a mat effect from early to mid-spring. The dark green foliage is evergreen. Plants grow about 1 foot high and 2 feet wide. Some shorter choices: Snowflake, about 8 inches tall; Kingwood Compact, 6 inches;

Little Gem, 4 to 6 inches. Botanically, the name is Iberis sempervirens.

Black-eyed susan. One of the most popular garden flowers, the black-eyed susan named Goldsturm grows 2 to 2 1/2 feet tall and 1 1/2 feet wide. It blooms from midsummer to early autumn. Other good choices in its genus, rudbeckia, are two late bloomers: Herbstonne (Autumn Sun), which has bright green centers and can hit 6 feet; and Goldquelle, which has fluffy double flowers.

Anemone. Though their colors aren't typically fallish, the hybrid anemones will brighten the late-summer to early-autumn garden with a dash of spring pink, rose and white. Most rise about 3 to 4 feet tall, and about that wide. They're easy to grow and reliable. Popular varieties include Honorine Jobert, notable for its clear white petals and yellow stamens; September Charm, with rosy-pink blooms; Whirlwind, which has solid white, semi-double blooms; Queen Charlotte, which bears pink blooms; and Prince Henry, notable for its white, semi-double flowers.

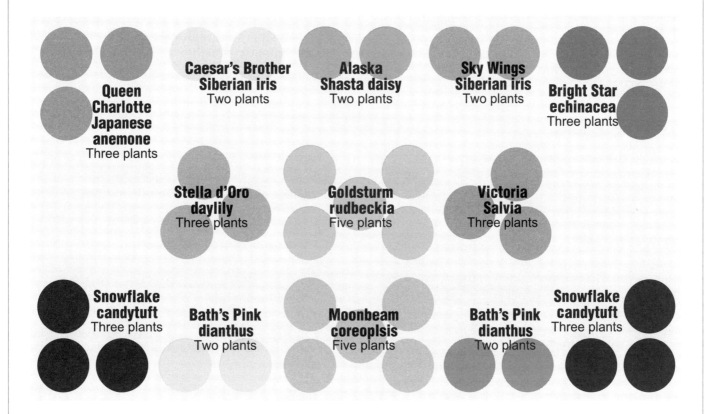

Winter

Siberian iris. An all-time favorite for late spring, Siberian irises come in a wide range of colors. Their tall, swordlike leaves rise in early spring and look good through the summer. The flowers, mostly in stunning shades of blue and violet as well as white, are smaller than the better-known tall bearded irises. The Siberians are much easier to grow, every bit as lovely and less likely to be attacked by borers and rot. They usually grow 2 to 4 feet tall. Notable varieties include Caesar's Brother and Sky Wings. No perennial is worth space in the garden more than Siberian iris.

Echinacea purpurea. The purple coneflower, ranks among the easiest of the summer daisies and prospers in warm, sunny areas. Flowers of this long-lived perennial have a domed center and purplish-pink petals. Bright Star, Magnus, The King and White Star are among the notable varieties of this genus. Plants grow about 3 to 5 feet, and are usually pest-free.

Bath's Pink dianthus. One of the top choices for Piedmont gardens among the dianthus clan, Bath's Pink possesses spicy scent, blue-green foliage and candy pink flowers. Plus it tends to stay with us despite hot summers that wear out other kinds of dianthus. It is reasonably tolerant of drought and humidity. but like all members of the dianthus genus, requires well-drained soil that is neutral to slightly alkaline.

PERENNIAL PLEASURES FOR THE SHADE

Shade-loving perennials are a different challenge from the sunny perennial border. With a wide range of choices, the challenge for a sunny location is not what to put in, but what to leave out. The colors are bright and bold; their drama peaks in early to midsummer. The color palette for shade is more subdued, and, I'd argue, more elegant. It contains sky blues and pale lilacs, calmer pinks, softer yellows and lots of snow white. Combining these gentle colors with dappled sunlight and the lush green foliage of hostas produces a scene both cooling and restful.

The long season of bloom starts with winter's Lenten roses and hits its stride with spring's forget-me-nots, lily of the valley and wild sweet william. The season continues through summer with the wonderful foliage of hostas and the charm of foxglove and spiderwort. Finally, it moves into late summer with hardy begonias and bright red cardinal flowers.

Meet the Plants

Forget-me-not. A low, spreading plant with tiny light-to-dark blue flowers with yellow centers. Pink and white varieties are also sold. Sow seeds or buy young plants. Botanically, the genus is myosotis.

Lily of the valley. Intensely scented but fleeting of bloom, stems of white, bell-shaped blooms rise in mid-April. Grow from little roots called pips, which spread rapidly in moist soil. The less well-known name is Convallaria majalis.

Wild sweet william. Long-lasting, fragrant sky-blue flowers rise in loose clusters about 1 foot tall. Grow from young plants and divide the clumps occasionally. Often listed by the botanical name Phlox divaricata.

Lenten rose. An evergreen perennial, this isn't a rose, but it produces long-lasting blooms in late winter that resemble purplish or greenish white roses. Start your collection of this outstanding perennial with young plants. Helleborus orientalis will expand from self-sown seeds.

Bleeding heart. The common bleeding heart (Dicentra spectabilis) bears heart-shaped, pink flowers arrayed on stems that rise among the frilly, bluish-green foliage. Let other plants such as hostas or hardy ferns sprawl into its spot when the plant fades in summer.

Spiderwort. The tradescantias grow about 1 to 2 feet tall producing narrow leaves and a long sum-

Winter

mer season of pretty white, purple, blue or pink flowers with three oval petals.

❀ **Foxglove.** The old cottage garden favorite, Digitalis produces white, yellow, rose or purple tubular flowers arrayed along tall spikes, usually 2 to 3 feet tall. Start with plants, but save and sow seeds for the next generation.

❀ **Cardinal flower**. A native wildflower of swampy areas, cardinal flower is named for its bright red flowers that rise as spikes in late summer. Botanically named Lobelia cardinalis. Grow from plants or seeds.

❀ **Turtlehead**. Aptly named, the flowers of the turtle-heads (Chelone) resemble their common name, but the blooms are a pretty clear pink, white or rosy purple. Stems rise 2 to 3 feet tall. Start with plants.

❀ **Hardy begonia**. The hardy form of the better-known annual begonia, it produces stems about 2 feet tall bearing clusters of small pink flowers. Start with plants that grow from tuberous roots. Its botanical name is Begonia evansiana.

Foxglove

❀ **Hosta.** More to choose from than you ever imagined, hostas come in a range of greens from light chartreuse to deepest forest and bluish-green. Leaves come small, just an inch or so wide, to mammoth, a foot or more. Hostas can make a shady garden.

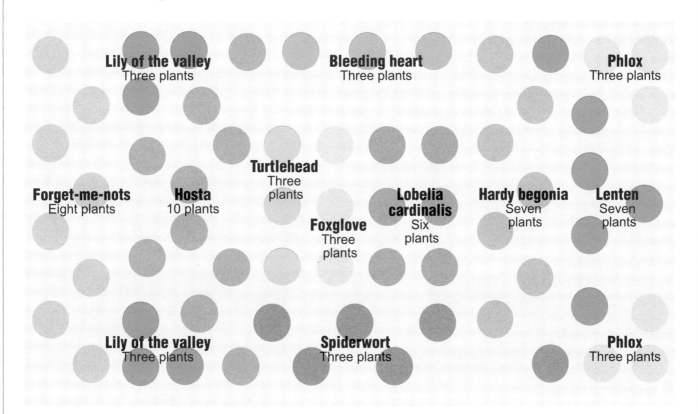

HOW TO HELP SHADY PERENNIALS PROSPER

- **Give them shade**, of course. Most often, gardeners place shade-loving perennials along the edges of shrub borders. Yet a flowerbed planned just for them is one way to give them a stage of their own. The shade could be cast by nearby trees, a building or a tall hedge. It should not be dense shade, the kind left for ivy, pachysandra and other ground covers. It needs dappled sunlight, the kind let through the tree-tops in broken streams, or half shade, where the harsh rays of summer afternoon sun are blocked by walls or hedges.

- **Give them moist soil**. A few brave plants prosper in dry shade, but most of the perennials shown here require moist – but not soggy – soil. Keep the hose – and, naturally, your favorite slug deterrent – within reach, especially during summer's dry days. Good soil that is rich and woodsy helps, too.

- **Give them care**. Some of these plants are so easy and so reliable, you simply plant and enjoy. Those are lily of the valley, hostas, spiderwort, wild sweet william and hostas. But foxglove will need renewal every couple of years. In the right spot, it will renew itself with self-sown seeds that produce new plants each year. Bleeding heart tends to disappear above ground in early summer, leaving a blank spot in the bed that you can fill with – why, of course! – annual impatiens or begonias.

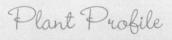

Plant Profile

DRACAENA

NAME:
Dracaena *(drah-SEE-nuh)* is a good choice for offices and homes with low light. Varieties of dracaena come in many styles and colors: narrow-leaved, broad-leaved, striped, solid and even spotted.

VITAL STATS:
Short forms will stop at 4 feet; bigger varieties can hit 15 to 20 feet, so plan to raise the ceiling for them.

FAVORITE SPOT:
Let the sun shine on dracaena through a light curtain. Or give it a bright spot without direct sunlight.

GROWING TIPS:
Keep the soil moist. Fertilize established (not freshly repotted) dracaenas every six months.

IF YOUR PLANT LOOKS DRAGGED OUT:
Take a deep breath and cut the plant well back, removing old stems and leaves. This should stimulate fresh growth.

MAIN PROBLEM:
Some people think this plant is dull looking. Tell them to take a gander at Sansevieria zebrina (commonly known as snake plant). Now *that's* dull.

Winter

It's time to...

- Mow or trim the monkey grass — well before it starts growing.

- Decide whether — and where — you're going to plant a garden of early vegetables, including peas, leaf lettuce, spinach, beets and carrots, later this month.

- Give your pansies a boost with liquid fertilizer.

- Make sure your perennials weren't dislodged or heaved from the soil after the last snow or ice storm. If they were, dig up the roots and reset the plant, dividing if necessary.

- Plant peonies, making sure the top of the crown, where the buds emerge, is at or just above the soil line.

- Save take-out food boxes with clear plastic lids to use as little greenhouses for starting seeds.

- Dig up wild onions and wild garlic as the plants emerge.

- Shop for lilies, gladiolus, dahlias, tuberous begonias and other summer-flowering bulbs to plant this spring.

- Look for cabbage, broccoli and other hardy vegetable plants to set out in the garden.

- Check out your tools. Are they sharp, rust free and ready to go?

Ask Nancy
Answers to some common problems

HOW DO I TAKE CARE OF MY ANGEL WING BEGONIA?

Isn't it wonderful how descriptions of plants turn into their names? Angel wing begonias are named for the descriptive, asymmetrical shape of their broad leaves. They have fibrous root systems, like the bedding begonias we plant outdoors in summer. But similarities end at the soil line. The main stems of angel wings are straightish and resemble bamboo stems. They can grow quite tall for a houseplant, maybe even 5 feet, but most people keep them pruned to a tabletop size.

The plants bear hanging clusters of pink, red, orange or white flowers, usually from spring until autumn. They need light, but not a heavy dose of undiluted sunshine and protection from wind to avoid stem breakage. Bring them indoors when night temperatures drop below 50 degrees in the fall until the weather is dependably warm outdoors in the spring.

Starting in the spring, fertilize the plants lightly and regularly. Use a liquid fertilizer for houseplants diluted to half strength when you water the plants.

And about those heavy stems: You can indeed cut them back in early spring. To tame a tall plant back to size or make a leggy one bushier, cut the stems back to just above the third or fourth joint on the stem. Try to keep the plant's shape balanced when you do this.

Ask Nancy
Answers to some common problems

WHY ARE MY RHODODENDRON LEAVES CURLING UP?

Rhododendron leaves curl up like long green cigars during stretches of cold weather. Somehow, they "know" when it's cold and, like humans, when it's time to curl up and protect themselves. By curling up, the rhodos reduce the amount of leaf tissue exposed to the winter sun and wind.

So why is this important in cold weather? When the ground is frozen, the plants cannot get water from the ground to replace the moisture that sun or wind draws out of the leaves. That's why evergreens need mulch to help keep the soil from freezing and shade from the sun, especially morning sun in the winter, which hits before things have a chance to thaw out. By curling its leaves, the plant loses less water and should show less browning from desiccation, which usually appears at the tips and edges of leaves.

When you see rhododendron leaves curled on a cold morning, watch for them to unroll as the temperature rises during the day. They're a bit like humans after all.

WHY DO MY RHODODENDRONS LOOK LIKE THEY'RE DYING?

Your sad rhododendrons, with their drooping, browning leaves, are probably suffering rhododendron dieback, which is caused by a fungus. Buds brown, leaves droop and roll (as they do in the cold; but with this, they don't unroll when the temperature rises), stems shrivel. All of this creates a browning effect, and the affected stems and leaves soon die.

It's time to amputate. Prune away the sick stems and leaves. Make your cuts a couple of inches below the sickly areas; if the tissue in the center of the remaining stem looks brownish or off-color, amputate a bit more.

You can move the disease around with infected shears, so dip your pruners in a solution of water with 10 percent bleach after every cut. I have seen rhododendrons affected by this problem recover their health and even their shape following such amputations.

MY DAFFODILS ARE COMING UP AND IT'S STILL WINTER. ARE THEY IN DANGER?

Only if you step on them. This happens every winter about this time of year. Leaves and buds are very cold hardy. Don't panic.

HOW DO I TAKE CARE OF LENTEN ROSES FOR A NEAT LOOK?

You can safely remove the old, tatty, non-neat leaves, now that the new ones are pushing out. This will remove any leaf disease and keep the leaves from whipping around in windy weather (meaning March) and possibly marring the emerging flowers.

Once you get those leaves out, add a topping around the plant of something delectable, such as mushroom compost. Nothing's too good for Lenten roses. An annual taste of lime in the fall will help keep the soil pH closer to neutral, which hellebores prefer.

As for the rest of you out there, if you're not growing Lenten roses, start looking for them. They grow beautifully in part-to-full shade, in soil that's neither dry nor wet. New plants will pop up from seeds dropped by older Lenten roses, but I would never characterize this as an invasive plant. By the way, a Lenten rose isn't a rose; it actually belongs to the buttercup family.

March

WAKE UP; IT'S SPRING

March arrives, sometimes stormy, sometimes mild, but always

welcome. As the sun gets stronger, the days longer and the sky bluer, the

urge to dig stirs in even the most laid-back gardener. So we turn our

back on cold, even though the calendar still proclaims winter for a few

more weeks. We descend on the garden to dig and till, sow early crops

and set out plants, all the while remembering the finicky nature of

March. One day calm and gorgeous; the next, windy and wretched. But

that's March. And always we have the daffodils to remind us that

spring is really here.

Spring

THE 3-SEASON GARDEN

This plan for a 12-by-15-foot plot should keep you in vegetables from spring's spinach right on through summer's tomatoes to autumn's last leaf of lettuce.

Select the location

Before you buy a seed or purchase a plant, think about location. A typical bed should go in a sunny, well-drained spot on the high side of a slope and well away from the shade and roots of large trees and hedge-rows. It should also be beyond the shadow of buildings. Don't think the garden must be in the backyard. I have seen lovely flower and vegetable beds or combinations in front and side yards. A vegetable garden requires full sun. That means six hours a day minimum; eight hours is better.

While a garden needs consistent water for good plant growth, it must not be soggy. Don't plant your garden where water collects in wet weather. It will kill the plants. A well-drained area is essential, preferably one higher instead of lower. Even if they don't stay damp, areas on the low side of a slope tend to warm up later in the spring and cool off earlier in the autumn. That shortens the growing season.

Make sure the garden is within hose-reach of a faucet.

Plotting your plot

1. **Decide on size.** Small is good. If there's one main error new gardeners make, it's digging up the whole backyard and planting everything they see on the seed racks. A small plot, perhaps 10 by 15 feet, is a good start. Shape the garden as a rectangle so you can tend it from both sides without stepping onto your well-prepared soil. Outline the area with stakes at each corner and stretch string.

2. **Check the soil.** First, make sure the soil is not too wet. Sink your spade in; then pick up a handful of soil and squeeze it tightly. When you open your hand, the soil should fall apart into clumps, not remain in a tight ball. If it does, put your garden fork and spade away and let the soil dry out for another day or so.

3. **Dig and till.** If the turf is thick and well developed, dig it up in sections. Remove any stray rocks, large roots or other debris. It is difficult to use a tiller on soil that has not already been dug, so use a garden fork or spade to loosen the soil first. Then dig up the soil at least 8 inches – 10 to 12 inches is even better. Next, cover the ground with as much good topsoil, well-rotted compost or peat as you can get your hands on, and work it in. The easiest way is to put a layer of several inches on top of the bed, work it in well and deeply, then add another layer and work that in. If you have good topsoil, work that in as well.

Lime improves the soil by making it less acidic and allowing fertilizer to work better. If you're making a vegetable garden out of lawn that has been limed in recent years, plan to dig in about 7 pounds of lime per 180 square feet, which is the size of the plan for "The Three-Season Garden." Add 4 to 8 pounds more lime on soil that hasn't received lime recently.

4. **Set out plants and sow seeds**. Look for plants that aren't spindly or skinny. They should have a healthy green color, be well branched and shapely. Mark the rows with short stakes and string. When you take them out of the pot, if the roots seem wound around and around, tease them out a bit with the tip of your finger or trowel. They will settle into the soil faster.

Space the plants just a tad closer than the distance recommended on the tag accompanying them. That will help to shade the roots a little from the hot summer sun. Put the fertilizer on at planting time. For each 40 square feet, you'll need about 1 pound of complete fertilizer such as 8-8-8 or 10-10-10. If using a special fertilizer formulated for vegetables, follow the rate directed on the package.

Liquid fertilizer sprayed onto the plants through the season will keep them growing and producing flowers and vegetables.

Spring

WHEN TO PLANT FOR A 3-SEASON GARDEN

It takes careful planning to keep a garden producing spring through fall. Here's how..

In March ▶

Plant your spring garden. Cool air and cool soil prevail in early spring, so choose crops that thrive in mild weather and won't suffer if there's frost. These are easy-to-grow salad crops. Look for onion bulbs (often called "sets"). Get seeds of the popular edible-podded peas such as Sugar Snaps, as well as spinach, mesclun, carrots, beets and leaf lettuce. And save some of those seeds for planting again in late summer for a fall crop.

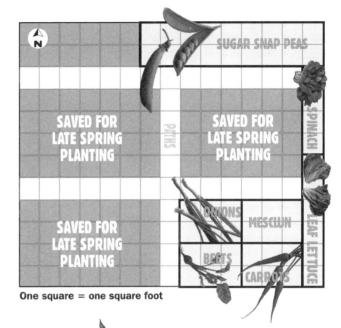

One square = one square foot

In mid-April ▶

Plant your summer garden. Now, it's tomato time. Get plants, at least two kinds, and set them out with stakes or cages for support. Put out hot and sweet peppers, too, to liven up your cooking. Since this is a small garden, choose bush-style cucumbers and bush-style zucchini or yellow squash to avoid sprawl. Look for plants or seeds. Choose pole beans that will climb a trellis and make a green curtain for the back of the garden. When the soil is really warm, in early May, set out your eggplants.

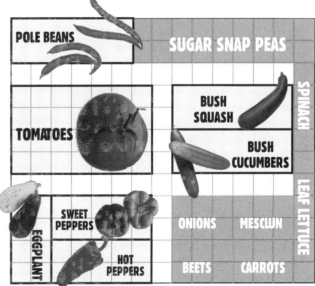

One square = one square foot

◀

In early fall

Plant your autumn garden. Though it's still hot, think about a new season of crops that will mature in the cooling days of autumn. Set out plants of broccoli and cauliflower by Sept. 1, and sow new crops of leaf lettuce, spinach, beets and carrots, as well as a new crop of onions. Watering is especially key during these hot weeks to ensure good germination and growth.

One square = one square foot

Spring

What to Plant in March

These vegetables all prosper in the cool of early spring.

Beets: Sow seeds 1/2 to 1 inch deep. Thin seedlings to stand 2 inches apart. Harvest in 55 to 60 days.

Carrots: Sow seeds 1/2 inch deep in very loose, deeply dug soil in early March. Thin seedlings to stand 2 inches apart. Begin pulling carrots in about 70 days.

Cabbage: Set out plants 12 to 18 inches apart. Harvest in 65 to 75 days.

Leaf lettuce: Sow seeds 1/4 to 1/2 inch deep. Thin seedlings to stand 3 to 4 inches apart. Begin harvesting the outer leaves while plants are quite young. Stagger sowings every 10 days to lengthen the harvest.

Mesclun: Sow seeds of this mixture of greens 1/4 to 1/2 inch deep in short rows every week or so to keep the harvest going. Thin seedlings to stand 1 to 2 inches apart and use the young leaves you pull in salad. Harvest the leaves while young and tender.

Onions: Set out onion bulbs 1-2 inches deep and 4 inches apart by March 15. Begin harvesting in about 60 days.

Peas: Sow peas by March 15, about 2 inches deep and 2-3 inches apart. Taller ones require support such as string and stakes, a net strung between posts or a wire trellis. Faster varieties such as Sugar Bon (56 days) and Mr. Big (58 days) should be ready before summer heat hits.

Spinach: Sow seeds by March 15, about 1 inch deep; thin seedlings to 4 inches apart. Harvest in about 45 to 55 days. Save some seeds for planting in late summer.

KNOW YOUR TOOLS

Garden fork
Sink those sharp tines into the garden to dig and loosen soil and work compost, manure and other ingredients into the bed. Use it to dig up clumps of perennials, even to separate large clumps.

Spade or shovel
Shovels, with their concave bowls, are meant for moving soil and mulch. Spades, with their sharp-edged flat blades, will dig and turn soil.

Trowel
Use this little scoop to set out single plants in beds or pots, move potting soil, add small amounts of fertilizer.

Hand fork
Dig and turn the soil in pots or beds. Set out plants. Even more versatile than a trowel, except when you need to get potting soil out of a bag.

Hand cultivator
Fingerlike prongs will loosen the soil and pull up weeds. Just push or pull. You can really get close to plants with a little cultivator.

Pruning shears
For trimming and tip pruning and a myriad of other tasks to encourage shapely plants.

Also good to have
Lightweight cotton gloves (heavier ones are for cleaning gutters and pruning thorny shrubs); a watering can; a ruler to help you get plant spacing and depth right until it becomes second nature; long-handled lopping shears; a leaf rake, especially one whose sweeping area is adjustable from narrow to wide; a hoe to murder the weeds that sneaked past the mulch.

FEAR THE FROST?
GET SEEDLINGS GOING INDOORS.

If you can't wait to get started, plant some seedlings inside now. While some seeds such as spinach can be planted outdoors safely now, most of the popular flowers and vegetables require warm soil and air to germinate and grow. The possibility of frost will hang around until early April. That's why we sow some seeds indoors in March – to get an early start on tomato and pepper plants, even marigolds and petunias. It's a way to stock your garden with plants you grew yourself and stay useful until tomato time in mid-April.

The equipment for this project is simple.

Garden centers are already stocked with this year's seeds, enough to force some hard choices about this tomato or that marigold. Just consider that part of the drama. You also will need sterile, packaged growing mixtures, an essential ingredient to prevent attack by soil-borne fungi that cause seedlings to drop dead overnight. Not a cheerful outcome for your effort.

Fill the container – a shallow pot or box with drainage holes – with the growing mixture and dampen it before sowing the seeds.

Maybe it sounds obvious, but you should read – and keep – the seed package. If the seeds have special requirements for light or darkness during germination, the package will say so. If the seeds require darkness, you must sow the seeds at the right depth. Those that require light may be sprinkled thinly on top of the planting mixture. The seed package should also give distances the plants should be set apart in the garden, another reason to keep the envelope.

If you have bought seed trays with individual cells, sow two seeds in each, and prepare to sacrifice the smaller, less vigorous one after growth begins.

Label the trays. It's easy to forget whether you have petunias in one pot or zucchini in another. That makes a difference when you set out the plants.

The normal household temperature of about 70 to 72 degrees should suit most seedlings. During germination, the top of a TV or refrigerator should make a warm spot for the pot or box holding the seeds during germination. But once germinated, the seedlings must have some warm sunshine. Move them to a window. A sunny window and regular gentle misting will provide the light and humidity seedlings need, in addition to your daily check to make sure the soil does not dry out.

The mister can also serve as a means of watering the seeds and seedlings; it will not dislodge them the way pouring a direct stream of water will.

After the seedlings grow two pairs of true leaves, transplant each to an individual peat or plastic pot, then fertilize regularly and lightly. Keep the little plants in a warm, sunny spot until planting time outdoors in early to mid-April.

WHAT TO SOW INDOORS

If you are keen to sow seeds indoors, here is a list of some popular flowers and vegetables that are suitable. It includes the approximate number of weeks it takes for each to grow large enough to set outdoors. Except for leaf lettuce, these are warm-weather flowers and vegetables best planted outdoors in mid-to-late April, when the weather is settled and the soil warms up.

• Hot and sweet peppers, tomatoes, eggplant – *eight weeks.*

• Ageratum, snapdragon, dianthus, echinacea, gomphrena, impatiens, rudbeckia, salvia, tithonia – *six to eight weeks.*

• Cosmos, portulaca – *five to six weeks.*

• Alyssum, celosia, zinnia, watermelon, summer squash – *four weeks.*

• Leaf lettuce – *four weeks* (may be set outdoors in cool soil during late March to early April).

Spring

PUT YOUR GARDEN IN A POT

For apartment and town house dwellers without a lot of room to plant, getting into the swing of spring is as down-to-earth as a terra-cotta pot. There you can have tomato plants accented by a frill of herbs, a hanging basket overflowing with pentas and verbena, a big pot of daisies or coleus. Practically anything (well, maybe not corn).

Think of your containers as a shrunken garden. Where others spread out their flowers and vegetables across many square feet, yours will spread across many square inches. Where others garden with spades, garden hoses and tillers, you will garden with trowel, watering can and pruners. Where others struggle to improve their soil to suit the plants, yours will be loose, rich and quite perfect – straight out of a bag.

So here we go. Into the shrunken garden, where not a square inch goes unplanted.

What to grow

You can't have it all, so choose carefully. First, evaluate how much sun your garden will get once the leaves come out and cast their shade.

For places with limited sunshine, choose such flowers as begonias and impatiens and such beautiful foliage plants as coleus or hosta.

For the really hot spots that get the scorching afternoon sun, go for lantana, the mandevilla or allamanda vines, pentas, creeping zinnias, celosia or vincas.

In between those two extremes, consider miniature roses, marigolds, verbena, salvia and long-blooming marguerite daisies.

Most vegetables such as peppers, tomatoes and bush-type yellow squash, zucchini and cucumbers require full sun for a minimum of six hours a day. But leaf lettuce, mesclun and many herbs will do well with a few hours of sun in the morning.

How much space do you have to make this garden and still have room to sit down and enjoy it? Start small, with perhaps a pair of 12-inch pots, each planted with durable, long-blooming flowers, or a particular color you love or the tomato plants you can't live without.

Water your plants

Will rain fall on your shrunken garden? Or is it blocked by a ceiling or shade over the balcony, deck or stoop? Face it, a container garden requires daily attention once the heat hits in May and rainfall gets even more erratic in the summer. Plan to water, either by hauling water to plants from the kitchen sink in a traditional can or by using a special hose you connect to the indoor faucet and run outside to the plants where you turn on the sprayer. I have one of these and find it works quite well. It runs from the kitchen, out the back door and to the steps, all within the reach of the 50-foot lightweight hose. If you opt for one of these, make sure it's long enough before you buy it.

A third watering option is to start with pots with a separate reservoir in the bottom, from which the soil draws up water as needed. You just keep the reservoir filled. The soil and plants sit above it, but the outward effect is of one sleek container.

Terra-cotta pots will dry out faster than plastic ones. If you're serious about container gardening and know you won't be around to water every day, consider plastic pots, which are widely available and nice looking.

Plant roots must make maximum use of every inch of growing room they can get in the pot or container. That means they need really good soil. Start with fresh potting soil each spring for best results. And plan to fertilize your plants with water-soluble fertilizer that you apply at the rate directed on the package when you water.

Combinations make container gardens more colorful and interesting. If you're doing a 12-inch pot of flowers for a sunny spot, consider two pentas plants for the center and three verbenas to trail over the side. Or, think about a pair of white or pink osteospermum daisies or yellow marguerite daisies coupled with trailing lantana.

Coleus, with its incredible patterns of colors, is rather hard to mix with other plants. But they mix well with each other, creating dynamic arrays of greens, golds, yellows and reds for a kaleidoscope effect in shade to light sun.

Spring

It's time to...

- Plant new shrubs, ground covers and perennials.

- Prune hybrid tea, grandiflora and floribunda roses.

- Look over still-leafless trees for broken or cracked limbs while they're easy to spot.

- Finish the winter pruning of evergreens.

- Finish the winter fertilizing of your lawn.

- Finish repairs to lawn mowers and tools and the cleanup of outdoor furniture.

- Apply pre-emergent crabgrass prevention to the lawn by the time dogwood trees bloom.

- Finish setting out broccoli, cabbage and cauliflower plants.

- Dig, divide and replant clumps of chrysanthemums that are growing vigorously.

- Transplant potted plants to larger containers for the new growing season.

- Hit the weed patrol while the plants are small and tender.

Plant profile

PIERIS JAPONICA.

NAME:
Pieris japonica (py-ER-is ja-PON-i-ka) It's named for the ancient region of Macedonia in Greece called Pieria and the muses who worshiped there.

ANCESTRAL ROOTS:
Pieris japonica hails from the mountains and forests of East Asia, particularly Japan.

VITAL STATS:
A slow yet steady grower, Pieris japonica will, after many years, go 6 feet and higher, spreading about 4 feet. Many named varieties of Pieris japonica, called cultivars, exist, so gardeners are sure to find one that suits the size of their landscapes. Some cultivars are shorter, more compact and produce particularly bright foliage and pink orred flower buds.

FAVORITE SPOT:
Pieris prospers in a partly shaded spot, in moist but well-drained soil liberally enhanced with acidic peat moss. Give it shelter from blasts of winter cold and summer's blazing sun.

CARE AND FEEDING:
Fertile soil will keep the pieris growing, but a yearly dose of fertilizer formulated for acid-loving shrubs, such as azaleas, will give the plant an extra kick. Keep this shapely plant spiffy by pruning off dead twigs that occasionally intrude on its loveliness.

BEST REASON TO PLANT ONE:
It's a shrub for year-round beauty: white, pendulous flowers resembling an upside-down, lily-of-the-valley about 6 inches long in spring; reddish-bronze new foliage adds color into the summer; new flower buds form in late summer and remain attractive through the fall and winter.

Spring

A WALK ON THE WILDFLOWER SIDE

Out of the chilled earth and into the cool air come the wildflowers, these supporting players of spring's biggest names, the dogwoods and azaleas and rhododendrons. Some are native wildflowers. Others, such as the spring starflower, originated elsewhere but settled down and spread like they were born here. Some, like the dwarf crested iris, possess endless charm. Others, such as the Carolina jessamine, impress you with their robust growth and prolific blooming, not to mention their ability to climb trees. Though sometimes called "wild," this group has a place in the city. Under the canopy of the Piedmont's trees or lurking around the sunny perimeter of natural areas, they remain wild things with a civilized touch.

• **Ranunculus ficaria**, commonly called lesser celandine, produces the brightest yellow flower of early spring. The daisies, about 4 to 8 inches tall, rise above rounded tufts of glossy green leaves. This ranunculus, native to Europe and western Mediterranean regions, loves moist soil and may become too rampant in the cozy conditions of a well-cultivated flower bed. Give it a spot in the woodland, under trees whose leaves emerge after the plant blooms.

• **Ipheion uniflorum** is commonly called spring starflower. Though native to South America, the starflower grows and spreads happily in the Piedmont's fertile but well-drained soil. The star-shaped blooms appear briefly in mid-March, always signaling that spring is here. Plant the little bulbs at the sunny edges of lawns or shrub beds. Dig and divide clumps in early summer.

• **Erythronium americanum** is commonly called trout lily for its green leaves with purplish brown speckling. The flowers possess a curious color combination of sulfur yellow on the inside of the petals and reddish yellow or purple on the back. Give this native of the Eastern woodlands of North America a spot under your trees where spring sunshine will filter through. They require deeply dug, moist organic soil.

• **Chrysogonum virginica** is a little ground cover that originated in the eastern United States. Its common names, green-and-gold and golden star, come from the bright yellow, daisy-shaped flowers that nestle among bright, semi-evergreen leaves. Grow in moist but well-drained soil liberally enriched with compost

Ranunculus ficaria

Ipheion uniflorum

Erythronium americanum

Chrysogonum virginica

Iris cristada

Mertensia virginica

Spring

What's blooming in March

- Pieris japonica
- Camellia japonica
- Star magnolia
- Saucer magnolia
- Carolina jessamine

- Yoshino cherry
- Forsythia
- Hyacinth
- Daffodils
- Dutch crocus

- Pansies
- Bradford pear
- Bluebells

WILDFLOWERS...

in sun or partial shade. Divide and replant clumps in fall or winter.

- **Iris cristada**, the dwarf crested iris, blooms for a week or so in early April, longer if the weather stays cool. The violet-blue flowers rise a few inches tall. The foliage, a shorter version of typical iris leaves, rises about 6 to 10 inches. Native to the South and Midwest, the dwarf crested iris needs moist but well-drained and rich soil, in sun or partial shade. Divide clumps in late summer or early fall.

- **Mertensia virginica**, the Virginia bluebell, is an American native that bears clusters of pink buds that open to bell-shaped flowers in shades of sky blue to purplish blue. This perennial rises about 18 inches tall, begins to bloom when just out of the ground and has bluish-green leaves. Give it moist soil and light shade; dig and divide plants in late spring or early summer, just as the plant goes dormant. Make hardy ferns their companions to conceal the bluebell's disappearance during its long dormancy.

- **Gelsemium sempervirens** is commonly called Carolina jessamine. A vigorous evergreen vine suited for cascading over walls and fences and climbing sturdy trellises, the jessamine, state flower of South Carolina, does us a big favor by starting to open its golden yellow blooms in late winter. But the big show is in early to mid-spring. Grow in full sun, with good, well-drained soil. Some people may try to tame this vine into tight quarters by pruning, but the plant looks best when allowed to sprawl and cascade naturally. A severe winter may mar the glossy green leaves, but the jessamine should rebound nicely.

Gelsemium sempervirens

Under the canopy of the Piedmont's trees or lurking around the sunny perimeter of natural areas, they remain wild things with a civilized touch.

Ask Nancy
Answers to some common problems

WHEN DO I PLANT AZALEAS AND CAMELLIAS?

Despite abundant encouragement to plant in the fall, people still like to select, buy and plant their camellias (plus azaleas and rhododendrons) in the spring. That's when they can see the size, shape and color of the flowers. It's OK. You can buy these plants now, plant them and succeed. Planted spring or fall, camellias require moist but well-drained soil that is high in organic matter. Partial shade under trees or a northern exposure is best. Be sure when you set out the plant to keep the base of the trunk even or slightly higher than the soil level. Once you plant, water the root zone and check the level. If the trunk base sank below the soil level, raise and reset the root ball to the right depth. Then put on 2 to 3 inches of mulch, such as pine needles. While the plant gets established this year, and even next, pay close attention to watering it during the growing season, especially when rainfall proves erratic in the summer. Don't fertilize the plant until next year.

HOW TO PICK THE RIGHT SHRUBS FOR UNDER A POWER LINE

Your goal should be a set of shrubs that will provide you privacy but reach their mature height without bumping into the power line and requiring cutting. The power line will win this contest every time. Take a look at these types of evergreens in a garden center:

• **Cleyera japonica**. This is not – repeat, not – the infamous red-tip photinia. Cleyera doesn't get sick with leaf fungus like the red-tips, which had their day and went – a decade ago.

• **Dwarf Burford Holly**. This popular, dense and beautiful shrub usually tops out at about 8 feet. Be sure you get the dwarf; the regular Burford can soar to 20 feet.

• **Ligustrum japonicum**. Before we had Leyland cypresses, we had red-tips, and before we had red-tips, we had Japanese ligustrum. Ligustrum is a better screen and healthier plant than either of its successors. Shearing will make it a dense formal hedge; gentle pruning will keep it a loose, informal screen. It grows rapidly.

• **Camellia sasanqua**. With tip pruning, the fall-flowering camellia will turn into a dense screen. Some varieties, such as Apple blossom, grow faster than others. The sasanqua is an excellent plant, rarely beset by problems. Severe cold will set back a plant.

HOW DO I PRUNE A BUTTERFLY BUSH?

Cut back a newly planted buddleia this month by removing weak growth and shortening the main stems to about 1 1/2 feet tall just above where you see strong buds or shoots developing. This will be the framework for the plant. Flowering wood will develop from it. In subsequent years, cut the prior year's growth back to just above one or two pairs of this framework. The butterfly bush blooms on new growth.

THE MESSAGE IS OUT THERE:

In flower buds opening daily, in grass so robust it demands a

twice-a-week cut, in early pickings of lettuce and peas, in dark

and damp soil that gets under your nails. Even when April

regresses into chilly and gloomy – the message remains: Spring is here.

The message says savor the moment, yet it tantalizes us with

images of what's ahead: home-grown tomatoes, richly

colored daylilies, fragrant roses. Gardeners hear the message in April.

They are getting ready: picking out plants, selecting seeds,

putting finishing touches to flower and vegetable beds.

The dreaming and thinking are done. The message is here.

The time for doing is now.

Spring

THESE BEAUTIES BLOOM BY THE CLOCK

From morning glories at daybreak to moonflowers at dusk, flowers that bloom by the clock add special effects to the garden.

❀ **Dawn's morning glory.** Easy to grow from seeds sown in warming soil from late April to early May, morning glories produce fast-growing, twining vines. The funnel-shaped flowers usually close by mid-afternoon. Vines do best on a sunny fence, trellis or lamp post. Soak the hard seeds in warm water for about eight hours before planting to soften them and speed up germination. Sow seeds where you want them to grow in ordinary soil; transplanting is difficult and risky. Vines of the common morning glory grow about 8 to 10 feet long. The best-known variety is Heavenly Blue, whose sky-blue flowers are breathtaking. For a different look, try growing morning glories in a hanging basket and let the vines trail instead of climb.

❀ **Afternoon's four o'clocks.** Waning daylight in late afternoon signals that four o'clocks (actually, they're more like five o'clocks in the Piedmont) are ready to open. Easy to grow, seeds germinate best after the soil is thoroughly warmed in May; plants

grow fairly rapidly and start blooming about mid-summer. Space plants about 3 feet apart in sun. The plant, botanically named Mirabilis jalapa, is probably a Mexican perennial; it won't survive most Piedmont winters. Flowers are red, pink, yellow or white on plants that grow 2 to 3 feet tall. Try planting them where daffodil or tulips grow so that the new growth of four o'clocks can conceal their dying foliage. They will also fill up the eventual blank spaces of the bulbs.

❀ **The evening's primrose.** Lemon yellow and evening bloom tell the story of Oenothera missourensis. Flowers open slowly at day's end, but fast enough for you to sit and watch without getting bored. The round, yellow flowers, which can be a dramatic 5 inches or more in diameter, usually remain open until the following day; that evening, you get a new show. Plants grow about 9 to 12 inches tall and need ordinary soil in a sunny spot. The evening primrose won't tolerate wet soil and will spoil your show by rotting. In the right spot, it's a long-lived perennial. Start with plants from garden centers. For a dramatic combination, plant a row or cluster of evening primroses with purple-leaved basil.

❀ **The night's moonflower.** A relative of the morning glory (both belong to the same plant genus), the moonflower is a tidy vine that grows 8 to 10 feet. Its flowers open in late evening and remain open in the dark, usually until mid-morning. The flowers are white, fragrant and big, about 5 inches in diameter. Sow seeds (soaked like the morning glory) where you want them to grow or get young plants at garden centers and set out in the sunny, warming soil in late April. Moonflower requires a trellis, preferably one near the chair or bench where you enjoy sitting on summer evenings. Collect and save seeds for next year.

For real flower power, combine morning glories and moonflowers on the same trellis and spend some time at daylight and dusk watching them.

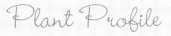

Spring

Plant Profile

COLUMBINE

NAME:
Botanically named Aquilegia (a-kwee-LEE-jah), columbines come as both wild plants and brightly colored hybrids.

HOME GROUND:
The eastern columbine, Aquilegia canadensis, is native to many counties of North Carolina and a few counties of South Carolina. The Rocky Mountain columbine is a native of America's West.

VITAL STATS:
The eastern columbine has nodding, red and yellow flowers and grows 1 to 2 feet tall. The Rocky Mountain columbine, which is Colorado's state flower, grows over 3 feet tall. Hybrids can reach 3 feet. Flower size ranges from about 1 1/2 inches wide (the eastern columbine) to 2 inches wide (the hybrids and Rocky Mountain columbines).

FAVORITE SPOT:
Columbines prosper in moist but well-drained, slightly sandy soil and light shade. Summer's too hot in the Piedmont to grow columbines in full sun.

PLANTING TIP:
The eastern columbine, though short-lived as a plant, is prolific and regenerates from seeds dropped from the flowers. Give this columbine a place to call its own and develop a colony.

Aquilegia

HOW TO COAX AN EASTER LILY TO BLOOM AGAIN

In the mild South, you can turn your Easter lily, Lilium longiflorum, into a garden flower. Here's the plan. Once the flowers are done, cut off the spent blooms and take the plant out of the pot. Set it, with the soil and roots attached, into a well-drained, sunny part of the flower garden. The top of the root ball should be 3 inches below ground level. Once it's planted, mound some soil around the stem for a couple of inches for stability. Water the plant immediately and fertilize it with one teaspoon of slow-release, water-soluble fertilizer every six weeks through the summer. If you have more than one plant, set them about 12 to 18 inches apart. Outdoors, these plants bloom in early summer.

Easter lily

Spring

CREATE A GARDEN AROUND YOUR MAILBOX

There's a spot in your front yard you may not think of as a garden spot. Something you look at every day. Visit six days a week. Of course, it's the mailbox. Make it part of the garden with plants chosen for beauty and durability – and for keeping the mailbox accessible. Here are three plans, from elaborate to simple, to get you started.

Plan 1: All dressed up

The goal:
A permanent array of woody vines, ground-cover shrubs and spots of summer color, all enclosed by an evergreen edger.

What you see here:
Scatterings of low-to-the-ground junipers are enclosed by deep green, almost black, mondo grass. Golden yellow blooms of the perennial black-eyed susan named Goldsturm liven up the scene. It grows 12 to 18 inches tall. An elegant clematis blooms in late spring on the post.

Other choices:
Clematis comes in a huge array of colors, from white to yellow to pinks to purples. Perennial salvias, veronicas or coreopsis could replace the black-eyed susans. And there's room for accents of late-winter crocuses or snowdrops and some summer annuals in your favorite color. Monkey grass could also be the edger.

Plan 2: Big and bold

The goal:
A dramatic, colorful display with bold vines and annuals, all with a long flowering season.

What you see here:
The popular mandevilla vine with its bright pink, trumpet-shaped blooms wraps around the post. At the base, white daisies with sparkly blue centers bloom on bushy plants about 18 inches tall. They belong to the genus osteospermum and used to be known more commonly as African daisies. Remove the spent flowers to keep the plants blooming. The outer circle has lilac-flowered pentas. The plants grow 12 to 18 inches tall and also come in

clear and rosy pinks. None will survive winter outdoors.

Other choices:
For the post, the yellow-flowered allamanda vine, which, except for color, resembles the mandevilla. At the base, lantana, melampodium, heliotrope, ageratum, verbena and vinca. All require sun and range from 8 to 18 inches tall.

Plan 3: Sweet and simple

The goal:
A simple planting of two to three dozen long-blooming, colorful annuals at the base of the mailbox post.

What you see here:
Concentric circles of low-growing, spreading golden zinnias (Zinnia angustifolia) that bloom all summer and hold up well through hot, humid weather. There are also white and orange varieties. Unlike many other zinnias, these zinnias resist powdery mildew. Flowers are about 2 inches wide and grow about 8 inches tall. This zinnia likes sun and soil on the dry side.

Other choices:
For sunny spots: short to medium marigolds, scarlet sage, Swan River daisies, portulaca, gomphrena. *For shade:* wax begonias, impatiens and, though they don't bloom, caladiums with their colorful leaves.

**Plan 1:
All dressed up**

Spring

Tips For Success

- Prepare the soil well. First, outline the planting area with a garden hose or short stakes and string. Then dig the soil to about 10 inches deep. If the soil seems crumbly and brown, it should be good enough for planting. If it's hard-packed and clayish, add copious amounts of bagged topsoil or compost to loosen it up. The digging and the soil amendments will raise the level of the soil slightly.

- Plan for rain runoff. Even a slight slope could cause heavy rain to push soil and mulch, particularly shredded pine bark or wood chips, into the curb or street. To avoid this problem, make a good-looking edger with bricks or rocks, or plant a rim of monkey grass or mondo grass. A permanent ground cover such as pachysandra, vinca or ajuga will help hold in soil and serve as mulch.

- Be sure the box remains accessible and visible. Don't bury it in shrubbery or hard-to-control vines like wisteria. If people must step on the ground in front of the box to place or retrieve mail, put a stepping stone there so shoes won't get wet and muddy.

- Don't choose thorny vines or shrubs such as climbing roses or barberry that might scratch arms or legs of people at the mailbox.

- Get a watering can if your mailbox is beyond reach of the hose. Plants will have to be watered in the summer. Count on that.

- Choose plants based on the site. Is it hot and sunny? Warm but shady? When you look at plants in the garden center, read the tags. They should tell you the correct environment. They will also tell you how tall the plants should grow and how far apart to space them.

- If you plant annuals such as zinnias or tropicals such as pentas that will not survive freezing weather, plan to replace them in the fall with pansies and a collection of bulbs such as daffodils and tulips. That will make your mailbox garden a year-round beauty spot.

**Plan 2:
Big and
bold**

**Plan 3:
Sweet and
simple**

WINDOW DRESSING: A BOX BRIMMING WITH FLOWERS CAN BRIGHTEN THE VIEW

For pure charm, look to the window box. Filled with flowers, nothing makes a prettier summer sight, particularly if you choose long-blooming annuals. With the right combinations for sun or shade, your box will become a miniature flower garden. Perhaps your window box is already there, bracketed sturdily to a wall. Perhaps it's still an idea after you've seen the large range of lightweight, ready-made boxes in garden centers. Look for ones close to the width of the chosen window, an inch or two either way. If you don't have the right window, set your box on your stoop, deck or patio. Here's how to get started on being a window box gardener.

Exposure: Study the exposure to the sun your box will get. Morning sun is much gentler in summer than afternoon sun. A hot afternoon exposure will mean you'll have to water daily in summer. Has the newly emerged canopy of trees put the spot in dappled shade? Then you'll want to choose plants that flourish in partial shade.

Soil: Lightweight, very loose potting soil will reduce the weight of the box and allow plants to make maximum use of their confined space. Start with fresh potting soil every year; plants deplete the nutrients in soil quickly in tight quarters. Don't even think about shoveling soil out of the garden into the box; it will be too heavy and dense. The box must have drainage holes for water. Cover the holes with shards from a clay pot to keep soil from washing out.

Plant selection: Look for flowers and colors you like and that suit the paint or brick of your house. Don't forget about the exposure to sun or shade. Look for some trailing plants such as petunias or ivy-leaf geraniums to spill over the front. This cascade will have the effect of expanding the size of the "box garden." For the middle of the box, choose annuals that mature short, about 10 to 12 inches; use slightly taller ones for the back. Plant labels sold with flats or pots of annuals should tell you the mature height of the variety. Don't be afraid to combine colors, even in a small space. The essence of a summer garden is a mix of

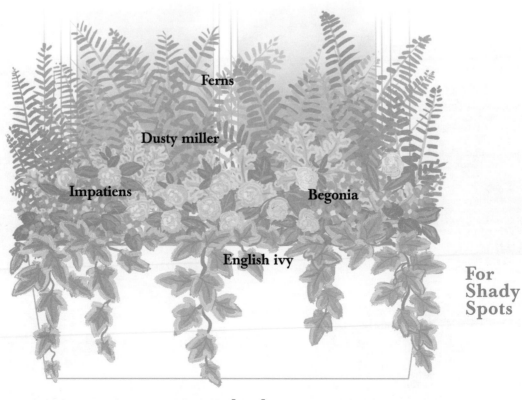

Ferns

Dusty miller

Impatiens

Begonia

English ivy

For Shady Spots

Spring

lovely color – pinks, reds, yellows and greens. They won't clash. But if a monochromatic color scheme of white or pink or yellow is your wish, go for it, and let the green of foliage provide the lush contrast.

Arrangement: Place the shortest or cascading plants at the front or sides. In the middle section, try to stagger the plants slightly for a more natural effect than straight rows provide. Once the front and mid-section are planted, place the taller selections. The box shouldn't be full at first. The plants need room to grow.

Care: Don't count on the rain to water your box. The roof may divert rainfall away, so plan to water regularly during hot weather. Add liquid fertilizer for flowering plants to the watering schedule weekly throughout the summer. Pinch off spent blooms as often as possible and groom the plants to keep them in top form.

In winter: A window box doesn't have to go dormant in winter. Fill it with pansies in the fall for bright bloom; even add some small bulbs such as crocuses or snowdrops to spark up the late-winter scene.

CHOICES FOR A WINDOW BOX

In shade, the range of plants for window boxes is small. Look for colorful foliage in coleus and caladium plants to add spark and diversity to plantings of shade-loving begonias and impatiens. For sun, a wide number of trailers and short varieties of garden flower offer many choices:

- African daisy
- Ageratum
- Celosia
- Gazania
- Gomphrena
- Lantana
- Madagascar periwinkle (vinca)
- Melampodium
- Nasturtium
- Ornamental pepper
- Portulaca
- Swan river daisy
- Sweet alyssum
- Verbena
- Narrowleaf and creeping zinnias

Victoria salvia

Dwarf dahlia

Marigold

Trailing petunia

Ivy-leaf geranium

For Sunny Spots

What's blooming in April

❧ Camellias	❧ Early irises	❧ Dianthus
❧ Azaleas	❧ Scillas	❧ Fringe tree
❧ Clematis	❧ Crab apple	❧ Kerria
❧ Late daffodils	❧ Tulips	❧ Spirea
❧ Dogwoods	❧ Columbine	❧ Weigela

HOW TO PLANT A CUTTING GARDEN

For beautiful indoor flower arrangements this summer, plant easy-to-grow flowers well suited for cutting and making bouquets. A simple cutting garden possesses two qualities.

First, it's out of sight, tucked behind the garage or beyond trees or shrubbery so that it's not under your nose or in clear sight of guests eating barbecue on your deck or patio. Because it isn't a garden for viewing, you'll feel free to pick the flowers.

Second, it is stuffed with a wide variety of flowers suited for vases over a long season. This is not a situation where colors, shapes and textures have to be planted to please the eye. You'll do that with the arrangement.

The bed requires the same attention to preparation as any flower garden. Dig it deeply, at least 10 inches or so, then add lots of good topsoil or compost. Make the bed narrow enough to reach the flowers at planting and cutting times without stepping on the soil. A long, narrow bed is easier to tend. And it is easy to build in stages. Start with a 3-by-8-foot section this spring, then see how your enthusiasm for cut flowers grows this summer. You can expand the bed with another 3-by-8-foot section in the fall or next spring, either of them designated for a particular season or even a particular type of flower, such as daisies, chrysanthemums or irises.

Tips For Success

- **Variety.** The most important thing is to have a lot of flowers to choose from to create the mixed, colorful bouquet that says summer. Some of your selections will be annuals, planted every spring; others will be perennials, which live for three years or longer. Planting will be easier if parts of the bed are dedicated to the perennials, the rest to the annuals. Some good choices are plumed celosia, dahlia, yarrow, annual and perennial sunflowers, coneflowers, gomphrena, marigolds, zinnias, snapdragons, echinops, salvias lilies, Shasta daisies and cosmos.

- **Keep the bed working for you**. When annuals such as the early zinnias are spent, replace them with something new. By then, it may be too late to start from seeds, but garden centers remain stocked with flowers well through the summer. Or you can put in fall's chrysanthemums.

- **Resist the urge to keep it tidy.** Part of the charm of the cutting garden is the random, even wayward, way the plants grow. A snapdragon may be tilted toward the dahlia in a friendly sort of way. A bunch of cosmos may spread all over. The black-eyed susans are in lily's face.

- **Think about the colors** that go with your furnishings. If harmony is important to you, plant flowers in colors a step brighter or a bit paler than your indoor colors. A neutral decor lends itself to many flower colors, including the brightest shades of midsummer.

- **Choose plants that succeed.** There is one reason some flowers, such as marigolds, snapdragons, cosmos, black-eyed susans and sunflowers, are planted so often by so many people. They grow and they

produce. These are not temperamental; they don't get eaten alive by pests; they perform as expected. That's what you want in your cutting garden.

- **Don't forget foliage.** Foliage is an important part of any arrangement. But you don't have to devote part of your cutting garden to foliage. You can snip stems here and there from your evergreens to tuck into the arrangement. Hardy ferns grow beautifully, usually in shady areas. Don't be afraid to cut them.

HOW TO CREATE A JOLLY GOOD ENGLISH GARDEN

When most people think "English garden," they see a magnificent mixture of colorful, mostly summertime blooms, varying shapes from round to spike and textures smooth to prickly. The entire thing is laid out without a definite pattern in a long but narrow garden called a border and backed up by an evergreen screen or brick wall.

People go to England, where they see the beautiful perennial borders of Hampton Court, Sissinghurst and Wisley, and come home determined to replicate them, at least in a small way.

And then our climate intervenes. Really hot summer days, very hot summer nights. Stretches of drought. High humidity. The delphiniums don't prosper, the lupines are so-so; the tree peonies and primroses come and go in no time flat.

The hoped-for effect just isn't the same in southern America as it is in southern England. Yet still we try. And we can achieve a reasonable facsimile of the revolutionary idea put forth by garden writer William Robinson in the late 19th century. He believed that gardens "should not have any definite pattern to weary the eye but quiet grace and verdure, and little pictures month by month." Robinson was the founding father of the movement to embrace hardy perennials instead of exotic bedding plants. It took hold to create a classic style that is informal yet sophisticated and applicable elsewhere in the world, including here. The key is picking the right plants.

Pick the right plants

Choose perennials that perform best here. Many kinds of perennials do beautifully in the Piedmont.

They bloom a long time and live a long time. They stand up to heat, tolerate humidity and aren't ravaged by insects and diseases. Make them the backbone of your border. The idea is to create a mix of color, shape and texture. To help decide, visit public gardens that grow perennials, such as Daniel Stowe Botanical Garden in Belmont, and Wing Haven and the UNC Charlotte Botanical Gardens, both in Charlotte.

Supplement the planting with annuals and tropicals. Though delphiniums don't perform very well here, larkspur, grown from seeds sown in the fall, does. Red corn poppies grow easily from seeds and perform better and longer than the perennial Oriental poppies. Tropical and subtropical hibiscus, pentas, lantana, canna and gingers can help keep the show going through the heat of July and August.

Select plants for every season. Even if late spring to midsummer is prime time in your perennial garden, there is no reason for it to look dull the rest of the year. Supplement the summer plantings from the wide array of perennials and bulbs that bloom early and late.

Plan the design

Round, oval or rectangular? A narrow rectangular bed about 5 feet wide is easier to tend from either side, and you can make it as long as space, energy and budget allow. Run a green lawn between two narrow beds for a really authentic look. Round and oval beds are a more recent look for perennial gardens, but perfectly OK if your space and sunshine dictate a garden in the center of your backyard. They are, however,

Spring

harder to take care of because you have to walk on the garden to weed and tend it.

Plant in clumps and drifts. This is not Noah's ark, where you want everything marching in line two-by-two. Think random and curving instead of soldier straight. Think casual rather than formal.

Repeat and repeat. Limit the number of varieties you choose and repeat them in clusters at various points here and there in the border. It's not a zoo, where you want one of everything possible. Repetition achieves both continuity and unity within the design.

Fill in for structure. The flowering perennials cannot do all the work. Accent plants such as ornamental grasses, cannas with interesting foliage, artemesias and even dusty miller can help calm down a garden before it gets too busy and help link sections. And don't overlook shrubbery, even trees (the limbs cut high to let the sunshine in), as a means of adding year-round structure to the garden. It's not classic English, but the look brings in the Southern fondness for shrubs.

CHOICES FOR AN ENGLISH GARDEN

❀ **Sunflower.** Helianthus is the genus of the ever-popular sunflower. Perennial sunflowers come in many forms, most producing great masses of yellow daisies in late summer and autumn. Most are tall, 6 to 7 feet, so they make great background plants. Some good named varieties are Flore Pleno, which reaches 6 feet and bears blooms that resemble a dahlia; Loddon Gold, 3 to 5 feet tall, with double daisy blooms; and Sheila's Sunshine, a pale yellow daisy that may grow above 8 feet (staking probably required).

❀ **Yarrow.** The most popular varieties of achillea, commonly called yarrow, produce flat-topped, yellow blooms in summer. Varieties include Coronation Gold, about 3 feet tall, with golden blooms; and Moonshine, a shorter (1 to 2 feet), sulfur yellow variety. Both are well suited for drying for use in arrangements. Red, copper and pink varieties will also light up the garden. Set these vertical plants 12 inches apart.

❀ **Verbena.** Perennial verbena may eventually cover the landscape, thanks to the popularity of such varieties as Homestead Purple, 8 inches tall; rosy pink Sissinghurst, just 3 inches tall; and the pink and white Texas Appleblossom, 6 inches tall. Most will spread about 2 feet wide. Their sprawling, floriferous nature makes them well suited as front-of-the-garden edgers. Watering will help them spread with vigor.

❀ **Spiked speedwell.** The spiked speedwell, a member of the veronica genus, brings dignified, vertical bloom in blue, lavender, white or light pink to the summer garden. Plants grow to 1 1/2 to 2 feet, depending on the variety. To extend bloom, remove spent flowers. Some top varieties are Blue Spires, 18 inches tall with deep blue blooms, and Red Fox, rosy red blooms on 15-inch plants. Other good veronicas are Sunny Border blue, 18 to 24 inches tall, with violet-blue flowers, and long-blooming Goodness Grows, 12 to 14 inches, with cobalt blue flowers.

❀ **Shasta daisy.** A classic perennial garden favorite, the Shasta daisy adds a fresh, cool effect to the garden. White daisies with yellow centers appear in spring and summer, depending on the variety. If you need a short, compact Shasta, consider Snow Lady, which grows and spreads only about 1 foot tall, or Snowcap, which grows 12 to 18 inches tall. The hot Shasta, though, is Becky, which starts to bloom at midsummer on sturdy, straight stems, about 3 to 4 feet tall. For the longest season of Shasta bloom, plant several kinds and cut off the spent blooms.

❀ **Salvia.** If you like blue flowers, salvias offer a lot of choice, ranging from pale sky blue to boldest indigo. You can find lots of good kinds on the market that are hardy in this area. Even the marginally hardy are worth planting for their dramatic bloom. Some are short, such as May night, an

Spring

early bloomer (mid-April) that grows 18 inches tall with dark indigo blooms. Others are quite tall, such as Salvia guaranitica, which can hit 6 feet and has deep blue flowers; in between is the long-blooming Indigo Spires, 4 to 5 feet. The variety, beauty and usefulness of the genus may turn you into a salvia hobbyist.

Echinops. Not so well known, but worth growing, Echinops ritro bears round, prickly, blue blooms that look like its common name, globe thistle. *Good named varieties:* Veitch's Blue, a deep blue, about 3 1/2 feet tall; and Taplow Blue, a metallic blue, 2 to 3 feet tall. Plants spread 2 feet. Blooms dry well for wreaths or dried arrangements.

Daylily. Daylilies come in thousands of colors from white to nearly black on plants usually 2 to 3 feet tall, though dwarf and taller varieties exist. Daylilies bloom in late spring to about midsummer, depending on the variety. Each bloom lasts just a day, but each plant produces many buds on arching stems called scapes. To stretch the blooming season, plant as many varieties as you have space to grow.

Candytuft. A great edger for flowerbeds, candytuft bears white flowers in clusters for a mat effect from early to mid-spring. The dark green foliage is evergreen. Plants grow about 1 foot high and 2 feet wide. Some shorter choices: Snowflake, about 8 inches tall; Kingwood Compact, 6 inches; Little Gem, 4 to 6 inches. Botanically, the name is Iberis sempervirens.

Black-eyed susan. One of the most popular garden flowers, the black-eyed susan named Goldsturm grows 2 to 2 1/2 feet tall and 1 1/2 feet wide. It blooms from midsummer to early autumn. Other good choices in its genus, rudbeckia, are two late bloomers: Herbstonne (Autumn Sun), which has bright green centers and can hit 6 feet; and Goldquelle, which has fluffy, double flowers.

Baptisia. Baptisia australis, commonly called false indigo, bears spikes of deep bluish purple blooms in early summer. Its other assets are longevity and drought tolerance (thanks to the deep taproot that makes moving established plants risky.) It grows 3-6 feet tall and about 3 feet wide. Baptisia alba bears white flowers.

Butterfly weed. The butterfly weed of eastern North America, Asclepias tuberosa, has increasingly moved from the roadside and meadow to perennial flowerbeds. That's because this vibrant beauty draws butterflies to its vivid orange blooms. The seedpods that follow the flowers will produce seed for more plants, possibly with yellow or red flowers. Butterfly weed tolerates both heat and drought. Plants grow about 2 feet tall.

Anemone. Though their colors aren't typically fallish, the hybrid anemones will brighten the late-summer to early-autumn garden with a dash of spring pink, rose and white. Most rise about 3 to 4 feet tall, and about that wide. They're easy to grow and reliable. Popular varieties include Honorine Jobert, notable for its clear white petals and yellow stamens; September Charm, with rosy-pink blooms; Whirlwind, which has solid white, semi-double blooms; Queen Charlotte, which bears pink blooms; and Prince Henry, notable for its white, semi-double flowers.

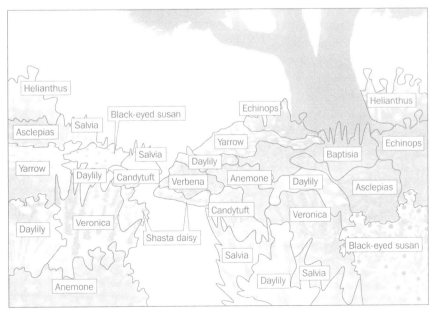

Spring

WHAT'S BUGGING YOU

THE AVID APHID

NAME: Aphids are small insects, less than an eighth of an inch long. They appear as the weather warms up in springtime in many colors, including green, pink, red, dark brown and blue-black. Some have wings; many kinds do not.

Aphids

FAVORITE HANGOUTS: The undersides of leaves, and packed onto the tender tips of new growth of countless kinds of flowers and vegetables. They are less apparent during the hottest weather of summer.

DAMAGE DONE: Aphids suck plant juices from the plant's tissue, reducing its vigor. The result may be wilted plants and oddly malformed foliage. Aphids may also transmit viruses from plant to plant. Often the honeydew-like substance exuded by aphids results in a black coating on leaves.

BIOLOGICAL CHARACTERISTIC: Prolific, thy name is aphid. Aphids reproduce continuously through warm weather at an amazing rate.

SOME WEAPONS AGAINST APHIDS: Lady beetles, parasitic wasps and green lacewings are natural predators. A forceful spray of water will dislodge and drown some. Insecticidal soap will also kill aphids.

WEIRD FACT: Certain female aphids are capable of bearing nymphs continuously - without mating. Such prolific reproduction explains why the battle against aphids goes on and on and on.

Tent caterpillar

CATERPILLARS TO WATCH FOR

The tent caterpillar and the inchworm, or cankerworm, particularly vex gardeners at this time of year.

The green cankerworm, or inchworm, has infested trees in parts of Charlotte for many years, causing serious damage through defoliation. It especially favors oaks. Bands covered in a sticky substance called Tanglefoot are put up around tree trunks in affected areas in late autumn to trap the wingless female moth en route to the treetops, where she lays eggs.

The eggs hatch in early April, and gardeners can spray young cankerworms with Bacillus thuringiensis; older populations should be sprayed with Orthene. The infestation usually lasts about six weeks.

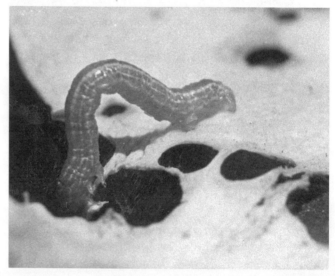
Cankerworm

The tent caterpillar is distinctive for the silken webs and tents it spins in forks of trees and the white stripe along its back,

Early March, before the caterpillars emerge, is an ideal time to remove and destroy the nests. So file away a reminder for next year. The caterpillars are out and roaming now. You can still fight them. Use a broom or tall pole to pull out the tents they build in trees. Cold, drizzly weather is when they're most likely to seek sanctuary in their tents. You also can capture caterpillars crawling on tree trunks with a trowel. Just drop them into a jar or can and put them into the trash.

Spring

It's time to...

- Finish planting cool-weather vegetables such as beets, cabbages and leaf lettuce by early April.

- Plant caladiums, tuberous begonias and elephant ears in pots indoors to get them growing early; plant outdoors when the ground is warm, in early May.

- Make collars from strips of light cardboard or stiff paper about 9 inches long and about 4 inches wide. Staple the ends of the paper together, or cut the bottom off paper cups. Set the collars 1 inch or more into the soil at the base of young vegetable transplants to protect them from destructive cutworms.

- Buy tropicals, mandevillas, allamandas and hibiscus, to plant in big pots outdoors and make a colorful splash.

- Move houseplants outdoors to a shady porch or spots under the trees when the night temperature stays above 50 degrees.

- Look out for slugs headed toward your leaf lettuce, pansies and other tender plants. Catch them in traps or shallow pans of beer.

- Start sowing seeds of green beans, melons, corn, cucumbers, pumpkins and squashes at mid-month. Set out tomato and pepper plants.

- Plant summer flowers, including marigolds, impatiens and begonias, after mid-April.

- Plant warm-weather ornamentals that grow from bulbs and tubers, including gladiolus, canna, dahlia and caladium.

Ask Nancy

Answers to some common problems

WHEN DO I PRUNE MY AZALEAS?

With the bloom season nearing its end for most azaleas, you can prune. Cut the wayward stems back to the interior of the plant, stopping just above the junction where one stem meets another. Try not to leave stubs. To encourage a denser, more compact plant, try tip pruning. By gently pinching out the tips of new growth all over the plant, you can promote side growth on the stems and make the plant denser. While you are at it, look for any dead or broken stems to trim away.

WHEN CAN I MOVE MY PEONIES?

Must you? Peonies benefit from staying put, and a peony plant that's growing well should not be moved without a very good reason. Of course, if it's an heirloom handed down for two or three generations and you're moving, that's a good reason.

Fewer flowers, a lack of vigor and shorter flower stalks all could indicate that the plant needs the rejuvenation of division. Do this in the fall, while the plant is dormant. Dig up the plant and separate the crown into two or more divisions, then replant.

If you must dig the plant now, plant it in a pot until fall, when you can divide and replant it in the ground.

Spring

Ask Nancy
Answers to some common problems

SHOULD I BRAID OR TIE BACK THE FOLIAGE OF DAFFODIL LEAVES AFTER THE BLOOMS FADE?

No. For best bloom in future years, daffodil foliage needs maximum exposure to sunlight to develop new buds. When you tie back or braid the foliage, this shortens the life of the leaves and reduces the amount of sunlight they get. Let the leaves stand, then lie naturally until they are nearly brown. Then you can cut and remove them. They will have done their job.

WHAT IS WRONG WITH MY AZALEAS?

The leaves are rough and have yellow dots on the top and brown dots on the bottom.

Your problem is the lace bug, a bad insect with a pretty name. This insect, named for the lacy appearance of the adult insect's transparent wings, makes itself at home on the undersides of leaves.

As it dines on the plant's sap, the leaf loses its green color and becomes yellowish or even grayish white. The appearance is mottled. The dark brown spots are their excrement. But its presence is what separates lace bugs from other problems such as mites.

Get your glasses on and examine your plants, including the succulent new growth, for the early bugs. Both the wingless nymphs and the lacy-winged adults feed on the leaves.

When you see infestations begin to develop, spray the plants with insecticidal soap, Orthene or malathion, taking care to get the undersides of the leaves. Spray again in 7 to 10 days. Infestations may build up again in the summer, particularly on azaleas growing in full sun. Watch the plants carefully, but spray only as needed. The damaged leaves will probably not recover their nice green color, but the new foliage should cover this up.

WHY DID THE BLOOMS OF MY CAMELLIAS TURN BROWN AND THE BUDS FALL OFF?

Cold weather probably burned the buds brown and led to their demise. But a fungus caused the discolored flowers. The problem, named camellia petal blight, results in enlarging brown spots as the petals unfold and expand. It causes a distinctive netted appearance and a dry, leathery feel to the petals. The dead flowers fall off, usually intact. And that keeps the problem going year after year.

The fungus rests in the soil just under the camellias, just awaiting the moment to splash up and infect blooms next year. Rake away all the fallen camellia debris promptly so the fungus doesn't get into the soil and mulch. Remove and dispose of infected blooms before they fall off the plant. Removing the old mulch and replacing it with fresh mulch late each winter should help.

Because you've had a serious problem this spring, next spring spray the plant with a fungicide such as Bayleton. Do this at 14-day intervals from the time the buds start to show color through the bloom season. It may take several years to get this problem under control. It isn't impossible, just tedious.

It may take several years to get this problem under control. It isn't impossible, just tedious.

May

IT'S MAY, THE LOVELIEST MONTH.

The grass is its greenest, the roses and irises their brightest;

the trees are an expanding canopy of welcome shade.

May brings calm to the garden. Surely we're done planting.

Or are we? Isn't May for enjoying and tending, to search for watering

cans and insects that dare invade the flower and vegetable beds?

Yet trips to the garden center tempt us to get just a few more

perennials, more shrubs, even more annuals to add to the garden.

It will keep that to-do list fully packed and never done.

May is like that. Its loveliness always tempts us to do more.

The heat of summer ahead will finally call a halt.

But for now, enjoy yourself.

Spring

HERBS: FROM THEN TO NOW

If, by a large stretch of imagination, you could transport a resident of the 15th century into the late 20th, what type of garden plants do you think she would recognize first? Not most roses, not most annuals or perennials and probably not the vegetables. It would be herbs. Important then, important now.

Our visitor from the 15th century would know many of the common herbs we use today. Herbs have been used for centuries for culinary, medicinal and other household purposes. Today, gardeners grow and enjoy mainly culinary herbs such as basil, dill, marjoram, parsley, thyme, sage and chives. Herbs also make an attractive addition to any flower or vegetable garden because of their scents, textures and colors.

Anyone can have an herb garden. You can put potted herbs on a windowsill, group several plants in a large pot on your front steps, line the front of your vegetable garden, even include them in flower beds.

Any good, well-drained soil will do for herbs, and fertilizer is rarely, if ever, needed. Too much fertilizer will limit the development of oil in herb plants.

Dig the bed about 8 inches or so deep, break up clods and rake the surface smooth and level. Peat moss may be added to heavy clay soil to improve its internal drainage. Most herbs require full sun, although chives, basil, catnip, chervil, lemon balm and mint will tolerate partial shade.

5 herbs to get you started

It would be easy to go overboard and plant a few of every herb you can find, but I suggest you start with five, easy-to-grow and easy-to find culinary herbs. Get young plants because you only need one or a few of each type.

• **Basil**. Sweet basil is popular for many dishes, especially Italian cooking. Dark basil is often used in vinegars and jellies. Basil requires warm weather and warm soil, so don't put it outdoors until about mid-May. Plants purchased now must be protected from temperatures under 60 degrees. Bring them indoors at night or keep them in a sunny window in the daytime until planting time.

• **Chives**. One plant of chives will expand and be with you forever. Chives like fairly moist soil but are not otherwise particular. They produce interesting globes of purple flowers at mid-spring, but the leaves are valued for their onion-like flavor. This is a good plant for growing in pots.

• **Parsley**. Easy, easy, easy. Parsley is the best-known garnish and beautiful as a garden ruffle. Look for curled and flat-leaved parsley. The flat-leaved type has a stronger flavor than curled parsley, the popular garnish.

• **Thyme**. A hardy herb for pots. Try more than one kind: lemon, as well as common thyme, to discover the variety of this wonderful herb. They also make a lovely addition to a sachet or bouquets garni.

• **Rosemary**. A perennial herb that is marginally hardy in the Piedmont, but valuable to grow for its many uses in the kitchen. Well-drained soil is mandatory.

Rosemary

Once you have succeeded with this fantastic five, expand your collection to include more kinds of these wonderful plants. And if someone from the 15th century drops in, show her the garden.

Spring

BRANCH OUT TO OFFBEAT HERBS

When you plant herbs, don't be afraid to go beyond the basics. Here are some herbs that are beyond the regular palette:

- **Annie Hall/Creeping thyme**. This herb bears tiny pink flowers and proves very suitable for growing in a shallow pot, creating the appearance of a ground cover. It grows just a few inches tall.

- **Sage**. This golden variegated sage, named Icterina, bears yellow and green leaves. It brings good color contrast to the herb garden and a different look to this popular culinary herb. It grows about 2 1/2 feet tall.

- **Spanish lavender**. This herb originated in Spain and southern France and can grow 3 feet tall. It bears dense spike of purplish-blue flowers. It requires well-drained soil, preferably in a raised bed.

- **Golden feverfew**. The yellowish-green foliage of this golden feverfew, named

Aureum, makes a distinctive sight, and bears white flowers tinged with yellow. It grows 2 to 3 feet tall. It is sometimes grown for its ornamental qualities.

- **Lavender mint**. This is useful in a variety of culinary ways. Though mints tend to be invasive, you can contain them by growing plants in a plastic pot sunk into the ground. Remove the bottom of the pot.

Creeping thyme

Sage

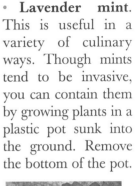

Spanish lavender

Golden feverfew

Lavender mint

HOW TO GROW MINT

Taste mint, that old reliable chewing gum flavor. See mint. There it is, racing out of the garden and into the lawn. Think mint. Do you think boring? Don't. Think interesting. Leaves with curls. Leaves with white margins. Leaves with golden marks. Fruit flavors such as apple, pineapple and lemon. Even names recalling places like the Mediterranean isles. All kinds of mints will tempt the gardener as well as the cook. Granted, mints aren't roses or rhododendrons. But they still possess a variety of styles and scents that will make your garden more interesting.

Ask anyone who's seen spearmint run rampant in the garden and you'll know that mints rank among the easiest plants to grow. Despite their differences of flavor and appearance, the mints – botanically, they belong to the genus Mentha – share common needs. Most mints require full sun to light shade and good garden soil well-enriched with compost. While some

mints will tolerate dry soil and neglect, you will get better color and growth by keeping the soil evenly moist and the plants nourished. Use a balanced liquid fertilizer diluted to half strength every month or so during the growing season.

Mints grow very well in containers, and not only because they keep the wandering spearmint confined. You can place pots just outside the kitchen door, where they'll be handy at harvest time. And herbs look pretty in pots. The look and the scent of herbs in terra cotta pots combine to give a patio, deck or steps a real Mediterranean flavor.

Harvest the leaves as you need them for recipes and garnish, taking care to cut stems just above the point where a pair of leaves meets the stem.

Every few years, rejuvenate established plants by digging up, dividing and replanting. Discard the older, woodier portions.

Spring

MOVE BEYOND SPEARMINT

There's more to mint than spearmint and peppermint, both well-known pungent and invasive types. Spearmint, botanically named Mentha spicata, will grow 2 feet tall; peppermint, botanically named Mentha piperita, stays a little shorter. Peppermint is a naturally occurring hybrid of spearmint and the wild water mint. Curly mint is a fancier, more decorative form of spearmint named Crispii. Hybrid variations of peppermint emit scents of oranges and lemons.

Try these, too:

- **Apple mint,** Mentha rotundifolia, possesses an apple flavor that is usually on the mild side. Plants can reach 3 feet, but if grown in a pot and harvested regularly for garnishing and cooking, will stay a shorter, more attractive 1 to 2 feet. By resisting the mint tendency to sprawl, the round-leaved apple mint ranks among the better-looking potted mints.

- **Pineapple mint** is a variation of apple mint that produces leaves with white or cream markings. The pineapple aroma is often quite faint, but it makes a long-lasting garnish. It grows about 1 foot tall.

- **Corsican mint,** Mentha requienii, is an odd-looking mint with very small – maybe 1/8-inch – leaves tightly packed on the plant and hugging the ground. This is a ground-cover mint for shade, more decorative than useful, with a fresh, slight peppermint scent. The plants rise a mere 1 to 2 inches, and that's under good, moist conditions. Plant it where it won't get stepped on, dried out or covered by bigger ground covers such as ajuga, ivy or pachysandra. Growing in pots is risky because Corsican won't tolerate drying out.

- **Ginger mint,** Mentha gentilis, bears red stems with leaves striped or flecked with golden markings. The leaves possess a ginger flavor. It grows about 1 foot tall.

HOW TO TAKE ALONG PLANTS WHEN YOU MOVE

So you're moving. But you don't want to leave your cherished plants behind. Here are some tips for taking along seeds, bulbs and cuttings of your favorites.

- **Learn the art of "heeling-in."** This is a temporary replanting in ground. Roots of herbaceous perennials and shrubs that you've dug up are covered loosely with light soil or mulch to protect the roots from drying out, but the plant is easy to pull out once the permanent site is ready.

- **Save seeds.** Many annuals, such as bachelor's buttons, poppies and sweet peas, are easy to propagate from seeds. Save the seed pots in an envelope or jar and replant them in the new location.

- **Take cuttings.** A shrub such as a viburnum, boxwood, rhododendron, rose or other woody plant that is impossible to move because of its size can go with you, too. Take cuttings to root and make new plants. Cuttings of half-ripened wood, about 3 to 4 inches long, taken in early summer and treated with a rooting powder, give the best results. If the time for making a cutting is wrong, ask the new owner if you could come back later for cuttings of a treasured plant.

- **Check the seasons.** Some long-lived flower bulbs, such as daffodils, are worth moving by digging them up in late spring or early summer, trimming off the foliage and storing in a paper bag until fall. Short-lived bulbs, such as tulips and small, inexpensive crocuses, may not be worth the effort, except where there is a strong sentimental attachment.

Spring

HOW TO MOVE DAYLILIES

Daylilies are among the easiest perennials to transplant successfully, whether you are moving or simply changing your gardens.

- To start, loosen the soil in a circular pattern several inches from the base of the plant; the bigger the plant, the farther out you go. Then sink your spade or fork at several points on the circular pattern to gently loosen the roots from the soil.

- Raise the clump of roots, as shown at right, shake off as much soil as possible to reveal the daylily's roots, then decide if it is ready for division. If there are several individual plants seen at the base of the clump, gently pull them apart.

- Place daylilies and other perennials and shrubs that will be replanted within a day or so in a cardboard box with their roots dampened. Keep the box in a shady area or covered to protect the roots from drying. Wrapping the plants in several layers of newspaper will also do the job if you moisten the roots first. When plants must stay out of the ground longer than a couple of days, replant them in pots holding good potting soil.

TURN ON TO SUMMER BULBS

One season of bulbs – the crocuses, hyacinths, tulips and daffodils – is over, just as a new one begins. That means it's time for the well-known lily, gladiolus, canna and dahlia, as well as the lesser-known nerine and agapanthus. Even though they emerge from different types of underground plant structures – bulbs, corms, tubers and rhizomes – they all fit into a loose confederation known as summer bulbs.

These reliable hot-weather flowers are easy to find and grow and come in an array of pale to bright colors. Because they originated in warm, sometimes tropical regions of Asia, South Africa and South America, they're right at home in our warm-to-hot and humid summers. Fortunately, too, our winters are mild enough for most of these bulbs to stay in the ground,

Dahlia

though wet soil in cold weather can cause rot.

Now that the soil is warming, you can plant these bulbs, then relax in anticipation of pretty flowers this summer. Their uses are as varied as their shapes and colors.

- Incorporate bulbs such as dahlias, cannas and lilies into beds of perennials or ornamental grasses.

- Combine tall lilies with ground covers to spark up dull plantings of ivy or vinca.

- Supplement spring-blooming shrubs such as azaleas with the summer color of lilies or dahlias.

- Grow them in large containers with annuals in complementary colors to create a focal point at doorways and steps. The agapanthus, with its tall stalks of blue flowers and strap-shaped leaves, looks wonderful in a half-barrel on a pool deck or patio.

- Plant the bulbs in well-drained soil. They rot in wet soil. Look at your proposed spot and try to recall if water still stood there a day after the last

Spring

What's blooming in May

- Deutzia
- Roses
- Clematis
- Irises
- Dianthus

- Peony
- Rhododendron
- Poppies
- Coreopsis
- Early alliums

- Madonna lily
- Fernleaf yarrow
- Foxglove
- Thalictrum
- Verbena

intense rainfall. If so, look for another area. The amount of light is also important. Most bulbs require at least morning sunlight and benefit from protection from afternoon sun. But cannas can take the rigor of hot afternoon summer sunshine.

Some Choices

Agapanthus, a native of South Africa and member of the lily family, grows from a rhizome that should be planted just below the soil line. It looks best in a large pot; heights range, depending on the variety, from 2 to 4 feet. Give it full sun. Flowers come in light blue to deep blue and white. Dig rhizomes and store in a frost-free area during the winter.

Dahlias originated in Mexico and offer as much variety of form and color (pure white to deep purple) as any garden flower. Dahlias make superb plants for the cutting garden. They grow from tubers (a slimmer version of a potato) set 2 to 3 inches deep. Dahlias need at least morning sun. The shorter varieties are well suited for containers. Increase the bushiness of plants by tip-pruning the main stems about three weeks after planting. Pluck spent flowers to keep them blooming. Some gardeners dig the tubers in the late fall and store them in a frost-free area; others leave them in the ground.

Gladiolus is an old favorite, loved for the rich blooms of pink, red, yellow, white and blue. The glad originated in South Africa but has been hybridized extensively (over 10,000 named varieties exist) to create the enormous range of colors we have today. A long-lasting cut flower, the gladi-

olus grows from a corm; the flower spikes grow 2 to 4 feet tall, depending on the variety. Set the corms four inches deep, 5 inches apart, in full sun. For a long season of bloom, set out corms, a dozen at a time, every other week. Leave them in the ground in winter. A variation on the traditional garden gladiolus is the Abyssinian gladiolus, which originated in Ethiopia. It bears white flowers with mahogany centers in late summer and grows about 3 feet tall. Dig the corms and store in a frost-free place. It is often sold under the genus acidanthera.

The **lily** represents another huge category of bulb plants, bearing showy, trumpet-shaped flowers in the entire color spectrum from white to nearly black. The Oriental and Asiatic hybrid lilies make particularly good garden flowers, bearing such well-known names as Casablanca, Star Gazer and Enchantment. Lily heights range from 2 to 10 feet tall, so check the heights carefully when you plant. The shorter ones are suited for containers. Plant the bulbs 6 inches deep and space them about a foot apart. They need sun, but shade during the hottest part of the day is important. Let them stay in the ground during the winter.

Nerine is another bulb from South Africa. It bears a cluster of flowers in late summer on a leafless stem. The flowers – white, pink, red or orange – are trumpet-shaped, with the petals curled back in an interesting way. The leaves come up after the flower stalks. Plants grow 14 to 36 inches tall. Set the bulbs 8 inches apart, so that the tops (the necks) are just above the soil line. They need a spot with morning sun and mulch to protect the bulbs from winter cold.

Spring

10 FLOWERS THAT BEAT THE HEAT

Spring is when you make choices about your garden. Some of those decisions ought to zero in on annuals and perennial flowers that can take the heat of Piedmont summer and, once established by regular watering in the spring, can tolerate a stretch of dry weather. Here are 10 that do that -- and do it beautifully. I call them "My Top 10 Summer Heroes." They're a mix of easy-to-grow, easy-to-find flowers. Many are well suited for containers, but those will require closer attention to watering, since pots dry out quickly. All but one require sun, but that's the point, isn't it? They can take it. And if it isn't really, really hot, and if the rain falls evenly, they'll be happy about that, too.

- **Begonias**. A superstar in light shade, the bedding wax begonia, 8 to 12 inches tall, bears white, pink or red blooms in nonstop fashion that would impress a NASCAR driver. In full sun, choose the varieties with bronze foliage, whose names came out of a bar: Brandy, Whiskey and Vodka. It's a long-blooming annual that sometimes survives winter in the Piedmont.

- **Canna**. An old-fashioned Southern favorite, the canna has fresh appeal thanks to relatively new, named varieties. These include Tropicanna, which is short enough for pots, and Bengal Tiger, with its distinctly striped foliage. Take care about placement. Some soar to 6 feet; the colors are strong yellows, reds, oranges and pinks. Don't try to pair them with some shy violet. Perennial in the Piedmont.

- **Coneflower**. Native of dry American prairies, the coneflower (Echinacea purpurea) bears beautiful daisy-shaped blooms that are pink, white, purple or rosy red. An easy-to-grow, long-lived perennial, the coneflower requires sun, grows 12 inches to about 4 feet tall, depending on the variety. Magnus is probably the most popular variety; it bears deep purple blooms about 7 inches in diameter with orange centers.

- **Cosmos**. Cosmos grows in beds along interstate highways, which tells you something about its fortitude in difficult conditions. Sow seeds where you want them to grow, or set out bedding plants about 12 inches apart. The color range is big: white, pink, rose, red, burgundy, yellow and orange. The height ranges from the compact Bright Lights, which grows about 12 inches, to Gazebo, which can hit 4 feet. It's an annual.

Canna

Cosmos

Coneflower

Gazania

- **Creeping zinnia**. It doesn't look like the traditional, upright zinnia. This one, Zinnia angustifolia, is lower, bushier, more floriferous and less subject to disease than the typical zinnia. Plants, about 12 inches tall, spread gracefully, making them suited for baskets, pots or the front edge of the sunny flowerbed. Flowers are small white, orange or gold daisies. Grow from seeds or plants.

Spring

- **Gazania**. Long popular in Florida, the gazania worked its way north in recent years, showing up increasingly in garden centers. They don't survive winter here, but prosper in the bright summer sun. The colors of hybrid gazanias are vivid solid reds, yellows and golds or interesting bicolors that give the effect of striped daisies. Set out plants when the soil is really warm in May.

- **Lantana**. One of the most useful tropical plants for hanging baskets, pots or flowerbeds, lantana shows up in an increasing range of gorgeous colors, including salmon pink, creamy white, and juicy orange. Most varieties usually grow 2 to 4 feet. Lantana plants sometimes survive warm winters in the Piedmont if they are well mulched.

- **Mandevilla**. Mandevillas came to the Piedmont area some years ago, and found their place – climbing mailbox posts – almost immediately. They also grow well on trellises and fences. The mandevilla most often seen here is the Alice du Pont, which bears funnel-shaped, bright pink flowers. Bring indoors before freezing weather or treat it like an annual. Pinch a young plant to make it fuller.

- **Pentas**. The plant for which many gardeners left geraniums in the dust, pentas hail from the tropics. A perfect plant for containers on sunny patios or steps, pentas produce light pink, orchid, white or red flowers for many months. The blooms attract butterflies. If grown in containers, you'll have to water pentas regularly.

- **Vinca**. Also known as Madagascar periwinkle, annual vinca comes in a wide range of colors, including white and many shades of pink, purple and red. Easy to grow in a sunny spot, vinca will bloom all summer with moderate watering during dry weather. Don't expect it to survive winter after all it's done for you since May.

WILD IN THE CITY: ADORN AN URBAN GARDEN WITH FLOWERS OF FIELD AND FOREST

Sometimes, wildflowers just appear. A Queen Anne's lace among the marigolds. Sky-blue chicory at the edge of the lawn. Butterfly weed along a country road. But usually we plant them. Even in the city, where sun-drenched areas laced with pavement cry out for something natural.

Wildflowers – the common term for native perennial plants – are both easy and difficult to grow. Some resist even small changes in their native environment; others are so adaptable that success is practically guaranteed. Interest in these native plants has grown so in recent years that most garden catalogs and many garden centers usually offer a selection. To grow wildflowers, keep some things in mind:

- **When shopping**, either by catalog or in person, find out how the plants were propagated, or multiplied. Horticultural propagation by growing from seed, root division or stem cuttings is acceptable for multiplying the stock. But digging up plants in the wild, and potting and selling them depletes the native population and should always be discouraged.

- **If you own land**, such as a family homeplace that is being developed for residential or commercial purposes, do not hesitate to dig up and move the native plants growing there. Even if they are on the fringe of the property, their chances of surviving the heavy equipment and construction work are probably nil.

- **Learn about these plants as you acquire them**. Some woodland plants, such as the white trillium, prosper in moist shade. Grow them near azaleas and rhododendrons. Others, such as Indian paint brush, do better at the edge of the woods, where they get some sunlight while in bloom. Put them with the dogwoods. Wildflowers of prairie origin, such as sunflowers and black-eyed susans, prosper in sunny, warm areas. Put them along the driveway, where heat rises in summertime.

- **Understand their nature**. Many wildflowers, such as the trilliums and the dwarf iris, have very short bloom seasons. Some, such as Virginia spring beauty, disappear in the summer, but return the following spring. Accept it and enjoy it. Make up for short blooms and disappearing foliage with the long-lasting Queen Anne's lace and the sunny daisies. Throw in the cardinal flower for a late-summer blast of fire-engine red.

SOME GOOD WILDFLOWER CHOICES

❀ **Monarda didyma**. Through the summer, bee balm produces colorful blossoms on plants that can reach 4 to 5 feet. Butterflies and hummingbirds, as well as bees, are enticed by this flamboyant plant. It needs moist soil and benefits from division and replanting every few years. Discard the aging center of the plant.

❀ **Hemerocallis fulva**. Though originally from Eurasia, the orange daylily settled down like a native and blooms extensively in summer along roadsides and in meadows. Though less appreciated than hybrid daylilies, the orange daylily is a natural winner, too. Propagate by dividing the roots.

❀ **Arisaema triphyllum**, known to most as Jack-in-the-pulpit, gets its name from the solitary figure standing under a green hood that resembles a pulpit. It grows about 2 feet tall and does best in a damp, wooded place. Constant moisture makes better plants. Sow seeds from the ripened "Jack" about 1/4 inch deep in the fall. It should bloom during the second spring.

❀ **Aquilegia canadensis**, the Eastern columbine, bears nodding blossoms above deeply cut foliage in late spring to early summer. Flowers are long-lasting when cut for bouquets. Plant in moist soil that isn't too rich. If given a place of their own in the garden, columbines self-sow and produce new plants that bloom the next year.

❀ **Trillium grandiflorum**, commonly called great white trillium, will prosper in moist shade with woodsy soil. Its parts – petals, sepals and leaves – are arranged in threes, giving rise to the name. White flowers, which fade to pink, appear in early to mid-spring. Plant the rootstock, called rhizomes,

Jack-in-the-pulpit

in the fall, about 2 inches deep. Grows about 1 foot tall.

❀ **Caltha palustris**, the marsh marigold, bears golden yellow, buttercup-shaped flowers in spring on plants about 2 feet tall. Marsh marigold flourishes in very damp soil.

❀ **Dicentra exima**, the fringed bleeding heart, requires filtered sunlight and bears stems lined with drooping flowers in mid- to late spring. Divide the roots very carefully every few years.

Spring

❀ **Echinacea purpurea**, the purple coneflower, ranks among the easiest of the summer daisies and prospers in warm, sunny areas. Flowers of this long-lived perennial have a domed center and purplish-pink petals.

❀ **Hepatica americana**, round-lobed hepatica, will prosper in the shade of trees or a shady rock garden. The flowers are less significant than the attractive foliage. New foliage appears right after the flowers bloom and lasts through the winter.

❀ **Lobelia cardinalis**, the cardinal flower, bears tall spikes of red flowers in late summer. It requires damp, rich soil and light-to-full sun. Lobelia isn't too difficult to grow from seeds sown in early spring.

❀ **Mertensia virginica**, the Virginia bluebell, produces stalks of dangling flowers that start out as pink buds and turn into blue, bell-shaped flowers. The foliage is gone by July, so give this plant a neighbor that will sprawl and conceal the blank space. Part shade is best.

❀ **Thalictrum dioicum**, meadow rue, is a graceful perennial that bears flowers in mid- to late spring. The combination of lacy leaves and feathery flowers creates a dainty effect. It needs light shade and soil on the dry side.

❀ **Tiarella cordifola**, the foam flower, is among the most popular wildflowers for gardens. It bears a fluffy, white stalk of flowers in late spring and makes a nice edger because the medium-green foliage is long lasting and attractive.

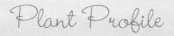

Plant Profile

ALOE VARIEGATA

NAME:
Aloe (AL-o) is a succulent plant usually grown indoors; in fact, it won't survive winter outdoors.

HOME GROUND:
Aloes are natives of dry, sunny places in Africa and the Mediterranean region.

VITAL STATS:
The common aloe, Aloe vera, grows pale green leaves 18 to 20 inches long. Smaller forms, such as Aloe variegata, grow only about 12 inches tall. This variety has heavily striped leaves and is the best-looking aloe.

HISTORICAL REFERENCES:
Aloe is mentioned in the Gospel of John and writings of the first-century naturalist, Pliny.

GROWING TIPS:
This good indoor plant will prosper in bright household light. When replanting, don't set the plant deeper than it grew before transplanting. Fertilize lightly: An established plant needs a dose of half-strength fertilizer once a year, in the autumn. Let soil dry out between waterings.

WOULDN'T YOU LIKE TO KNOW?
How did somebody figure out that juice of aloe eased the pain of a small burn when a cut stem is rubbed against the wound? That's why a potted aloe is a common sight at kitchen windows.

HOW TO CARE FOR HYDRANGEAS

Lots of potted hydrangeas go to mothers and grand-mothers on Mother's Day. I'll bet some of you are already wondering what to do with these beauties after they've graced the living room. And perhaps you are wondering about that ageless hydrangea issue of keeping the blue blooms blue and the pink ones pink.

Unlike the Christmas poinsettia, your hydrangea should stay with you for many years, a happy symbol of love.

Plant it outdoors in a partly shady spot in good, well-drained soil. Don't be misled by its current size; it has been treated with a growth retardant to keep it short and shapely. Planted outdoors, hydrangeas usually sold for Mother's Day (Hydrangea macrophylla) will grow, and rather rapidly, about 3 feet tall and wide, and possibly bigger, depending on which named variety it is. So give it space. Keep the plant well watered through the summer after you put it outdoors.

This type of hydrangea blooms on the prior year's growth, and the buds are susceptible to freeze damage in early spring. Covering small plants with a cardboard box on especially cold nights (under 20 degrees) may help avoid this. Choosing a spot where the plant is protected from winter wind also helps.

Now the color issue. Most varieties of florists' hydrangeas tend to be either red/pink or blue, although some can go either way, depending on the soil's pH, its acid-alkaline balance.

Soils in the Piedmont are on the acidic side, which is why most of these hydrangeas appear pale blue after some time in the garden. Acidic soil encourages aluminum uptake into the plant and bluer blooms. Using fertilizer formulated for acid-loving plants may be all you need to do to keep the blooms blue. But small additions of aluminum sulfate to the soil will encour-age a deeper blue. Buy a small amount, and follow the directions and recommended amounts to the letter. If your potted hydrangea is pink, that means it has been treated with high levels of phosphorus to keep any aluminum in the soil from moving into the plants.

Outdoors, that is a trickier thing, but if your pink hydrangea begins fading to blue, sprinkle about 1 cup of ground limestone per 10 square feet around the plant. That should help move the soil toward a neutral or slightly alkaline state.

Unlike the Christmas poinsettia, your hydrangea should stay with you for many years, a happy symbol of love.

Spring

ONE-POT WONDERS:
MAKE A GARDEN IN A SINGLE CONTAINER

When spring comes, too many apartment gardeners are digging deep into their souls and coming up with – guess what – one lonely red geranium.

No offense meant to geraniums. But you could do more with your stoop, deck or patio than a single pot of geraniums (or impatiens or petunias or begonias), which by July might get a tad boring. Instead, think about an artful combination – small-scale, of course. A variety of herbs or flowers, just like the big gardens have. All in one large pot you'll enjoy looking at every day. Successful combinations result from

- Choosing plants that grow well together because they have similar needs for water and sunlight. Put the sun lovers – petunias, pentas, marigolds – together. Make the shade lovers – impatiens, begonias, coleus – good companions in a pot.

- Arranging them to best advantage, mixing plants of different heights. The taller choices, such as pentas or rosemary, grow to a majestic 18 inches or so; the mid-sized ones, like marigolds, huddle around the middle. The low sprawlers drape gracefully over the pot's edges. Plant labels often tell you the plant's mature size.

- Mixing colors and textures boldly. A mixed bouquet of colors is one of the prettiest sights of summer. Don't be a wimp about this. Choose flower colors you like and amaze yourself at how well they go together. Herb combinations produce fascinating arrays of curled, ridged and scalloped

textures – and wonderful scents, too. Some will even surprise you with their blooms.

- Paying attention to the everyday details of watering and grooming. A garden in a pot is like your pet. Feed and water it carefully. Keep it trimmed. But you won't have to take it to the vet.

Marigolds, petunias and pentas share a pot.

Tips For Success

- Bigger pots, 12 inches in diameter and up, allow you to choose more kinds of herbs or flowers.

- Use packaged potting soil because it is lightweight and will allow the roots to spread best, even in tight quarters.

- Pots, especially the classic terra-cotta ones, dry out fast. In warm weather, plants will require watering daily, even more often when it's blistering hot and dry. Even plants in plastic pots, which hold moisture longer, demand close attention in hot weather.

- Plants whose roots are packed into the tight quarters of a flower pot especially need the boost of liquid fertilizer. Use it all summer in the watering can.

- Because you'll look at your potted garden close up, keep it neat and tidy by picking off spent flowers or yellowing leaves. Many annuals, including petunias and marigolds, bloom longer if you regularly pinch off spent flowers. Harvest the herbs regularly to enjoy and keep them from outgrowing the pot.

- Choose flowers that bloom for a long time. But when something's done, take it out of the pot and replace it with a fresh plant.

Spring

It's time to...

- Plant okra and lima bean seeds, and keep setting out young vegetable plants, including tomatoes, peppers, eggplant, cucumbers and melons.

- Check your rose bushes to see if any suckers are sprouting below the graft union, that knobby spot at the base of the plant. Cut them off neatly with your pruning shears.

- Make your last plantings of gladiolus and dahlias. Pinch tips of your chrysanthemums once they get about 6 inches tall. Pinching every month or so until early July will produce better plants.

- Check azaleas for iron deficiency. If azalea leaves appear yellow but the green veins are visible, spray with iron chelate.

- Fertilize rhododendrons with an acid fertilizer as blooms fade, at the rate directed on the package. Prune spent flowers.

- Begin looking over vegetable plants every day and picking off harmful insects.

- Pull out the pansies and plant summer flowers.

- Sow seeds of zinnias, cleome, portulaca, cosmos and morning glory directly in the garden for summer bloom.

- Finish filling pots for steps and balconies with pentas, geraniums, heliotrope, lantana, begonias and other flowers good for containers.

- Start practicing the fine art of deadheading – the timely removal of spent blooms from annuals and perennials. It makes the plants bloom longer.

- Put mulch on the vegetable garden, now that the soil is warm.

- Remember to wear sunscreen when you work outdoors.

- Prune the tips of chrysanthemums to keep them low and compact and encourage branches.

- Stay on the lookout for bagworm bags on evergreens, particularly arborvitae and junipers; cut off the bags with scissors or knife and discard in the trash.

AN OLD FAVORITE: GERANIUMS

The geranium is a flower even nongardeners can grow. This potted plant, botanically named Pelargonium, blooms all summer, except during stretches of high temperatures. But it doesn't survive Piedmont winters outdoors. The Pelargonium is a native of the warm and sunny climate of South Africa; traders took them to Europe at least 300 years ago.

What do geraniums require? Not a lot. But they do need well-drained soil and full sun from spring through fall. To confuse matters, they need protection from the hottest summer afternoon sun. Geraniums growing in pots perform best if the roots fill most of the pot, so don't move them up to larger containers very often. The plants also prefer soil that is on the dry side, so let the pot or bed dry out slightly before watering. Their fertilizer of choice is low in nitrogen, high in phosphorous and potassium. Although this is an annual, people often save their plants through the winter by placing the pots in a frost-free sun porch. Just don't expect much bloom in the dim light of winter.

Spring

Ask Nancy

Answers to some common problems

WHAT ARE SOME SHRUBS WHOSE FOLIAGE I CAN USE IN FLOWER ARRANGEMENTS?

Many popular evergreens are quite useful in arrangements. Some, such as red-berried hollies and nandina, are so identified with Christmas decorations that they aren't used much at other times of the year. But there are plenty of other choices, starting with, dare I say it, the glossy-leafed or variegated ligustrums. The leaves are small enough to suit a medium-to-tall arrangement, and the stems are bendable enough to work with.

Some other good choices are eucalyptus, aucuba (looks good solo in fireplaces), broom (the flowers are pink or yellow in spring). English laurel, kolkwitzia, deutzia and spirea. All are vigorous shrubs that would not be harmed by judicious cutting through the year and have foliage that looks interesting enough to go in an arrangement.

WHAT IS THE BEST WAY TO STORE LEFTOVER SEEDS THIS SPRING?

Some seeds have a long shelf life, some a very short one, but all seeds need good storage conditions to remain viable. Put the seed packets in a glass jar; place the lid on tightly and put the jar in a refrigerator.

Once you decide to use the seeds again, test their viability this way: Put a dozen or so seeds between damp paper towels placed in a closed plastic bag. Keep the bag at room temperature and check in a few days to see if the seeds are germinating and the towels still damp.

To make planting the seeds worthwhile, the germination rate should be over 50 percent. This should occur by the expected germination time stated on the package for that variety of flower or vegetable.

WHAT IS A PERENNIAL VINE THAT WOULD BLOOM SPRING TO FALL? HOW ABOUT WISTERIA?

Sorry, but wisteria blooms just in the spring. Untamed, it gets out of control. And seedling plants may take years to produce blooms.

That said, I have some other ideas. There's a great Chinese trumpet vine on the market named Morning Calm. It bears peachy tangerine blooms in summer, grows quickly and offers a far more dramatic display (less invasive, too) than the American trumpet vine of the roadside.

Still, that leaves spring and fall to take care of. If you have space, why not consider a mixture? You could put in a spring-flowering clematis to get the show going.

And, for sheer drama, nothing beats the moonflower, a relative of the common morning glory. The annual plant, which you can grow from seeds or young plants from a garden center, bears big white blooms up to 6 inches across with a shape resembling morning glories. They open in a matter of minutes during the late afternoon and stay open all night. It's a sight to behold as the white flowers unfurl. Really worth scheduling a party.

Two other choices to consider:

Mandevilla, which will bloom spring to fall on vines that grow reasonably fast. The flowers are usually bright pink. The disadvantage is that mandevilla won't survive freezing weather. Kept in a pot, mandevilla can come inside for the winter.

Gold Flame honeysuckle, which bears coral and yellow blooms for much (but not all) of the time between late spring and autumn. It grows vigorously.

All these vines are reasonably easy to grow.

June

THE BAD AND THE BEAUTIFUL

Break out the sprinklers. Go on a slug-bashing crusade.

Massacre those beetles. Hold it. This is not war; it is

gardening. The daylilies are beautiful, the hostas lush and

tender. The emerging perennials a pleasure to anticipate.

It's June. So much good. Some pretty bad stuff to deal with.

Like caterpillars and beetles. It may rain nicely. It may not.

The perennials may do as you expect. Some may sulk, in their

own way demanding cooler or hotter, wetter or drier weather.

Still, it's June. Beautiful June. Cool enough to enjoy gardening

and get things done. Warm enough to say the T-shirt-and-

sandals season is here for good. The potential

of tomato plants set out in April, of marigolds

planted in early May, is here.

Let's enjoy it.

Summer

DAYLILY MAY BE THE PERFECT PERENNIAL

The colors: ice-cream-delicious shades of peach, raspberry, tangerine, lemon and grape.

The time: early summer. Put them together and you get ... daylilies.

And no perennial makes life easier. Got to move? In the chill of January or the heat of July, daylilies will pack up and go with you. Need to cover a steep bank? Daylilies will do the job.

Hanker for an all-pastel garden? A bed of vivid reds and rich purples? Take your pick among the 30,000 named varieties.

And no plant ranks as easier to grow.

New leaves emerge in early spring, turning into arching foliage that looks good well into fall (if slugs don't take their bite out of it). The earliest varieties bloom in May, but daylilies really star in June and early July.

The common name of daylily describes the flower's life span and its appearance. The bloom resembles a lily because it belongs to the lily plant family, liliaceae. Each bloom lasts just a day, but a well-established plant produces many stems, and each stem produces many buds to keep the show going.

Combine early, mid-season and late varieties, and you get a longer show.

While daylilies require much less care than many plants, they prosper with attention. Give them good, well-drained garden soil and at least six hours of sun a day for good growth and bloom. I never get very good bloom from daylilies planted in partial shade. Slow growth, less vigorous plants and fewer blooms result. However, the darker colors do better if kept away from hot afternoon summer sun. Grow them in morning-to-noon sun.

Plant daylilies anytime -- and I am not kidding. People tell me amazing stories about digging up their grandmother's plants just before the home was sold and keeping the roots in bread wrappers for weeks, even months. The plants survived – and bloomed.

Still, fall ranks as the best time to move daylilies. Simply dig up the clumps and separate the crowns at the base of the plant. Use a knife or pruning shears. Dig, divide and replant when the clump gets crowded, or when you want to share a plant. When you replant, set the crown about 1 inch below the soil line.

Except for slugs, pests don't bother daylilies much. Where these leaf-eating menaces appear – the evidence is chewed young leaves – sentence them to capital punishment. Use a slug remedy, such as a shallow pan of beer or slug pellets. Thrips, a type of insect, also can show up, usually deforming the flower buds and leaves. Spray with Orthene.

Summer

COLORFUL SHRUBS CAN BRIGHTEN SUMMER'S GREEN

While many gardeners are diversifying their plant collections to create a year-round landscape, many others still see spring as the season for flowering shrubs. They stock up on azaleas, camellias and rhododendrons and neglect to put in vitex, abelias, hydrangeas and rose of sharon. All these bloom in summer, when much of the landscape is green. They add drama and color, are easy to grow and usually free of pest problems.

So step right up and meet beautyberry, clethra, caryopteris and buddleia. You can work them into your landscape as accents -- either solo or in three of one kind, such as by a bold stroke of beautyberry's ripe purple berries or caryopteris's feathery blue blossoms in late summer.

All are deciduous, meaning they lose their leaves for the winter, but don't let that discourage you. Forsythia is also deciduous and ranks among the area's most popular shrubs. Plant these shrubs where their leafless form won't bother you in winter – the back fence, among the perennials also asleep for the winter, or in a corner. I would not hesitate to buy any of these plants while they are in bloom or the berries are out. That's when you can see their summer beauty, which would not be so obvious in spring or fall.

If you plant them now, pay careful attention to watering through the summer and the dry weeks of early autumn, since roots won't be well established.

Buddleia

Hydrangea

Callicarpa (beautyberry)

MEET THE SHRUBS

Callicarpa dichotoma. Often called purple beautyberry, it bears small, pinkish-lavender flowers in midsummer on a 4-foot shrub that spreads about the same width. The purple, inedible berries appear in late summer. Beautyberry requires full sun and will tolerate dry soil.

Caryopteris clandonensis. This shrub is also called bluebeard. It grows 2 feet tall and bears feathery-tipped flowers from mid- to late summer. Dark Knight is a deep blue variety that grows about 2 feet tall. Bluebeard requires sun and loose, well-drained soil.

Buddleia. It has recently become extremely popular for gardens because it is easy to grow and the flowers attract butterflies. Buddleias require sun and are easy to move. Many varieties offer gardeners a choice of colors including white, pinks, lilacs and violets, such as Nahno Purple.

Clethra alnifolia. This is one of those rare plants that prosper in shady, very damp areas. The fragrant flowers, white or pale pink, last a month or longer in midsummer. Clethra grows slowly to about 8 feet in moist soil. Leaves are golden yellow in autumn.

Summer

HOW TO ATTRACT HUMMINGBIRDS AND BUTTERFLIES

To attract butterflies, think of flowers that smell good and grow in colorful clusters that give butterflies a spot to land. Good choices are buddleia, lantana and verbena.

For hummingbirds, look to blooms that are red, tubular and odorless, such as cardinal flower or pineapple sage.

And plant in the sun.

Other good choices include abelia, achillea, columbine, butterfly weed (Asclepias curassavica), Tangerine Beauty bignonia, Shasta daisy, cleome, Moonbeam coreopsis, dill, Joe-pye weed, gaura, gomphrena, helianthemum, lobelia, scarlet mallow, Snowflake candytuft, lythrum, parsley, patrinia, penstemon, pentas, salvia, scabiosa, Autumn Joy sedum, goldenrod, veronica and zinnia.

When butterflies and hummingbirds turn up, you may find them as interesting as flowers.

A hairstreak butterfly on a Verbena bonariensis

Gomphrena

Butterfly weed

WISE WATERING TECHNIQUES

Summer has arrived, bearing a long stretch of hot, usually dry weather. So shake the dust off those watering cans, drag out the sprinkler and hose and lay down that drip-irrigation system. Your flowers and vegetables, new lush lawn, young trees and shrubs are depending on you.

If you haven't mulched your flowerbeds and vegetable gardens, do it this minute. This is important because mulch keeps the soil evenly moist and reduces the rate of evaporation. It also cuts down on weeds and looks nice. About 3 inches of grass clippings, shredded bark, straw or decomposing leaves should do the trick.

Still, watering is essential. But you will have choices to make about what to water, how and when.

"When" is easy. Water in the morning, when the air is cooler and evaporation lower. This will also give the leaves time to dry off before nightfall, reducing the risk of disease.

"What" to water means picking the plants and crops whose survival and productivity depend on a steady stream of water. These include your vegetable garden, which will simply shut down or develop kinky problems without a predictable inch of water a week. For example, tomatoes, the home gardener's favorite vegetable, especially suffer from erratic watering in hot weather. The fruit may crack or develop a dark blemish at the blossom end, which is called blossom-end rot.

Also in the "must-water" category are trees and shrubs planted in the past year and a half, valuable plants that are still getting adjusted to their new surroundings. New lawns planted since last fall also fit this category.

It is the technique, the "how" of watering, that many people get wrong. Shallow watering – a quick sprinkle that merely wets the top inch or two of soil – encourages plants to grow shallow roots. That makes them even more vulnerable to drought.

Amazingly, gardeners tell me they think they are helping their plants when they sprinkle lightly every day. But a lot of that water is lost to evaporation, especially on hot days. With less frequent but longer watering, you push the water deep into the soil; 5 or 6 inches deep is good.

EFFICIENT WATERING WITH A HOSE

If you're using a hose, three pieces of equipment will help you water more efficiently: a "breaker" nozzle with many small holes designed to emit a gentle stream of water, an extension arm to reach close to the soil and a shutoff valve.

If all your plants are in containers, a watering can should suffice. Do not use the forceful gun-type nozzles that are better suited for washing cars; they can knock over plants, even dislodge roots; they also create a lot of runoff.

If hand watering is too time-consuming, use a soaker hose or drip irrigation system that will emit water right over the root zones and avoid wasteful runoff. Soaker hoses can be placed in the garden and topped with mulch.

Water should reach about 6 inches deep for optimum root growth. Use a trowel to measure how deeply the moisture is penetrating.

WHEN TO WATER

* If you walk across the grass and the blades don't spring back, the lawn needs water. Look for a telltale footprint.

* If you scratch the soil in your garden and it is dry before you get 2 inches deep, the bed needs water.

* Plants wilting in late afternoon may simply be suffering from the summer heat. But if they're wilting in the morning, they need water.

HOW TO CONSERVE WATER

* Use a watering can instead of a hose on container plants. You'll probably use less water.

* Get a drip, trickle or seeping hose for the flower an vegetable beds. Such hoses direct water to the roots and reduce runoff.

* Know how much you're watering. Mark a 1-inch depth on a coffee can and time how long it takes for your sprinkler to put out 1 inch of water.

* Aim for 1 inch of water a week.

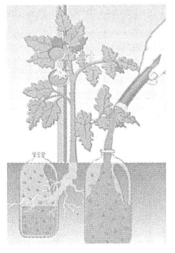

To make an easy, instant watering device, punch small holes in the bottom and sides of a plastic milk or juice jug. Sink it into the ground near your tomato plants. Keep it filled with water and liquid fertilizer.

Summer

INSTALLING A DRIP IRRIGATION SYSTEM

Before inserting ooze tubes
Place the irrigation hose between all the rows of plants to be watered. Make a smooth curve at each end.

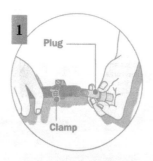

1

Inserting a plug
Slip a clamp loosely around one end of the irrigation hose. Insert the plug and tighten the clamp.

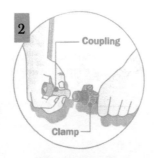

2

Garden hose coupling
At the other end of the hose, slip a clamp on loosely. Insert the hose coupling, tighten and connect to the garden hose.

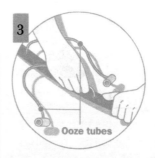

3

Inserting ooze tubes
Use an awl or a nail to punch holes in the irrigation hose at intervals for each plant. Insert ooze tubes into holes.

4

Watering the plants
To soak the roots, place the water-emitting end of the ooze tube on the ground by each plant. Turn on the water.

Shallow watering — a quick sprinkle that merely wets the top inch or two of soil — encourages plants to grow shallow roots. That makes them even more vulnerable to drought.

Summer

It's time to...

- Pick off spent blooms of daylilies, taking care not to disturb buds yet to open.

- Rake away yellowed or brown daffodil foliage, a sure sign that spring is over. Sow seeds of quick-growing plants such as zinnias or cleome on the bare ground.

- Set up a friendly competition to see who gets the first ripe tomato in the office or club, on the street or within the extended family.

- Pinch back the tips of main shoots on chrysanthemum plants to encourage branching and more blooms this fall.

- Replace your pansies in beds and containers with fresh bedding plants for the summer.

- Check to see which perennials need light-weight stakes to keep them neat and upright.

- Prune and shape climbing and shrub roses after they finish blooming.

- Finish planting summer bulbs such as gladiolus and dahlias.

- Check every day the hanging baskets and pots you keep outdoors. They'll probably need watering.

- Look for seedlings of Lenten roses, transplant to a shady area and keep them well watered through the summer.

- Snip off spent flowers of annuals such as snapdragons to keep them blooming.

- Pay close attention to harvesting vegetables at their peak.

- Protect your ripening figs from bird assault by covering the bush with a net.

SPRUCE UP LANDSCAPE TO ATTRACT HOME BUYERS

If you're thinking about selling your house this year, or if you'd just like to spruce up the place, now is the time to do things that will put your landscape in ship-shape condition.

Your goal should be to make it look neat. This neat exterior – an evenly green lawn, well-groomed shrubbery and freshly pruned trees – impresses potential buyers not just because it looks good. It also expresses a feeling of care for the property starting at the front edge of the lawn.

A presale spruce-up for the landscape shouldn't require much money. You can do some of the work yourself, but hire an arborist for tree trimming.

Rake the lawn, getting up all stray leaves and debris. Keep it mowed regularly. Keep the lawn's edges sharp along driveways and walks.

Are the shrubs getting in the way of the house? Overgrown hollies, boxwood and other broadleaf evergreens can be pruned to make them the right size and shape. Flowering evergreens such as azaleas, camellias and pieris should not be pruned until after they bloom because the flowers are an asset. Remove shrubs that detract from the landscape, such as a leggy ligustrum or diseased red-tips.

Are there any dead trees standing on the property? Is there deadwood clogging the beauty of your shade trees? Get them removed. Do low tree limbs prevent people from seeing the house well from the street? Get them trimmed.

Clean the gutters; sweep the roof of leaves and twigs. Put fresh pine straw around trees and under shrubs.

Plant colorful patches of annual flowers at the door, around the mailbox or lamppost and as a strip in front of the shrubs to give your home a fresh, welcoming look.

Summer

What's blooming in June

❀ Roses   ❀ Portulaca   ❀ Torch lily

❀ Hydrangeas   ❀ Gladiolus   ❀ Garden phlox

❀ Daylilies   ❀ Lilies   ❀ Purple coneflower

❀ Coreopsis   ❀ Butterfly weed   ❀ Rose-of-sharon

❀ Sunflowers   ❀ Shasta daisies   ❀ Vitex

SPOTS ON DOGWOOD LEAVES AREN'T FATAL

Don't panic if you see spots or grayish powder on your dogwood or crape myrtle trees. They aren't usually fatal, just bad to look at.

The problem sometimes occurs when there is a spell of cool weather well into early summer. A disease called powdery mildew appears. The grayish powdery fungus turns red crape myrtle flowers a mush gray, makes dogwood leaves gray and changes elm leaves silvery yellow.

Spray with a powdery mildew fungicide as soon as the problem appears. Many newer crape myrtle varieties are more resistant to this fungus and mildew than are red varieties. Kousa dogwoods are less affected than are native flowering dogwood trees.

FIGHT ZINNIA FUNGUS

Summer heat seems here to stay, and zinnias rank among the stars of the season. But, when the weather is rainy, one problem runs rampant on these colorful plants. It's a leaf blight, usually due to a fungus named Alternaria zinniae, that leads to small reddish brown spots with grayish centers on the leaves. The fungus sometimes affects stems and flowers. A plant seriously affected by this fungus turns brown, then dies.

The solution is to pick off leaves at the first sign of infection. Take out seriously infected plants or dying plants to reduce the risk that the fungus will spread to healthy ones nearby. Wind and raindrops spread the fungus.

Spray the plants regularly with a fungicide that states on the label it is effective against the problem. When watering the plants with a sprinkler can, try to keep from wetting the foliage.

Be on guard against this problem as soon as you get zinnia plants. Spray regularly to protect them. Some zinnias, such as the excellent spreading type named Zinnia angustifolia, resist the fungus to a remarkable degree, even without spraying. This zinnia, which bears gold, white and orange flowers, tolerates summer heat amazingly well.

Summer

LEAF GALL NOT AS TERRIBLE AS IT LOOKS

It appears in the best of gardens, shocking people when the leaves turn thick and fleshy or develop an ugly deformity that resembles nothing they've ever seen. It's enough to make a gardener run for cover.

While this problem appears truly awful, it is not difficult to deal with. You just remove the offending portion from plant society and put it in the trash.

That is after you've recovered from the sight of this weird growth, which is caused by a fungus named Exobasidium vaccinii. You can get by with the common, descriptive name of leaf gall.

Leaf gall usually shows up in the spring, with just a few on each plant, and becomes most noticeable after the flowers are gone and you have a clearer view of the foliage.

Azalea and camellia foliage grows thicker and becomes fleshy.

Oddly enough, sometimes only half a leaf may develop this thickened fleshiness, the other half remaining normal. However, the fungus may also affect the flowers or the seed pods.

The flowers turn into hard, often waxy, irregular gall, often covered with a white dusting. The seed pods turn fleshy. I notice this more often on the seed pods of camellia sasanqua, the fall-flowering camellias.

Except for disfiguration of the plant – and shock to the gardener – leaf gall should be handled simply. A quick snip of the affected leaf or bloom and its immediate neighbor will suffice.

If you have a severe infestation with many affected leaves, or if your plant is growing in a greenhouse, spray the plants with zineb or ferbam just before the leaves unroll in spring and 10 days later.

POLLINATE SQUASH YOURSELF

If your yellow squash or zucchini plants are not bearing, lack of pollination may be the cause.

Squash plants have male and female flowers, and if bees or other insects fail to pollinate the plants, the baby fruit of a female flower won't develop nicely.

But you can perform the bee's pollinating job yourself. In early morning, pick a male squash flower (long stem) and brush the pollen onto the stigma of female flowers (short stem, tiny yellow-or-green squash-to-be at the base).

INCREASE YOUR SHRUBS BY TAKING CUTTINGS

- Many old-fashioned shrubs, including shrub roses, spirea, hydrangea and azaleas, can be propagated by cuttings you will root in small pots for eventual planting in your garden.

- By early to mid-June, the new growth should be hardened enough for you to have a reasonable chance of getting the cutting to root. A rooting hormone powder in which you dip the cut end of the stem will aid the process.

- Make your cuttings about 3 inches long, and use clean shears that have been disinfected with household bleach (10 percent bleach and 90 percent water).

- The cut end should be semi-mature wood located just below the soft green wood at the tip of a branch. This green wood could rot before rooting; more mature hardwood won't root readily.

- It's best to plant the cuttings immediately, so they don't dry out. But pots don't have to be large, and you can enclose them in a plastic bag placed loosely over the cuttings and held up with a small stake. Keep the bag loose to prevent overheating the cuttings.

- Rooting will take some weeks; a gentle pull on the cutting will reveal how the process is going. When the cuttings take root, transplant them to individual pots.

Summer

PEST OR PAL?
HOW TO TELL GOOD BUGS FROM BAD

Crawling, hopping, flying, the bugs of summer are on their way to a flower or vegetable near you. Some, like the lady beetles, are worth keeping. Others, such as the tomato hornworm, deserve a quick exit. Identification is key; the battle, not terribly difficult.

Learn to identify insects, especially the beneficial ones, so you will recognize and not harm them.

And think about whether a harmful insect is actually doing much damage. This strategy of letting nature take its course can be successful with native insects, which have natural predators.

Adopt habits that encourage beneficial bugs to hang around. Unless you've been spraying a lot, most beneficials are out there naturally. Mail-order companies sell them; sometimes you see them at garden centers, in little bags, ready to go. Regular and often unnecessary spraying with insecticide will kill both harmful and beneficial insects. Even insecticidal soap sprays, one of the mildest approaches to garden pest control, can harm some larvae or adult beneficials. Insecticides will also eliminate the insect populations that beneficials need to live on. They will either starve or go somewhere else.

PESTS
Japanese beetle

Iridescent, bluish-green heads and shiny copper-brown wings could make these beetles the star of a sci-fi movie. Instead they aim for roses, plums, peaches, grapevines, cherries, raspberries and some vegetables.

Control: Use Sevin or pyrethrin or knock beetles into a jar of soapy water. Milk spore disease, spread onto lawns, is the natural enemy of the beetle's white grubs.

Colorado potato beetle
Ten black stripes identify these beetles, which can defoliate potatoes, tomatoes, eggplant and peppers. They also dine on the fruits of tomatoes and eggplants.

Control: Use a clean straw mulch; pick off beetles and their orange eggs from the leaves. For heavy infestations, use Sevin or pyrethrin insecticide.

Cucumber beetles
They're striped or spotted and affect most kinds of vegetables by feeding on foliage and new growth, as well as the crop.

Control: Clean out all plant debris at the close of growing season; pick off beetles; use Sevin or pyrethrum insecticide.

Tomato hornworm
This lime-green weirdo eats the leaves and fruit of tomatoes, potatoes, eggplants and peppers, but it's easy to get rid of.

Control: Simply pick it off the plants. Or use the caterpillars' natural enemy, Bacillus thuringiensis. Other controls: Sevin and pyrethrum.

Cabbage looper
Light green with pale stripes, the destructive cabbage looper caterpillar advances on cabbage, lettuce, tomatoes and other crops. Telltale signs are large, oddly

Japanese beetle

Colorado potato beetle

Cucumber beetles

Summer

Tomato hornworm

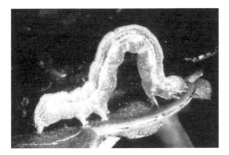
Cabbage looper

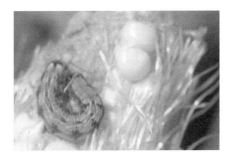
Corn earworm

shaped holes in leaves. The looper also puts holes in tomatoes and cabbage heads.

Control: Handpick the caterpillars. Use Bacillus thuringiensis or pyrethrum.

Corn earworm
Plump, destructive and easily recognized, this striped caterpillar is usually green or brown and grows up to 2 inches long. Chief targets are corn, squash, tomatoes, okra, strawberries, peas, peppers and eggplants.

Control: Apply a drop of mineral oil inside the tip of a corn ear once the silks wilt. Spray other crops with Bacillus thuringiensis.

Squash vine borer
This caterpillar does its damage from the inside out. It bores into vines of squash, pumpkins and other vining crops, causing the wines to wilt.

Control: Once the borer takes hold, slit the stem, remove and destroy the caterpillar. Bury the slit portion of the stem in moist soil to encourage new roots.

Bagworm
A tiny, wingless female moth, it attaches a tentlike bag to junipers, cedars, pines and arborvitae. After the caterpillars emerge, they eat the foliage.

Control: Spray them in early summer with Bacillus thuringiensis. Spray heavy populations with malathion. In winter or spring, pick off and destroy the bags.

Cutworm
A fat caterpillar that's 1 to 2 inches long and usually curled. They eat at night, usually through the stems of young transplants in the garden.

Control: A well-established favorite is to encircle seedlings or transplants with a paper collar made of heavy paper or plastic pushed an inch or two into the soil. You could also cut the bottom off a paper cup and press it into the soil.

Slug
A slug isn't a bug, of course, but it is definitely a pest, munching away on daylily foliage and other leafy fare.

Control: A small shallow pan of beer will draw slugs to death by drowning. Or use a pan with a teaspoon of brewer's yeast in a cup of water. Commercial slug jails can also lure slugs into fatal captivity.

Slug

Squash vine borer

Bagworm

Cutworm

Summer

PALS

Assassin bug

It's a voracious predator that seeks out many destructive garden pests, including caterpillars and beetles. Many North American species exist, some black, others brown, some marked with pink or red. The short, stout beak operates as a dagger.

Praying mantis

It's named for the prayerlike way it folds the front pair of muscular, grooved legs. Though seemingly in reverent repose, the insect is actually on the lookout for another insect to come its way. Look for foamlike, straw-colored masses of eggs in the fall in weedy growth along roadsides and in hedgerows and bring them carefully on their twigs to your garden. Attach them to branches off the ground for the winter. They hatch in spring. The praying mantis is the official state insect of South Carolina.

Lacewing

Brown or green, adult lacewings possess transparent, lacy wings held like a little roof while the insect rests. Lacewings grab the prey with their jaw and suck the juices through their hollow mandibles. Fortunately, the prey are destructive aphids, mealybugs, scale insects, mites, caterpillar eggs, corn earworms and other small soft-bodied creatures. The voracious grayish-brown caterpillar larvae also work the pest beat, wiping out corn earworms, mites, scales and mealybugs. It tends to stick around, whereas ladybugs are more likely to roam.

Lady beetle

Charmers of the insect world, lady beetles, often called ladybugs, are usually red or tan with black spots, sometimes black with red spots. Whatever color these insects are wearing, it's bad news for aphids. An adult will lay up to 1,500 eggs in one to two months. The larvae can eat 25 to 40 aphids a day. An adult lady beetle may eat 50 a day. They also work on scale insects.

Lady beetle

Assassin bug

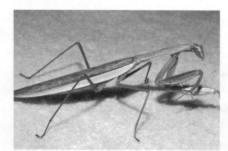
Praying mantis

Lacewing

HOW TO AVOID PESTICIDES

Try these methods and products to avoid using chemical pesticides:

Insecticidal soap. A commercial product made to kill certain pests, including aphids, mites and white flies, while not hurting plants and beneficial insects. It is most effective early in the season. When spraying, pay close attention to the undersides of leaves. Avoid using if plants are suffering from drought or severe heat.

Bacillus thuringiensis. A natural enemy of leaf-eating caterpillars. Use at the first sign of caterpillar infestation because bacillus lasts only about a week after exposure to sunlight. It is most effective on young caterpillars.

Garden cleanliness. Look for signs of insects or disease. Wash tools when you finish using them, especially if you've been working with a diseased plant. Dipping tools into a solution of water and 10 percent household bleach will sanitize them. In late fall, clear out garden debris such as plants that have borne their crops.

Handpicking. Pick off garden insects by hand and destroy them in soapy water. This is easiest with Japanese beetles, Colorado potato beetles and tomato hornworms.

PREPARE THE GARDEN FOR YOUR VACATION

Now, after weeks of giving your flower and vegetable gardens your total attention, you're ready. . . .

To leave them. For a summer vacation.

How can you do it?

Easy, you say. But just as the vegetables move into high gear of production, and the summer flowers hit peak bloom, it's hard to abandon them for mountain slopes or sunny beaches. Don't cancel the trip. You can get the garden ready to hold its own while you play. Here's how.

Vegetable gardens suffer most from summer neglect. To keep producing and remain healthy, plants need an inch of water a week and regular picking of ripe vegetables. So don't let tomatoes, squashes, peppers and other summer vegetables rot on the vine; the plants will tend to stop producing.

Go after the weeds, too. A weed that is a mere speck today will be huge in two weeks. Neighbors should be willing to water the garden if it doesn't rain, and happy to pick the vegetables. But weeding is probably above and beyond the call of neighborliness.

Flowerbeds also need weeding and weekly watering. And snipping off blooms (deadheading) that are passing their prime will keep the plants growing and producing.

Summer annuals such as marigolds, zinnias and petunias may look good now, but a week or two of inattention could put them in critical condition. Begonias and impatiens will take care of themselves.

If you fertilize the plants and snip off the flowers before you leave, a fresh surge of new blossoms should be ready when you get back.

Roses especially need a thorough working-over with pruning shears, fertilizer and pesticides before you depart.

Hanging baskets, which need water daily during hot weather, probably ought to be taken down and handed over to a neighbor who is willing to water

them. Otherwise, they will surely wilt and decline badly.

The simplest way to handle houseplants is to ask a friend or neighbor to water them.

If you have a lot of plants, an easy way to do this is to group the plants under a shower in the bathroom and ask a neighbor to turn on the faucet once a week for a good watering.

Or move them outdoors to the shade of a large tree. Shade is especially essential for tropical plants accustomed to growing in the dim light indoors. Choose a location outside that is not easily seen from the street. Houseplants are valuable and can be tempting to thieves.

Just before you hop in the car, cut the grass and water everything. A fescue lawn that is semi-dormant in July and August will stand two weeks without mowing. But if you have any doubt -- or you're leaving for longer than two weeks, ask a friend to look at it regularly and, if needed, hire someone to mow it. A lawn in need of mowing is another signal to burglars that no one is home.

Water vegetable and flowerbeds, shrubbery and young trees, even if it has rained recently. This will drive moisture deeper into the soil and reduce the likelihood of moisture stress on plants, which could cut short your garden's beauty and productivity.

Plant Profile

CALLA LILY

NAME:
Botanically, it's a mouthful, Zantedeschia (zan-te-DES-kee-a), but you'll know it as the calla lily. This swirling white or pink garden flower rises above deep green foliage spotted with white. The elegant flowers make long-lasting bouquets, often favored by brides.

HOME GROUND:
Mild-winter areas of South Africa.

VITAL STATS:
Plants usually top off at 18 inches, but some species may soar to 4 feet.

FAVORITE SPOT:
Calla lilies demand moist but well-drained, sandy soil. Semishade or just morning sun helps calla lilies prosper from spring until fall. In the Piedmont, it's best to cut off the remaining foliage in the fall, dig up the rhizomes and plant in a pot. (Or grow the plant in a pot all year.) Keep the pot in a cool, frost-free place through the winter, and water just enough to keep the light soil barely moist until new shoots appear in the spring.

WHO'S WHO:
Name confusion reigns between calla lilies and another garden plant, the canna, which blooms in many bright shades of red, orange, pink or yellow and is usually 4 to 6 feet tall. People sometimes call calla lilies canna lilies, and call cannas callas. It's an easy error. Neither plant should take offense.

SOW IT AND SEE IT: GARDENING FOR KIDS

Summer is a great time for parents to introduce their kids to gardening.

The project might be a small plot of flowers or vegetables, perhaps a large pot containing one or two kinds of flowers, or even just one tomato plant at the corner of the family's garden. But it should clearly be the child's own, from planting to picking.

The results, of course, may vary, but I think, for children, the process is as valuable as the product. By watching leaves develop and buds form, a child learns patience; by tending a plant, a child learns responsibility; by gathering the results, whether it is a pretty flower or something fun, like a pumpkin, the child feels the pleasure of growing things.

Parents and children should work together on this, the adult serving as mentor, teacher and encourager as the child learns to dig, sow, plant, water and weed.

Child-size hoes, shovels and rakes will make it easier for youngsters to tend their gardens, but they aren't essential. A regular trowel can serve as a little shovel, provided the soil has been dug and loosened.

You don't need a big backyard for a child's garden. Tiny bits of land make an excellent start. So do pots on steps, patios and decks.

Summer

The location will dictate the choice of plants. Tomatoes, pumpkins, marigolds and zinnias all require six hours of direct sun each day; impatiens, caladiums and begonias will do better in the shade. Don't hedge on this. A child who tends a tomato plant faithfully for weeks will be disappointed if it doesn't bear fruit because of inadequate sun.

The potential for success is raised by starting with young plants, such as tomatoes and peppers, or choosing seeds of plants that germinate quickly and reliably. In the latter category, I'd look for marigold, zinnia, bean, pumpkin or squash seeds.

An awareness and concern for the Earth should play a part in a child's summer gardening experience. Start a compost heap. Avoid pesticides; a tomato hornworm – a colorful creature that will probably fascinate a child – can easily be picked off a plant. If aphids intrude, a stout blast of water can dislodge them. Look for organic fertilizers, such as composted cow manure, to stimulate growth.

In addition to the lessons on responsibility that come with caring for plants (regular water is vital), a summer garden is also an experience in the interdependence of plants and animals. Each serves the other in unique and important ways. Food and beauty are obvious ones, but this is an opportunity to reinforce the idea that plants provide the oxygen we breathe and absorb the carbon dioxide we exhale. Some plants, such as vinca, are even important sources of medical treatment.

It's also a chance to emphasize that not all plants are edible, helping the child to distinguish between edible herbs and vegetables and nonedible ornamental flowers.

The vegetables will, of course, be picked for the family's table and perhaps even shared with others. Flowers, too, should be picked if the child wants to bring them indoors and tuck them into a vase. Let a few plants – perhaps a marigold or zinnia – go to seed so that the child can see a seedpod and understand how the wonderful circle of plant life continues.

HOW TO MAKE SQUIRRELS KEEP THEIR PAWS OFF YOUR TOMATOES

In the war against squirrels, many tomato gardeners would go nuclear if they could. Instead, they've devised many techniques they believe have deterred these urban pests from their favorite summer crop. Some examples:

- A circular cage of plastic Lucite, about 2 feet tall, that is too slick for the squirrels to climb.

- A hot pepper spray, sometimes laced with garlic, as a squirrel repellent. Commercial kinds are on the market.

- Human hair draped over and around the plants as a repellent. Check your local salon for freshly washed hair recently cut off someone's head.

- Humane traps, baited with bread or apple. Once the critters are caught, you can relocate them somewhere distant.

- A diversionary offering of dried ears of corn placed in feeders on trees and fences during the garden season.

If you want to concoct your own repellent, try these recipes suggested by the Clemson Cooperative Extension Service:

- Mix 2 tablespoons of hot pepper sauce, either homemade or a commercial type such as Tabasco, in one gallon of water and spray it on your plants.

- Blend two or three rotten eggs in a gallon of water to make a spray.

- Grind up dried red peppers or black peppers and dust onto plants. Chili pepper, which is already ground, could also serve as a dust.

Summer

Ask Nancy

Answers to some common problems

WHY IS MY MANDEVILLA WILTING?

Wilting tells you a plant is thirsty, and if you are watering that plant every day in the spring, it tells you another thing: The plant is probably root-bound. That means vigorous growth has filled the pot with roots, which are lapping up every bit of water you put down there, needing more and leaving none in storage.

I suggest you begin by transplanting the mandevilla to a larger pot. When you take the plant out of the pot, notice whether the roots are wound tightly around the root ball. If so, tease them away gently so they will grow into the soil in the larger pot. Use fresh potting soil.

In hot weather, expect to water a mandevilla in a pot on a balcony that gets afternoon sun every day. But the plant should not wilt within a day if the roots have sufficient space.

OUR ROSE LEAVES HAVE BLACK SPOTS. WHAT'S WRONG?

Black spot, a fungal disease, is the bane of rose gardeners and difficult to control once it gets going. Use a spray specifically targeted for black spot and applied at the rate and times directed on the label; otherwise, it isn't going to help.

What are your watering practices? Splashing water spreads the fungus from infected to healthy leaves, which is why a protective fungicide is essential and overhead watering discouraged. Nothing you can do, though, about rain falling.

I would not give in to this plague. Start by going over each rose bush and removing every infected leaf. Then look at the ground and pick up every fallen yellow leaf.

Next, check your fungicide for its ability to combat black spot, and get a soaker hose you can lay under the rose mulch and attach to your garden hose.

Apply rose fertilizer to get the plants growing vigorously. Some rose fertilizers are dual wonders, containing systemic pest controls that work from the inside out.

WHY ARE MY NEW HYDRANGEAS DOING SO POORLY THIS YEAR?

You were looking forward to big blooms, and your plants didn't perform. They're wilting because the plants haven't yet grown enough new roots to support the top growth and because of the stress of afternoon heat, which will be with us for weeks to come. Hydrangeas prefer a partially shaded location; morning sun, which is cooler, would be far better for the plants than an afternoon blast of summer heat. If the location is poor, move the plants while they are still young, if you have a suitable spot. If you can't move them, water the plants through the summers so they continue to grow more roots (and add a beach umbrella?). Put on pine-needle mulch to conserve moisture. Next year, the plants should perform better, but direct summer sun will continue to be hard on the leaves.

DOES IT HURT FOR IVY TO RUN UP A SHADE TREE?

Yes, because once established, ivy grows quickly and densely. Dense ivy can conceal any problems on the trunk. Once the ivy is up the trunk, it will grow onto the limbs and could eventually swallow up leaves and kill them. Loss of the leaves could lead to death of the limb and decline of the tree.

Pull down the ivy from the trunk. If the ivy is already well up the trunk and too difficult to pull down, cut the ivy stems near the ground and loosen the cut ends from the trunk. That will kill the ivy above the cut, and the dead leaves will eventually fall off. Don't expect this to happen overnight.

IT'S HOT OUT THERE.

July heat. Sweaty, steaming, energy sapping.

Yet vegetables grow and flowers bloom.

And then there's the shade – even in our air-conditioned world, we're

thankful for every cubic inch of it. You could kid yourself that

this summer will be different. The daytime temperatures

will be in the low to mid-80s, and exactly one inch of rain

will fall each week. Get real.

The gardener with more than two years of experience

under the trowel knows that won't happen.

Instead of falling gently, rain will hit as crashing thunderstorms.

Instead of mild, the air will be hot, hot, hot.

But despite it all, lovely things happen. Brightly colored

flowers and ripening tomatoes don't seem to mind.

But only if we take care of them.

Summer

SAY HELLO TO A HOST OF HOSTAS

At midsummer, take a lesson from hostas. They hang out in the shade, keeping cool while others sweat in the sun. All looks quiet in the hosta garden in July.

But not all green. Perhaps you recall hostas as simply a solid green, oval and smooth-leaved, low-growing perennial that you found merely useful to park in an odd corner as a ground cover. That was the hosta of old. A tad boring, if you'll forgive me for saying so. The new hostas get star treatment, and deservedly so, in prime positions of your garden real estate. That's because the variety of form, color and texture, as well as bigger leaves developed by hybridizers in recent years, raised hostas to the A list among perennials.

Hostas, sometimes called plantain lilies, arose as about 70 species in China, Korea, Japan and elsewhere in Eastern Asia, but American hybridizers created most of the newer-named ones. Hostas and daylilies – both members of the lily plant family – rank as America's most popular perennials. One reason for hostas' increasing popularity is its tolerance of shade; a second is its hardiness. It tolerates a bone-chilling minus-40 degrees, making it suitable for most of the United States.

But there's more to sensational hostas today than just a strip of white variegation that so impressed hosta fanciers not so long ago.

Size: Bigger varieties rise an impressive 5 feet tall, with leaves 18 to 20 inches wide. For rock garden enthusiasts, miniature hostas rise a mere 1 to 2 inches, the leaf width, a fraction of that.

Color: Of course, the deep green of the original hostas remains. But the hosta palette now includes bluish-green, chartreuse, golden yellow, pale lemon and almost white. Contrasting markings, including yellow and golden centers, margins, stripes and stipplings, also add to the new flair in hostas. The bluish-green and bluish-gray varieties tend to go green in midsum-

Choose hostas with a variety of color, texture and variegation.

mer in the South, when heat melts away the sheen that gives the leaves their blue tint.

Texture: Crinkled, dimpled leaves resemble seersucker. Deeply ridged leaves make solid green hostas more interesting. Wavy margins seem to flutter.

Form: New forms of hostas help them serve a variety of roles in the garden. Low, sprawling types make excellent ground covers. Upright, vase-shaped types create interesting mounds.

Such a range of features allows gardens to choose hostas for many purposes. Place large ones singly as specimen plants or group them in flower borders. Choose tiny varieties for crevices, rock gardens or along walkways. Place spots of hosta color anywhere a shady corner needs a bright touch.

Tips For Success

- Dig and divide hostas only if you must. Digging and dividing will cause the plant to lose size for several years while the plant grows new roots. Good reasons to dig and divide: You're moving, you want to share a special hosta or it outgrew the space. Know the plant's mature size when you plant, so it can stay put.

- Plant hostas in rich soil with lots of moisture-retaining organic matter such as compost or decomposed leaves. Fertilize in early March and June with a balanced fertilizer such as 10-10-10 at the rate of a couple of tablespoons per plant.

- Give hostas shade, with dappled morning sun. Filtered light, not direct sun, is what they need. Afternoon sun, especially in the South, will burn and disfigure hosta leaves. For better, faster growth, don't plant directly under shallow-rooted trees such as dogwoods and willow oaks, which will win the competition for water.

- Water them well during dry weather. Hostas demand water. In dry weather, drench the plants thoroughly at least once a week.

- Make up your own mind about removing the flower spikes, which some people do.

- Don't forget solid green hostas when planning your combinations. All-green hostas provide restful complements to the variegated types. An array of variegated hostas can look too busy without green ones as a calming foil.

STAMP OUT BROWN PATCH ON YOUR LAWN

If, where your lawn was thick and green, now stands an ugly brown spot, you've probably got the summer plague of fescue lawns: brown patch. It results from hot, humid weather and too much nitrogen fertilizer during late spring and summer. Light, frequent waterings, mowing the lawn while it's wet and heavy lawn seeding in spring also contribute to the problem. Spray affected areas with the fungicides Daconil and Bayleton to reduce the spread of the disease, about every two to three weeks during hot, wet weather. The diseased patches of lawn will likely require reseeding in the fall. Next year, to prevent the problem, mow your grass 3 1/2 inches tall and don't fertilize after mid-April. Water the grass one inch deep once a week or let it go semidormant.

Summer

OFFBEAT PERENNIALS ARE MIDSUMMER SHOWOFFS

Like all good dramas, the garden has its perennial stars. At midsummer, that means daisies and daylilies. But where is your supporting cast, a fleet of lesser-knowns to add color and life to the show? These secondary players possess a dramatic flair: globe thistle prickly in cobalt blue, the golden airiness of patrinia, crocosmia alive in luminous red blooms. They can deal with heat and humidity and even drought. All require sun.

❀ **Patrinia scabiosaefolia** at midsummer looks like it should be going to a coronation. The cup-shaped golden-yellow flowers are so loosely arrayed and airy, they seem to float above their stems and the foliage at the base of the plant. Plants grow about 3 feet tall.

❀ **Crocosmia** originated in South Africa, and its sword-shaped leaves rise 4 feet from small corms planted 3 to 4 inches deep. Besides red, crocosmias come in shades of yellow and orange. Each stem holds many funnel-shaped blooms. After blooming, the flowers produce interesting seed heads that continue to be attractive in the garden.

❀ **Russian sage** is too beautiful and long-lasting for the shadows. This upright plant, botanically named Perovskia atriplicifolia, produces aromatic gray-to-white stems with leaves that are green, tinged with silver. Plants grow to 3 to 4 feet tall. Blooms are soft violet.

❀ **Cardoon**, a native of the southwestern Mediterranean, bears long-lasting purple flowers

that look like thistles. The plant, botanically named Cynara cardunculus, produces clumps that grow about 4 feet tall. If cut back in August, it sends up new silvery gray foliage.

❀ **Globe thistle** gets noticed for the dramatic cobalt blue of its flowers. The long-lasting bristly blooms sit atop single stems rising above the grayish-green foliage. These undemanding plants grow 18 inches to 4 feet tall, depending on the variety. They belong to the genus echinops and the aster family.

❀ **Hibiscus coccineus** is a shrubby perennial distinguished by scarlet blooms that resemble the tropical hibiscus. The stems have an unusual reddish cast. It grows rapidly to about 6 feet tall and makes a good choice for the background or corner of a flower bed.

❀ **Maltese** cross is botanically named Lychnis chalcedonia. It bears flat clusters of scarlet, cross-shaped flowers. It is native to eastern Russia and grows 2 to 4 feet tall. A white variety also exists.

Cardoon

Patrinia

Summer

❀ **Indigo Spires salvia** is a shrubby perennial. It bears outstanding violet blooms on well-branched plants that can reach 4 feet. Put this vigorous plant in the background. It has a rangier habit than other, tidier salvias, but the color and vigor place it among the best of the blue ones.

❀ **Liatris spicata** is the flower commonly called blazing star or gayfeather. You've probably seen its purple spikes in professional floral arrangements. Native to the eastern and central United States, it grows 2 to 3 feet tall and spreads about 2 feet. The purple flowers blend well with summer's yellow daisies.

Globe thistle

Russian sage

Hibiscus

Crocosmia

They can deal with heat and humidity and even drought.

BLUE, WHITE GARDEN GIVES A COOL FEEL

Look at the flower garden in July and what do you see? Very likely, it's hot pinks, fiery reds, sunny yellows and blazing oranges.

That's a warm sight indeed for this, the warmest season. Summer seems even hotter when it is lit by the hot end of the color spectrum, with bright marigolds, sunflowers, coneflowers, zinnias, dahlias, coreopsis, pentas, petunias, daylilies and geraniums.

I prefer a calmer scene, one produced by the watery shades of blue and violet, accented by icy silver and snowy white and backed up by cool green grass, shrubs and trees.

This view is as restful as a walk on the beach, and not that hard to achieve, thanks to the array of summer annuals, perennials and shrubs that bear flowers ranging from the palest sky blue to the deepest violet. Add to that mix the white flowers of roses and Shasta daisies and the silvery foliage of artemesia, dusty miller and lamb's ear, and you have begun your alternative to summer's hot look.

For some years, I thought of blue and violet as minor players in the summer garden palette. There was really nothing to compare with the sapphire shades of Siberian irises or the clear-sky beauty of wild blue phlox in late spring.

But perennial salvias, veronicas, balloon flower, the annual Swan River daisy and the deciduous shrub buddleia have changed my thinking.

Two veronicas in particular, Sunny Border Blue and Goodness Grows, produce outstanding violet-blues that match so closely, one might think them identical. Height, however, separates Goodness Grows, which is about 1 foot tall, from Sunny Border Blue, which reaches about 2 feet. Either solo or paired, these veronicas make an impressive sight, particularly when set off by a plant with white flowers, such as the reliable Iceberg rose, or silvery foliage such as an artemesia. Yellow-flowered coreopsis will make the blues seem bluer – and add a touch of summer heat as well.

For ages, the salvia that people knew and grew was a red annual called scarlet sage. But the hardy and half-hardy perennial salvias are much more beautiful and interesting plants. Varieties such as Victoria with medium-blue flowers and the deep violet East Friesland have become popular for summer gardens.

Like the veronicas, the flowers are tall, narrow spikes rising gracefully above the low foliage. But their vertical appearance means that a more horizontal plant, such as threadleaf coreopsis or cranesbill, makes a pleasing neighbor.

An annual that I've come to love is the Swan River daisy, which produces tiny, lavender-blue daisies above feathery foliage that is low, tidy and spreading. This is

White flowers, such as petunias, add a cooling accent to the blue garden.

Summer

a fine plant for either pots, where it spills gracefully over the rim, or beds, where it makes a pretty edger.

I've not found it to survive even mild winters, but it blooms from spring to late fall with very little attention, certainly far less than the pinching and tending required of marigolds, petunias and zinnias.

The most permanent touch of lavender blue and violet for your garden could come from varieties of buddleia, the butterfly bush that comes in blues, pinks

and white. Blooming from early summer to autumn, the buddleia has become well stocked in garden centers. These are easy to grow and reliable, growing quickly into shrubs that will help create a cool look for the summer garden.

White flowers, such as petunias, crape myrtles, cosmos and Shasta daisies, add a cooling accent to the blue garden.

SPICE UP SHADY SPOTS

About this time of year, when the blaze of spring color has faded and the Piedmont's trees spread their limbs and leaves like a large, green umbrella, I hear the never-ending grumble: "I can't grow anything in the shade."

Though cherished for their grandeur and appreciated for the shade and oxygen they produce, trees take their licks for standing between the gardener and the perfect tomato.

Some of the very best flowers and vegetables – roses, tomatoes and dahlias – as well as much of the merely ordinary stuff – marigolds, zinnias and beans – require a long daily dose of sunshine to produce the desired results.

Even though many elegant plants are suitable for shade, they don't bloom long enough to satisfy the gardener who demands plants that produce like a factory working three shifts. For these gardeners, the rhododendron, azaleas and hostas, not to mention the vast assortment of native, woodland wildflowers, bloom and fade too fast.

Even more distressing than the tomato vs. hosta conflict is the belief that people who live in the shade are cut off from a life in the garden beyond raking the blizzard of leaves that fall every year.

That is not true. Shade is good.

The shade-loving impatiens is one of the most popular summer flowers sold in the United States today. It blooms longer – looks better, too – than either marigold or zinnia. Many leafy greens, such as spinach, kale and lettuce, grow better in the shade. Everyone who grows them is entitled to call himself a vegetable gardener.

Some of the best landscape plants – azaleas, rhododendron, pieris, leucothoe, glossy abelia, hosta, hardy ferns and Lenten rose – grow well in shade. (By

shade, I mean the filtered-light shade typical of the Piedmont's home gardens – not the dark, full shade of thick woods in summer.)

After the alleged limitations on the number and variety of plants suitable for shade comes the rap that a shaded summer garden is all green. In the heart and heat of summer, the shaded garden will not produce what the catalogues call "a riot of color." But, in July and August, when we need heavy doses of cool and calm, who wants a riot?

That's when green – itself a landscape color of many shades and intensities – dominates and other colors provide accent. Among the best and easiest accents are the purple spikes rising above ribbons and beds of liriope, also known as monkey grass. That's the same liriope you planted for the practical reason of putting an edge on the lawn or flower bed.

The great shade plants of impatiens, begonias, coleus and caladium tempt us in spring, while the blazing red and hot pink azaleas and tulips have us dazzled, to choose colors that will carry forth this colorful parade into the depths of summer's heat and humidity.

I think impatiens with white or soft pink flowers and the coleus and caladium in green and white look better in deep summer. The light colors look cooler in the daytime and stand out well in the twilight.

The ground around some houses may be so shaded, it gets insufficient light for anything to grow well. That is full shade. Such gardens are better called the woods. Turning the woods into a garden will mean taking out some of the less-attractive trees to let enough sunlight pass through the canopy to create a partly shaded garden, which is more common and offers the gardener more possibilities.

Summer

MADE IN THE SHADE
YOU DON'T NEED FULL SUN FOR A LOVELY GARDEN

Do you know your shade? **Some** shade is total; its dense canopy creates dim spots hospitable to few plants.

Partial shade is the less exclusive sort. It lets the sunshine leak through thinner layers of leaves or sneak in around the edges of the canopy for part of the day. More plants are welcome in this dappled environment.

And seasonal shade is the protective kind. In summer, leafy trees keep the hottest of afternoon sun off delicate flowers, and in winter, evergreen trees protect shrubs from morning sun that hits on while leaves are still frozen after a cold night. Many gardeners throw up their hands and moan, "I can't grow anything in the shade," but that's not true. You just need to evaluate your shade and pick plants to suit the spot.

Seasonal shade

Most broad-leaf evergreen shrubs need protection from the morning sun in winter to avoid damage to their leaves. And some plants that can stand the cooler morning sun of summer need protection from summer's hot afternoon sun.

Filtered shade

Sunlight slips through the lacy layers of pine and dogwood branches. The changing patterns of light through the trees also create lovely patterns of light and shadow.

Full shade

Mature trees with dense layers of leaves and a broad canopy create full shade in summer. By midsummer, these trees have full-size leaves and let little light pass through.

Plants:
Morning shade in winter –
aucuba, gardenia, camellia, leucothoe, azalea.
Afternoon shade in summer –
daylilies, tradescantia, cardinal flower, Lenten rose, hostas.

Plants:
Kerria, hydrangeas, rhododendron, pieris, impatiens, hosta, begonia, coleus, foxglove, violets, caladium, mahonia, vinca.

Plants:
Forget-me-not wintergreen, ivy, hardy ferns, ajuga, wild ginger, pachysandra, lily-of-the valley, liriope.

Summer

LET THE SUNSHINE IN

If the shade in your garden is too much for you, consider ways to let the sun shine through the canopy of trees. That doesn't mean cutting down your cherished oaks, maples and dogwoods. But it does mean taking a hard look at some less worthy or unhealthful trees that you could live without.

Ask yourself: "Would I rather have this grove of not-so-pretty pines and this group of ailing apple or plum trees, or would I rather have the sun shine on the flower garden I've always wanted?" Clearly the trees could be sacrificed to meet a personal goal.

But what if the trees are all gems, and you still want more than ferns? Action with a saw is the first step. Trimming off the lower limbs will bring more light to the ground below it and cause the tree no harm. The tree canopy will still keep the hottest noon-time sun off your head, while letting in the rays of early morning and late afternoon.

Cleaning out the deadwood throughout the tree can dramatically increase the amount of sunlight getting through. It also will contribute to the health of the tree by eliminating the home grounds for various pests.

Such work with the saw should expand the range of flowering plants. Still, you may not have enough sunlight to grow tomatoes. Accept it. Then get your neighbors with the same problem together, find a sunny spot and start a community vegetable garden. Or stick to leafy vegetables such as lettuce, spinach and other greens or root crops such as radishes and potatoes that will grow in less than six hours of direct sunlight a day.

CAPTURE MEMORIES THROUGH PLANTS

An ordinary sweet pea, an ancient peony, an elegant blue iris. Sometimes the favorite plant in a garden isn't the prettiest, the newest, the flashiest. It may be a pain to tend, bloom only briefly or suffer in the winter. But it is loaded with memories because it came from the garden of someone special to you.

While visiting family and friends this summer, you may see a daylily or a dahlia, an azalea or a poppy that is simply beautiful. If you take a bit of it home, you will also have something of your friends and families. That's because people are inseparable from their gardens.

Bringing plants home is not simply a matter of digging up entire plants and leaving your favorite aunt or best friend with nothing. You need to know basic propagation techniques. These include gathering seeds from pods, digging and dividing clumps of perennials and taking cuttings of woody plants.

And while spring or fall may be the better time to apply these techniques, if you're making just a summertime visit to the home place, go ahead and take the seeds in a paper envelope, get the clumps and take the cuttings that will provide a plant legacy you can take home.

Poppy

Summer

What's blooming in July

- Begonias
- Black eyed susans
- Canna
- Cleome
- Crape myrtle
- Dahlia
- Globe thistle

- Abelia
- Hibiscus
- Patrinia
- Hostas
- Salvia
- Zinnia
- Coneflowers

- Gazania
- Marigolds
- Moonflowers
- Celosia
- Crocosmia

NEED A QUICK SPLASH OF COLOR?
FILL A POT WITH FLOWERS

While gardening is a lesson in the art of patience, sometimes you simply need something fast. There's a gathering Sunday for friends on the deck. The front door looks unwelcoming without a bloom in sight. The balcony is as bare as it was last December. So you need something pretty, and you need it pretty fast.

An instant container, packed with flower power, would do the job. And it isn't hard to make. Because it's July, garden centers are filled with plants in bloom, ready to star at your door, on your porch table, hanging on the balcony.

Here are three ideas to get you going, even if you've never planted a petunia. All are plants that tolerate summer heat, will keep going for months and take little maintenance.

But you will have to water, no doubt about that. The hanging basket and the shallow pot will need watering every day; the big pot, probably three times a week. A gentle shower is more effective in wetting the entire pot than a strong gush of water that runs through quickly. Use water-soluble fertilizer (not to make the plants grow vigorously, but because they're in a tight spot).

A hanging basket for morning sun

What's in it? A descriptively named dracaena called Spike, two pink begonias, two lavender verbenas, two white bacopas, two gold lantanas, one helichrysum.

The effect: Cool colors dominate with only a spark of hot gold to stir up the lavender. The Spike dracaena and pink begonias provide the central, vertical elements, but the other plants were planted around the rim to take advantage of their trailing nature. New hanging baskets made of black metal with a natural liner look far more stylish than plastic ones.

Planting and maintenance tips: On their own, most of these plants could get quite large, but not when grown in this hanging basket. Let the sprawlers' branches sprawl over the side. Tip prune the begonias with scissors to keep them shorter and shapelier.

A hanging basket for morning sun

A shallow pot for a table in the shade

What's in it? One angel wing begonia, two white impatiens, five coleus plants, two asparagus ferns.

The effect: Tropical flair for a tabletop comes from the bright patterns on the coleus plants, the vivid red of the angel wing begonia and the feathery emerald green of the asparagus fern. A shallow, curved pot, 12 inches in diameter, is deep enough to hold the plants but low enough to make a porch centerpiece.

Planting and maintenance tips: Make the begonia the centerpiece, and arrange the other plants around it so the pot looks good from all directions. Place some of the coleus plants vertically and others horizontally for best effect. Tip prune the plants occasionally to keep them in scale with the pot. At summer's end, pull out the angel wing begonia and the asparagus ferns, plant in separate pots and tend indoors through the winter.

A big pot of flowers for the sun

What's in it? One tropical hibiscus plant, two Million Bells calibrachoas, three swan river daisies and two ornamental sweet potato vines.

The effect: It includes plants, particularly the Million Bells calibrachoa (the flowers look like very small petunias, but require no pinching off of dead blooms) that are somewhat new to the bedding and container plant market. The tropical hibiscus is a popular pot plant available in many colors. The ipomoea is a chartreuse form of the sweet potato vine (the nearly black leaf form called Blackie is better known) chosen to brighten the color scheme.

Planting and maintenance tips: Arranged with the taller hibiscus at the back, this pot could be set against the wall beside a door, along a sidewalk or on steps. The hibiscus blooms on new growth, so pinch the tips as blooms fade to keep it growing. Position the ipomoea horizontally to cascade the foliage over the side of the pot. Remove and replant the hibiscus at summer's end and keep it indoors during cold weather.

A shallow pot for a table in the shade

A big pot of flowers for the sun

Summer

IT'S EASY TO DESIGN A BEAUTIFUL BOUQUET

Bring the flower garden inside by making a bouquet that will say summer. Your first effort can be as simple as three stems of daisies or roses set at different heights in a tall, thin bud vase. A sprig of greenery will finish it off.

Do this and you'll be inspired enough to do a mixed bouquet for the dining room table. Pick a dozen or so red zinnias, and you're ready to arrange something quick and easy for a buffet dinner on the deck. Loosely arrayed in a bowl or vase, the zinnias practically arrange themselves.

But you don't have to stick to solid colors of the same flower. A mixed bouquet from the garden – marigolds, lilies, roses, zinnias, daisies, small sunflowers, accented by salvia, snapdragons and goldenrod -- is an easy one to make. Summer colors – purple, bright pink, red, yellow and orange – go together nicely. Tuck in some white flowers (baby's breath from the florist, perhaps), add green foliage, and you have a summer bouquet.

The tricky part is settling on the container and the height of your arrangement. If it's a round centerpiece for the dining room, the finished product should be short enough for seated diners to see over and appear similar from all directions. For a buffet-table center-piece, make it big and tall enough so that the flowers don't get lost in a long table of food and dishes. The choice of container dictates the size of the arrangement. The flowers and foliage should rise above the top of the container to about 1 to 1 1/2 times its height. A 1-foot vase will yield an arrangement about 2 1/2 feet tall; a shorter container, such as a 6-inch bowl, can produce a petite arrangement as short as 1 foot high for a table centerpiece. A round arrangement should be as wide as it is tall. A triangle-shaped arrangement should be roughly half as wide as it is tall.

Glass marbles make an anchor for stems in clear glass or crystal bowls; green florist foam is good for opaque containers.

When placing the flowers, first establish the height and width of the arrangement with the dominant flowers, such as the roses, lilies, marigolds, zinnias or sunflowers. Then fill in – staying within the height and width you've already set – with smaller accent flowers and stems of foliage. If you have stems of baby's breath, feathery goldenrod or frothy small asters, you can get away without using foliage. Let your eye be your guide on this. And don't forget to fill the container with water.

Tips For Success

- Cut flowers in the early morning or evening. Moisture content is highest then.

- Select blossoms that are about half open. They'll fill out quickly.

- Use a clean, sharp knife or shears. Don't use the type of shears that crush stems. It blocks uptake of water.

- Put cut stems immediately in a pail of warm water. As soon as possible, cut the stems again underwater to keep water flowing to blooms and the stems straight.

- Indoors, stand the flowers in warm water in a cool place for several hours. This increases the amount of water in the stem and flower.

- When ready to arrange, cut the stems at an angle at the desired length. Strip off all foliage that would go underwater. Add a commercial floral preservative to the water.

WIPE OUT WHITEFLIES

Whiteflies are a total nuisance. **Unlike** some insects that hang around, quietly causing damage, whiteflies make their presence known in several unappealing ways, from a cloud of insects to yellow leaves to a sticky residue that turns black.

The little adults travel upward; shake an infested plant and you will likely see clouds of insects that resemble tiny moths. They lay eggs on the undersides of many kinds of vegetables and ornamental plants growing indoors and out, while sucking sap. When the eggs hatch, the youngsters start feeding on the leaves as well. The result is mottled or yellowed leaves that may shrivel and die.

And then there's the sticky, honeydew-like residue that the whiteflies excrete onto the leaves.

Stay with me, it only gets worse.

That sticky residue turns sooty because it attracts a fungus that dines on the residue, which, because it is sweet, draws ants.

Try spraying with insecticidal soap regularly – every 10 days or so – to catch new generations of whiteflies as they hatch. A botanical insecticide containing pyrethrum should also be effective. If you have a bad infestation, stay with it to catch the emerging insects.

Another weapon could be the yellow sticky traps that are sold commercially. For reasons unknown, the adult whitefly is attracted to bright yellow; when the yellow surface is sticky, the whitefly gets trapped and dies, for which we will shed no tears.

These traps are used frequently in greenhouses, but with a bad infestation, they are worth hanging outdoors.

You can make your own sticky trap by laminating bright yellow cards and coating them with mineral oil before hanging them in your whitefly haven.

And next spring, when you buy plants, shake them a bit to make sure no little clouds of whiteflies arise, ready to come home with you.

BARE SPOTS? JUST FILL IN THE BLANKS

Blank spots start to show up in flower gardens in July. Pansies have had their day. The bulb foliage is gone. Filling these blanks isn't difficult, and you'll be rewarded with pretty blooms through the summer and into fall.

Walk into most garden centers these days and you'll find many kinds of annuals in bloom – or nearly there – that can transform your blank spot instantly.

I don't usually encourage the creation of instant gardens; it is fun to watch plants develop as their leaves grow and buds and flowers emerge. But in places where you are accustomed to seeing something pretty, particularly the most noticeable areas you see every day, there's no reason not to opt for instant beauty.

Marigolds, scarlet sage, cosmos, vinca and zinnias are colorful answers to this problem. In shady areas, impatiens, begonias, coleus, caladiums provide instant solutions.

These are plants that last, but they aren't maintenance free. Zinnias, in particular, are highly susceptible to fungus and require spraying with a fungicide to prevent this problem, which will ruin the foliage and cause early decline of the plants.

Most annuals, too, benefit from quick removal of flowers before they set seed. Setting seed is a signal to the plant that its days are over. But if you keep this from happening, the plant will continue to set buds and flowers.

Begonias and impatiens, which also perform in sun, provided they get enough water, need less bud removal, although the plants look better if they are tidied up occasionally. Coleus and caladiums, both valued for their colorful foliage, require very little work after planting – just the occasional removal of fading leaves.

If you are replanting an area occupied by pansies, remove the plants by pulling them up or by snipping the stem at ground level. If the area is a bed of tulips or daffodils, you must be very careful to avoid sticking a sharp trowel into the bulbs and ruining them. Look at the bulb foliage carefully as a guide to the location of the bulbs. Try to set the new plants between the bulbs.

Keep the soil damp as roots develop. A light mulch will keep the soil cooler and encourage better root growth.

Summer

CAUTION: CATERPILLARS

It's midsummer, prime time for two caterpillars that make their presence known by their droppings or unsightly webs. They're the fall webworm and the orange-striped oakworm. Neither is considered an alarming pest.

Orange-striped oakworm

The insect: The orange-striped oakworm, Anisota senatoria, irritates property owners because of the shotgun-pellet litter the caterpillar drops on decks, patios and walkways under its oak-tree habitat.

Vital stats: The caterpillar is black with eight narrow yellow stripes. It's usually about 2 inches long with a pair of curving horns.

Favorite spot: Mostly on oaks. Caterpillars will feed on leaves through August, but usually not cause great damage.

What to do: Spray smaller trees with Bacillus thuringiensis to get young caterpillars. Sevin and Orthene are chemical insecticides effective on older and larger caterpillars.

Fall webworm

The insect: Fall webworms, Hyphantria cunea, emerge in spring as a white moth, then lay eggs that hatch into the leaf-eating caterpillars.

Vital stats: The caterpillars are pale yellow to green, 1 to 1 1/4 inches long and covered with long silky hairs. There's a black stripe on the back and pale yellow stripes on the side.

Favorite spot: The moths mate in the spring and lay eggs (350 to 900 each) on the undersides of leaves. The caterpillars that emerge in summer feed on leaves and build webs in trees. Their favorite species are persimmon, pecan and sourwood trees. By autumn, the webs are quite noticeable; that's why an insect at work all summer is called fall webworm.

What to do: Unless caterpillars defoliate a tree year after year, the webworm doesn't usually affect a tree's long-term health. High-pressure spraying of water will dislodge the webs and drown some of the caterpillars. The insect produces two generations a year so they may show up again. Small trees affected by the insect may be sprayed with Bacillus thuringiensis while the caterpillars are young; Sevin and Orthene are chemical insecticides effective on older and larger caterpillars.

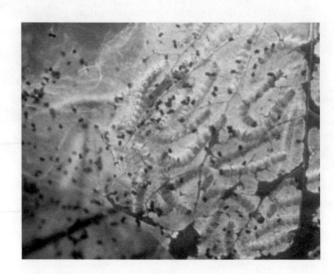

Summer

LEARN THE ART OF DEADHEADING

Deadheading is an art, the way to keep the flower garden neat and the plants blooming.

When spent flower heads of annuals and perennials are removed promptly by pinching them off with your fingers, it forces the plant to redirect energy away from making seeds. For perennials, this should mean stronger plants; for annuals, more blooms.

It also means a longer life for annuals such as zinnias. Setting seeds after flowers bloom is usually a signal that the plant has done its work of setting up a new generation and is ready to die.

Some plants, such as cosmos, bloom in clusters, so you should wait for the cluster to bloom out before deadheading. Trimming off single blooms of cosmos could prove too tedious.

As their season nears its end, however, let some annuals go to seed and drop seeds for next year's plants. These include alyssum, cleome, larkspur and poppies. Or collect the seeds in an envelope and save them to plant elsewhere in the garden.

Plant profile

AGAPANTHUS

NAME:
Agapanthus (*a-ga-PAN-thus*) is grown in large pots, tubs or half-barrels and admired for its many, long-lasting blue or white flowers. The name stems from Greek, meaning "love flower."

HOME GROUND:
Though sometimes called Blue Lily of the Nile, agapanthus is a native of South Africa. Today, it is popular on decks and around pools.

VITAL STATS:
The leaves, resembling an amaryllis, arch gracefully about 1 1/2 to 3 1/2 feet high. Globe-shaped flowers appear at the tips of stalks that rise a foot or more above the leaves.

A MOVABLE PLANT:
Agapanthus requires (and deserves) a sunny spot in spring and summer when the flower stalks rise and bloom. Don't let it dry out. In the winter, the pot or tub must be moved to a frost-free, well-lighted spot where the temperature is between 40 and 50 degrees. This will make the plant think it's winter and encourage dormancy. Water rarely in winter; soil should be nearly dry during dormancy.

SPRINGTIME WAKE-UP:
In early spring, about March, wake up the potted plant by watering it and moving it to a warmer location.

Summer

HOW TO DIVIDE IRIS

Poor bloom and crowded clumps are a signal it's time to divide rhizomes of most bearded irises. You'll need to do this every few years.

Digging up the clumps isn't hard because they grow right at soil level. Remove and discard the old rhizomes – the fat, rootlike horizontal stem from which the roots emerge – in the center that don't have leaf fans. What remains are the younger, fresher-looking rhizomes with leaf fans. Trim off the tops of the foliage as you go.

Separate the rhizomes with a sharp knife and replant them, making sure the rhizome lies horizontally on the soil. Be sure you can see the top of the rhizome just above the soil line. It will settle a bit to ground level.

DRESS UP A CHAIN-LINK FENCE

Though practical, secure and long-lasting, the chain-link fence isn't beloved for its looks. Fortunately, it isn't so hard to conceal this ordinary metal with plants. Maybe the result won't have the charm of a white picket fence laden with pink rambler roses, but it will look a lot better than it did bare.

You can dress up your fence with two kinds of plants: climbing vines and dense evergreen shrubs. And as with any planting project, the environmental factors of sun, shade, space and soil will guide your choices.

But first a word about climbing roses.

These lovely plants are widely used on chain-link fences, particularly by business and industry wanting to beautify their security fences. And though spectacular when in bloom from late spring until early summer, climbing roses don't look so great much of the year. I like climbing roses in small numbers, placed where they can steal the show when in bloom, but not in a location you look at all the time.

And if your chain-link fence surrounds a swimming pool or play area, where bare arms and legs may easily bump into thorny canes, climbing roses are definitely not the best choice.

The hard-edged look of a chain-link fence really calls for plants with a soft texture that will provide contrast. That's why ligustrum and Chinese hollies are not my first choices for this project, although they would do a fine job of concealing the fence.

I prefer such shrubs as the Southern Indica azaleas, which are dense yet possess a fine texture. A dwarf Burford holly, which is softer-edged than the Chinese holly, is another good choice.

But the shrub I like best for this task is nandina. Nandina is not the ordinary plant many people consider it. The ferny foliage possesses an interesting range of colors from darkest green to bright red. Cut it back hard, and it recovers nicely -- and rapidly. The winter berries are abundant and useful for Christmas decorations. It grows 4 to 6 feet tall, making it the right height for most fences on home properties. Its gentle stems and leaves grow neatly and gracefully into the fence, dense enough to conceal it on both sides.

Shrubs require space. If you have a narrow space next to a fence, you'd be better off with a vine, which won't get in the way.

In these cases, I like English ivy, which can be woven through the chain links and eventually cover the fence quite densely.

Our own Carolina jessamine (South Carolina's state flower), is another good choice. It is a strong, dense vine with semi-evergreen foliage that blooms for a month or more in the spring. It would not blanket the fence like a shrub or the ivy, but with training, could rise to the top, then spill gracefully over the sides. I like ivy better on a fence than on the ground.

Various honeysuckles, along with the deciduous silver fleece vine and dutchman's pipe, are other possibilities.

All of these plants will take several seasons to achieve your goal of hiding the fence. In the meantime, you might consider planting quick-growing annual vines such as sweet peas, morning glories or moon vine.

Summer

It's time to...

- Give your flower beds a midsummer dose of fertilizer, liquid or granular, at the rate directed on the package.

- Spray zinnias with fungicide to prevent attack by leaf diseases. Follow label directions.

- Cut off and replant runners of strawberry plants to expand your collection.

- Pinch back any leggy shoots of begonias, coleus and geraniums to create shapely plants.

- Keep your roses well groomed, sprayed and watered to encourage fresh growth.

- Install a protective net if birds are after your berries.

- Make a final pinching of chrysanthemums to induce compact, bushy growth.

- Remove stems of daylilies and yarrows as they finish blooming.

- Go over your potted plants and the flower garden, removing spent blooms.

- Take a close look at the blades of grass a day or so after mowing. Ragged edges mean you should get the mower blade sharpened.

- Sow broccoli seeds in flats or pots for transplanting into the garden later this summer.

- Cut back blackberry canes after fruits are harvested to stimulate new shoots and allow space for canes that will bear next year's crop.

- Look for browning tips and edges of houseplants – signals that the plant is losing more water than the roots are taking in. You'll need to water more often during these hot weeks.

- Keep tomato plants evenly watered to avoid cracking fruits, blossom-end rot and loss of plants that should produce for months yet.

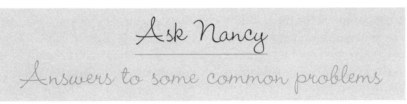

Ask Nancy

Answers to some common problems

WHY DIDN'T MY PEONIES BLOOM THIS YEAR?

The plants could be suffering from crowding, too much shade (Have trees or shrubs nearby stretched to shade the plants?), drought during the development of flower buds in the spring or from being planted too deeply. They require full sun, and the crowns of the plant should grow even with the top of the ground. If the plants have been in the ground a very long time, say eight or 10 years, they could benefit from digging and dividing, but don't do this until late summer. A thin layer of wood ashes from your fireplace may also help stimulate blooms.

I'VE PLANTED AJUGA. DO I STILL NEED PINE NEEDLES TO HOLD DOWN THE WEEDS?

Ajuga, sometimes called bugleweed, is a good choice for a ground cover in a deeply shaded, dry area. It grows quickly into a mat and bears white or bluish-purple flowers in the spring; the flowers individually aren't outstanding, but a spread of them is pleasing.

Ajuga, however, remains quite flat on the ground, the leaves barely rising. It is also susceptible to a disease called crown rot; to avoid this, the soil must not stay wet.

Ask Nancy

Answers to some common problems

Putting even a thin layer of pine needles on the bed of ajuga is likely to slow down the plant's rapid growth and retain moisture that could cause crown rot. Such a thin layer probably would not suppress many weeds.

So while the plants are growing, I think you are sentenced to pulling any weeds that emerge. Once the ajuga has grown into its mat, a few persistent weeds may still poke through crevices between the leaves. Pulling them out, especially before they set seeds, is the way to handle this problem.

WHY IS MY NEWLY PLANTED PLUM TREE DROPPING LEAVES?

Most likely, this problem is due to lack of water. The tree is shedding leaves to compensate for this. Newly planted trees, whose root systems are still settling into the ground, particularly suffer from dry weather their first and second summers. You must compensate for this by watering the trees. The entire root ball should be watered evenly and deeply at least once a week when it doesn't rain. Use a sprinkler or soaker hose to make sure the entire root ball gets wet. Your investment in this tree makes action mandatory.

WHAT DO I DO WITH HOLLYHOCKS NOW THAT THE BLOOM IS OVER?

With the last of the flowers faded on the main stalk, you can retrieve seedpods and get seeds for more plants. The seedpods are the knobby things where the flowers used to bloom along the stems. Pull them off easily and break open to get the seeds.

Sow the seeds now in a pot protected from hot summer sun and set plants out in the garden this fall. They'll survive winter and be ready to take off next spring.

Once you've harvested the seeds, cut off the main stalk to ground level. There may be signs of fresh growth at the base of the plant. This could rise and bloom in the cooler days of fall. Cross your fingers.

In our hot climate, hollyhocks are usually biennials, living only for two years – the first, to germinate and grow roots and foliage; the second, to bloom and bear seeds. In areas with cooler summers, they are short-lived perennials. But their prolific seed production should keep you well stocked with plants.

MY PETUNIAS ARE GETTING LEGGY. SHOULD I PULL THEM UP AND PLANT SOMETHING ELSE?

The plants you're ready to give up on in July could surprise you in August and September. Petunias grow quite nicely in the cooler weather of late summer and early autumn, provided they get enough sunshine and water.

Some kinds of petunias get leggy, particularly if they aren't pinched or tip pruned to encourage side growth and a bushier plant. If your plants are healthy, rejuvenate them by pruning off about one-third of the leggy growth, then watering and fertilizing the plants to stimulate them.

The plants you're ready to give up on in July could surprise you in August and September.

August

IT'S NOT ALL BAD

Oh, it's easy to say that August wears us out. Clothed in

summer's heat and humidity, it tempts us with visions of autumn.

It is still weeks until that golden season when we

will garden with gusto again. Yet August has its virtues. The vegetable

garden is still going strong, and there are new things to put in it. The

flower gardens get dressed up with fresh blooms of perennials and even

bits of new annuals put in to replace the ones ruined by

whatever July brought. So August moves along, and we

dabble in the evening light, getting shorter every day.

September is on the horizon. Until then, we will just

do small things in the garden.

Summer

FALL OFFERS A FRESH CHANCE FOR VEGETABLES

August means a fresh start for vegetable gardeners. Seedlings of such great fall crops as broccoli, cauliflower, collards and cabbage, and fresh seed packages of radishes, carrots, beets, leaf lettuce, spinach and other leafy greens await in garden centers.

But the autumn garden isn't without its perils. Late summer has warm soil, and that's good. But the sun remains hot, although noticeably less forceful each day, it seems. And rainfall tends to be pounding and erratic.

So pay close attention to watering seeds and seedlings while temperatures remain high. A daily check is mandatory to check soil moisture so that the plants don't dry out and wilt. Water as early in the day as possible.

Mulch is important, too, because it will keep the temperature of the soil cooler and moister during hot stretches in August and September. But it is difficult to protect young seedlings and plants with mulch without drowning them in it. Wait until plants are a few inches high, then add the mulch.

Placement of your fall crops should be easy. Remove summer crops that are spent, declining or diseased. Then dig the soil lightly and replenish it with a balanced fertilizer at the rate directed on the package. Tuck your fall seedlings into these places or sow rows or blocks of seeds.

Don't forget to watch for insects.

What to Plant

- **Beets**. Sow seeds by Sept. 1. Thin seedlings 2 inches apart. Detroit Dark Red matures in 55 to 60 days.

- **Broccoli.** Set out plants, 18 inches apart, now. Varieties such as Green Comet and Premium Crop mature in 70 to 80 days.

- **Brussels sprouts.** Set out plants now, 14 to 18 inches apart. Varieties such as Long Island Improved mature in 90 to 100 days.

- **Carrots.** Sow seeds now in light, porous soil; thin seedlings 2 inches apart. Danvers Half Long matures in 60 to 90 days.

- **Cauliflower.** Set out plants now, 18 inches apart. Early Snowball matures in 55 to 65 days.

- **Collards.** Sow seeds or set out plants now, 18 inches apart. Thin seedlings to same distance. Varieties such as Vates, Morris Improved Heading and Georgia mature in 90 to 120 days.

- **Kale.** Sow seeds between now and mid-September. Thin seedlings to 2 inches apart. Varieties such as Dwarf Siberian Improved mature in 55 to 70 days and taste best after exposure to frosty fall weather.

- **Leaf lettuce**. Sow short rows every two weeks until late September. Varieties such as Salad Bowl, Buttercrunch and Black Seeded Simpson mature in 45 to 50 days.

- **Mustard.** Sow seeds between now and mid-September. Thin plants to 2 inches apart. Varieties such as Southern Giant Curled and Tendergreen mature in 30 to 40 days.

- **Onions**. Plant onion bulbs 4 inches apart between Sept. 1 and Oct. 15. Varieties such as Silver Skin and Yellow Danvers mature in 60 to 80 days.

- **Radishes.** Sow short rows of seeds every 10 days or so between now and mid-September. Thin seedlings to 1 inch apart. Varieties such as Early Scarlet Globe and Cherry Belle mature in 20 to 25 days.

- **Spinach.** Sow seeds every two weeks until mid-September. Thin seedlings to stand 3 inches apart. Harvest usually begins in 45 to 50 days. A mild autumn and winter means a long harvest of spinach.

- **Turnips.** Sow seeds until mid-September. Thin seedlings to 2 inches apart. Varieties such as Purple Top White Globe mature in 40 to 60 days.

BEFORE FALL COMES, EVALUATE YOUR GARDEN

I like to think of mid-August as the evaluation season, a time to take stock and make plans for autumn, which, I am thrilled to announce, is just around the corner.

The busiest gardening season of the year is just ahead. September begins three months of nonstop gardening. Lawns will be rebuilt, shrub beds remade, tiny bulbs and majestic trees planted. The prospect is enough to tantalize the most experienced gardener, or overwhelm the beginner.

Between now and then, you should think. Think about what you have, and what you don't have in the garden.

Think about what's good and should be kept, what's bad and should go.

Think about how you use your property and how landscaping can make it a more useful place for entertaining and enjoyment. Don't trust your memory; keep a written record of your successes and failures. If you don't, you're likely to forget the name of that fabulous tomato as soon as you devour the last fruit. Worse, you'll forget about the purple zinnas that clashed so awfully with your red brick, and end up planting the same thing next year.

Evaluating the vegetable garden means rating your crops' production, both in length of season and abundance of produce. Also consider how much space the crops required and how much food they produced. Also, think about how they tasted compared with what is available at farmers' markets and groceries.

The fourth factor is the pest test. Were your tomatoes and peppers, beans and cucumbers reasonably free from pests? Or were some so badly affected by insects or fungus that they weren't worth the space? Write down the ones that didn't cause such grief.

This is also a good time to look over your trees and shrubs and decide where new ones should be

added. Some shrubs may need to be replaced, particularly if they are old and overgrown, badly diseased or simply not something you like. The garden is for your pleasure. Do not feel guilty about ripping out something you don't enjoy. You can get ahead of the game by doing some of this removal now.

It is also a good time to take a close look at your property. In the dog days, that takes no energy.

Decide if you want to reduce your lawn by adding shrub beds, natural areas and flower beds this fall. Use a garden hose to outline shapes and sizes of beds and study it.

Make note of problem areas in the lawn -- such as shaded places or slopes where grass is very hard to grow. You can deal with it in the fall by replacing the grass with evergreen ground covers.

Finally, determine if you need space used in a different way. Does the area where your children like to play need a shade tree? Will this be the year for a new deck or patio? Have you discovered a yen for perennials and want a long bed just for them? Will August ever end?

HOW TO DRY MONEY PLANTS

If you're growing the money plant, Lunaria annua, this summer, here's an easy way to preserve it for dried arrangements. When the pods change from green to brown, cut the stems, but don't put them in water. When ready, the brown membrane on the seed pod slips off easily to show the silvery pods. Let some of the seeds around in the garden. They'll drop to the ground, sprout and provide a fresh array of plants for next year. Money plant is a biennial, meaning plants germinate one year, bear seeds and die the next.

Summer

TROPICAL FEVER
PLANTS THAT LOVE THE HEAT ARE HOT

Tropical plants such as the mandevilla vine, as well as the hibiscus, pentas and plumbago and even coleus, can lend an exotic look to your garden in summer. However, the plants will not survive winter outdoors. If you want to keep them, grow them in pots and bring them indoors for the winter. Here are some popular choices for summer gardens.

❀ **Cape plumbago.** A popular shrub in the Florida landscape, cape plumbago bears clusters of sky – blue or white flowers on stiff stems with small leaves. Don't water too much. To produce fresh stems and flowers, cut back the plant when you bring it outdoors in the spring.

❀ **Coleus**. New types of this bedding plant, loved for its colorful foliage, tolerate sun. But forget about the flowers. Snip them off and enjoy this plant for the rich colors and patterns of its leaves. In fall, make cuttings and root them in pots for small plants you can keep indoors through winter.

❀ **Mandevilla**. A twining vine especially popular for lampposts and mailboxes, mandevilla has a season that's long and full of flowers. The pink variety, Alice du Pont, is widely grown. Mandevilla likes fertile, moist soil and sun. Another important tropical vine, bearing sunny yellow flowers, is the allamanda.

❀ **Pentas.** An evergreen perennial that won't stand freezing weather, pentas makes an excellent pot plant for steps, stoop or deck. The varieties on the market are usually red, pink, lavender or white. Bring the potted pentas indoors for the winter, and water sparingly.

❀ **Tropical hibiscus.** One of the leading plants for sunny decks in the Charlotte area, the tropical hibiscus plant bears large flowers in vivid reds, pinks, oranges, yellows and other luscious shades. Indoors, all winter, give it your sunniest place. Cut back the plant in early spring.

Cape plumbago

Coleus

Pentas

Tropical hibiscus

Summer

BEYOND PHILODENDRONS, TRY OFFBEAT HOUSEPLANTS

You may have seen this crop of houseplants and thought: Too hard. Too picky. Too demanding. They're not philodendrons or peace lilies that you can park on the coffee table and forget. But they have more style. And you can succeed with them. Now, while the heat and humidity are on, it's fun to buy and enjoy these plants indoors where you can enjoy the look – but not the feel – of a tropical summer.

Anthurium. Look at an anthurium – the common name is flamingo flower – and you can't help but think Florida. But this is a plant with a place in Piedmont homes, provided you meet its specific requirements of light and humidity. Native to Costa Rica and Guatemala, this anthurium grows slowly and prospers in a temperature range of 60 to 70 degrees year round. It requires the strong sunlight of a west window in the winter and the less harsh exposure of an east or north window in the summer. And don't let a draft blow its way. Keep the soil well laced with peat and sphagnum moss and evenly moist. Use a mister to keep the humidity up. Fertilize every couple of weeks with liquid plant food. Enjoy the distinctive, long-lasting red blooms. Even when the blooms fade, the leaves make an attractive houseplant. With luck, it will bloom again.

Calathea

remind some people of the peacock's fan. The undersides of the leaves, shades of pale to dark green on top, are a soft maroon. The calatheas, natives of Brazil, are about as picky as it gets concerning humidity. They demand high humidity. In an air-conditioned house, that probably means misting every single day. They also like light shade, so set them in the interior of a room where no sunbeams will hit the leaves. Fertilize plants with liquid fertilizer every two weeks. While the plant is growing, keep it well watered with warmish water. And if you don't want people to rub their fingers over the ribs and lines of the calathea's foliage, don't take it to the office.

Calla lily. Though sometimes grown as a garden flower, the calla lily performs better when planted in a pot and treated like a houseplant. Its light, temperature and humidity requirements aren't terribly exacting. It requires bright light and an hour or so of direct sun. As with most flowers, cooler temperatures will make the blooms, which are pink or white, last longer. A key factor in the plant's longevity is keeping the soil well watered. When the pot is packed with roots, and the plant is growing vigorously, that probably means every

Anthurium

Calathea. Forget about flowers; this a houseplant to love for its foliage. The plant, which comes in many colorful varieties, gets its common name, peacock plant, from the distinctive ribbing and lines that

What's blooming in August

- ❀ Ageratum
- ❀ Crape myrtle
- ❀ Liriope
- ❀ Black-eyed susans
- ❀ Cardinal flower
- ❀ Leadwort

- ❀ Lycoris
- ❀ Chelone
- ❀ Mandevilla
- ❀ Lantana
- ❀ Pentas
- ❀ Abelia

- ❀ Canna
- ❀ Sweet autumn clematis
- ❀ Hardy begonias
- ❀ Dahlias
- ❀ Helenium

day or so. Add fertilizer every couple of weeks. As blooms fade and leaves begin to die back, reduce the water and then let the plant spend the rest of the summer in a shady place outdoors, quietly gaining strength for another season. Bring it indoors for the winter.

Rabbit's foot fern. Gardeners have been struggling to succeed with tropical ferns indoors for decades, but this one should cause less suffering. It simply doesn't require rain-forest humidity, the lack of which causes many tropical ferns, such as maidenhair, to drop dead in heated homes. But rabbit's foot fern, botanically named Davallia fejeensis and native to the Fiji Islands of the South Pacific, should prosper with the level of humidity home gardeners can give it. Mist the frothy, delicately cut leaves occasionally and stand the plant on a tray of pebbles and water. The pebbles will keep the pot from standing in water, which will create the gentle humidity this fern needs.

Give the plant bright light but no direct sunlight, normal household temperatures and weak liquid fertilizer every two weeks. In winter, let the soil dry out a bit between waterings. The plant gets its common name from the distinctive furry rhizomes from which the fern fronds rise. These rhizomes climb over the sides of the pot. They are most apparent when you grow the plant in a hanging basket.

Calla lily

Rabbit's foot fern ·

HOW TO DIVIDE HOUSEPLANTS

If you've been taking good care of the houseplants you set outdoors this summer, you should have a bonus coming: extra plants.

Look closely at the base of a well-grown tropical plant, and you're likely to see tiny young plants rising around the perimeter of the pot or trailing over the side.

You can easily remove these small plants from the mother plant, replant them and grow a new generation of ferns, spider plants or African violets.

Others, such as philodendron, grape ivy, peperomia, Swedish ivy, geraniums or English ivy, are easily propagated by short cuttings from the stem tips that can be rooted and replanted.

Summer

These methods are basic propagation techniques that every gardener should learn. They are quick and cheap ways to expand your collection.

Once the young plants have grown a bit, they will also prove handy as gifts for friends and family. They're insurance, too, if the mother plant should suddenly drop dead. Plants do that. There are three simple methods you can use.

Division. Division simply means separating main stems or crowns into portions with attached roots that can be replanted separately in a small container with fresh potting soil. This is a very fast method of propagation. Take the plant out of the pot, then gently pull apart sections of the plant, with top and roots attached. If you need to cut apart some roots to separate the sections, don't hesitate. Many types of house plants, including ferns, most begonias, anthurium, African violets, peperomia, umbrella plant and palms, lend themselves to propagation by division, best done when the plant is at its peak of growth in the summer. Your new plants should be ready for dis-

playing or giving away in two or three weeks.

Plantlets. A few popular houseplants, such as piggyback plant, spider plant and strawberry geranium, produce plantlets at the tips of leaves or stems. Cut these plantlets off and and plant them in a fresh mixture. Keep them watered and humidified (cover the pot with a plastic bag) while they grow new roots, which should take three or four weeks.

Cuttings. Most houseplants can be propagated by cuttings. Some gardeners root cuttings in water, but I prefer to root plants in potting mixture. Simply take a cutting about 4 inches long, making sure there are at least two leaf nodes where roots will sprout. Trim to just below the lowest nodes and remove the lowest leaves. Then put the cuttings in a potting mixture. A bag covering the plant will increase humidity. Rooting powder will also hasten root development. Roots should form in two or three weeks. This method is commonly used with such trailing plants as pothos, ivy, grape ivy and philodendron.

The piggyback plant is an easy houseplant to propagate in summer.

HOW TO PRESERVE SEEDS

A young woman I know, new to gardening, was amazed when morning glories bloomed out of nowhere on her fence. Someone probably had planted the morning glories one previous spring, and the blooms dropped seeds that sprang into life later. That is nature's way.

Plants regenerate themselves by shedding seeds on the ground, seeds that lie dormant until the tem-

perature is right and they germinate, usually the next spring.

In the garden, that works for a number of popular garden flowers such as morning glories, impatiens, larkspur and poppies, whose seeds will survive winter's chill.

Some are even tougher. One of the famous plant stories of history is how, after World War I ended in

Europe, red poppies, their vitality not destroyed, germinated and bloomed on the battlefields of Flanders. Rather than just let seeds drop on the ground, then risk having them lost, a better choice is to harvest and save seeds for sowing next year.

Seed-saving works best with nonhybrid plants. These are plants whose seeds produce offspring that look identical or very closely resemble the parent plant. The plant has produced seed for many generations, so the offspring is a predictable match.

Hybrid plants, usually marked F1 on the seed packet, are the result of recent crosses and have a less stable gene pool. So their offspring are likely to be different and possibly inferior. A rich pink hybrid impatiens produces a muddy lavender one; or a cream hybrid marigold bears an ordinary pale yellow flower.

Even with nonhybrids, you should gather seeds from the healthiest, strongest plants. In most groups of plants, some will stand out for their obvious vigor.

Make a small label on a plastic stake to identify the chosen ones.

There is nothing magic about harvesting seeds at the right time. Some seeds, such as beans and tomatoes, are gathered from fleshy fruit, others from the seed pods that follow the flowers. The pods should be fairly brittle and on the dry side. If the pod looks quite delicate, cover it with a tiny paper bag tied gently to the stem.

Make sure to get the seeds before the pods of plants like lettuce, petunias and peas open and sprinkle them on the ground.

Fleshy fruits such as tomatoes should be overripe before harvest; then you can cull and wash the seeds.

Let your seeds dry while spread on white paper for a few days. Then put them in small, tight jars to keep out moisture for winter storage in a cool, dry place.

Don't forget to write the names down, or you will find yourself scratching your head about whether this jar has nasturtiums or that jar has lettuce.

Another caution about seed-saving concerns various squash and cabbage family plants. These are notorious cross-pollinators and should be kept separate in the garden to maintain a perfect strain. With these plants, it's better to start with purchased seeds.

Most flower and vegetable seeds hold their viability for at least two years, especially if they aren't exposed to high temperatures and moisture, which shorten their life. Don't count on the longevity and durability demonstrated by the poppies of Flanders fields.

Plants regenerate themselves by shedding seeds on the ground.

LATE-SUMMER BLOOMERS CAN REFRESH YOUR GARDEN

With summer on its downward slope, a cast of wonderful perennials blooms in August, giving the garden a new look as it makes the transition toward fall. These late-summer bloomers will also freshen up the garden in advance of the aster and chrysanthemum seasons.

Cardinal flower. This native plant likes damp, rich soil. Tall stems bearing scarlet flowers rise above rosettes of leaves at ground level. In good conditions, the plants will drop seeds and new plants rise. In less hospitable conditions (dry, poor soil), cardinal flowers tend to be short lived. Plants grow 3 to 4 feet tall and do best when shaded from hot afternoon sun.

Leadwort. I recommend this plant often because the color of its flowers – a beautiful cobalt blue – is so unusual. It is best suited for growing in corners of the flower bed, but it could also serve as an edger. Low and spreading, leadwort (botanically named ceratostigma) grows about 1 foot tall, prospers in rich soil and performs best in the South with afternoon shade. Leadwort demands excellent soil drainage in the winter and is famous for its slow start in the spring. Stems may not leaf

Summer

It's time to...

- Keep your azaleas, rhododendrons and camellias watered while they set buds this month.

- Look over your houseplants summering outdoors. Remove broken or brown leaves and stems. Fertilize the plants.

- Stay vigilant against attacks of mealybugs, spider mites and scale on houseplants.

- Sow seeds of beets, leaf lettuce, spinach, turnips and radishes.

- Start looking for young plants of broccoli, cauliflower and collards to plant for fall harvest.

- Repot houseplants whose roots fill the pot. Tip the plant out of the pot to check. If roots wind around the root ball, replant in a larger container.

- Take stock and list the changes you want to make in the garden during prime planting time this fall.

- Start thinking about which new shrubs and trees you'll select and plant this fall.

- Sow seeds of such hardy flowers as English daisies, coneflowers, wallflowers and forget-me-nots in pots or trays, but keep the seedlings protected from harsh sunlight.

- Hire someone to aerate the lawn in September (or find a place to rent an aerator).

- Start shopping for fertilizer and grass seed you'll need soon for lawn renewal.

- Groom the flower beds, removing spent blooms and plants, in anticipation of a revived fall garden.

out until May, which makes gardeners think it has gone to sleep for good.

Lycoris. Strap-shaped leaves of this bulb rise in spring and wither away in early to mid-summer, making people wonder if it is dead and gone. But – it seems magical – a flower stalk a couple of feet tall rises in mid-August. The stalk bears five to seven rosy-lilac flowers, each about 3 inches long. The pink color is more spring than August, but I couldn't hold that against such a reliable plant. Resembling lilies, these flowers also have a strong, sweet scent. Grow them in full sun with perfect drainage and leave them alone for years. They will surprise you every year.

Chelone. I love this plant because it bears flowers that are odd in shape but one of the loveliest shades of pink in the garden. Chelone is also called turtlehead, which may give you an idea of what the flower looks like. If it weren't such a

pretty, clear pink, turtlehead would be downright weird with its curved, tubular petals arranged sort of like a turtle's open mouth above shiny leaves. Chelone, however, does not look great as a single plant. For best effect, start with at least three plants; more is even better. Plants grow 2 to 3 feet tall; give it part shade and moisture. There is also a white form.

These reliable perennials are the stars of August, supported by zinnias, periwinkle, petunias, impatiens and other long-blooming summer annuals. Some of these annuals – such as impatiens, begonias and periwinkle – will last until the first frost.

Liriope. It, too, produces pretty white or purple, but liriope is more ground cover than garden flower. And sweet autumn clematis has a wonderful fragrance and pretty white flowers, but it may become a pest, springing out of lawns and flower beds faster than you can rip it out.

Summer

HARDY FERNS ADD FRESHNESS

In the parched world that is August, a few things stand out fresh as the daisies of May. One is the wonderful range of hardy ferns that still look green and lush even when everything else is dry with despair. At no other time of year do I appreciate these plants more. If they could speak, ferns might complain about the heat, but they sure don't show it. They've been around for eons, and they've rolled with whatever punches nature dealt them.

Too often, gardeners overlook these beautiful and interesting plants. I have heard people express surprise that (1) ferns grow in the ground as well as in pots; (2) they come with more than one shade of green; and (3) they survive winter. Perhaps that's because potted tropical ferns such as Dallas and Fluffy Ruffles are permanent residents of countless bathrooms and kitchens.

But hardy ferns are plants for woods and garden. Some are evergreen, some deciduous. They are practically indestructible. A large limb fell into a colony of ferns at my house one summer. Though a number of fronds were broken, the plants survived. They have also survived the coldest winters and the hottest, driest summers of the 1990s and a hurricane.

Naturally, among this huge class of plants, I have favorites. Here are four:

Christmas fern. Evergreen and vigorous, the fronds rise from the central crown in a circular pattern. This fern will take deep shade – mine is under an azalea that spread above it. It would have grown faster in damper soil, but the neighboring azalea's requirement of well-drained soil prevails. The Christmas fern, whose form is more upright in warm weather, tends to flatten in the winter, but that is only a small demerit for this marvelous plant. A bonus is that the fronds are large – 12 inches and up – and sturdy enough to cut and use as greenery in flower arrangements.

Maidenhair. The delicate appearance of the hardy maidenhair -- which resembles the popular tropical form sold as a house plant -- belies its nature. It is tough and reliable, provided it gets light shade and slightly moist soil. Fronds die down to the ground in autumn, and new growth rises in the spring. This is a real winner of a fern and well suited as a companion to the smaller woodland wildflowers that bloom in spring. The fern will keep the bed interesting – and cool looking -- through the summer and fall.

Cinnamon. Admired for its vertical fronds, the cinnamon fern is most notable for its dramatic fronds bearing fertile spores that are initially green, then turn cinnamon-brown as they mature. This is a big fern, and fronds may reach an impressive 4 feet in very damp soil. Cinnamon fern is also a plant for the sunny garden -- the middle to back of the sunny garden. But it will prosper in shade as well.

Lady. This is the kind of fern that recovered from a beating by my tree limb. And it is the fern that most people would say looks like a fern. Fronds are feathery and lacy and light to medium green. It requires light to medium shade and moist soil. My lady ferns don't grow quickly, because they are under a willow oak tree where the soil tends to be dry in summer. Yet even with this, they have prospered over the years, a testament to the remarkable adaptability of these ancient plants.

Lacy and tough, hardy ferns make even August seem cooler.

Native ferns are hardy and well suited to the shade garden.

Summer

PERK UP YOUR MEALS WITH EDIBLE BLOSSOMS

Take a second look at your nasturtiums, daylilies and violets. You might see them adding zing to your soups, color to your salads and a pretty touch to your dinner plates. They're part of the world of edible flowers. Once you batter-fry daylily blooms, chop pansies into salads and whip up nasturtium butter, they'll never look the same. Literally.

But consider two things first:

Not all flowers are edible. Some, such as the popular Carolina jessamine, are toxic and should never be put in a dish or on a plate. Keep to the specific lists of known edibles. Be sure you know what flower you're picking. The poisonous Carolina jessamine, for instance, looks a lot like honeysuckle, which is edible.

Don't use edible flowers that have been sprayed with chemical pesticides. Assume that a florist's flowers have been sprayed.

Perhaps the best way is to create a garden of edible blooms, with varieties chosen for a year-round harvest and grown from seeds yourself. With a bed dedicated to edible flowers, you can ensure that nothing poisonous gets sprayed on it. Even if that means you're down on your knees beating the brains (what brains?) out of a slug or insect en route to the tender petals of a Lemon Gem marigold or Whirlybird nasturtium, it will be worth it.

Nibble on violets.

Organic farms, which don't use pesticides, should also prove a reliable source of edible flowers.

The choices may surprise you. Marigolds aren't famed for their scent, but the Mexican Mint marigold and the Lemon Gem marigold have appealing flavor.

Harvest the blooms at the freshest moment, which means in the cool of the early morning. Keep them cool and moist in a damp paper towel in the refrigerator until you're ready to use them later that day.

Here are seven common and easy-to-grow plants that produce edible flowers:

Squash. The big, orange-yellow, star-shaped blossoms of the yellow squash or green zucchini plant may be stuffed with rice or cooked as fritters.

Violet. Tiny violets make crystallized flowers for beautiful decorations and irresistible nibbling. They combine with sweet geranium leaves and lemon balm for a fragrant salad.

Honeysuckle. White, coral or yellow blossoms garnish cold chicken salad with white grapes. The flowers also look especially pretty in desserts, soufflés, ice cream or custard dishes.

Rose. Petals decorate desserts. They also make jams, ice cream and sorbet.

Pansy. Pansies go into fennel salad with calendula blossoms and vinaigrette, add color and elegance to pasta, go into a pepper quiche.

Chrysanthemum. Use blanched and dried chrysanthemum petals for watercress, apple and walnut salad or garnish a red cabbage and apple casserole.

Nasturtium. Zesty, bright yellow, orange or red spicy flowers and tangy green leaves are delicious in salads and sandwiches. They also make wonderful garnishes.

Summer

A Private Paradise
FIND CALM IN A SECRET GARDEN

*"She held back the swinging curtain of ivy
and pushed back the door, which opened slowly — slowly.
Then she slipped through it looking about her
and breathing quite fast with excitement, and wonder,
and delight. She was standing inside the secret garden."*

—*The Secret Garden* by Frances Hodgson Burnett

Call it whatever you please — a secret garden, a garden room, a garden in the garden, a destination garden.

It's a secluded hideaway outdoors, a different place than deck, patio or lawn where you can hear the phone and you're an easy target for anyone who wants to talk or get something done.

The small, secret garden of Burnett's famous novel was set in a mammoth estate in Yorkshire, England. Like the story's unloved children, Mary Lennox and Colin Craven, it was in dire need of a guiding hand. Yet, its secrecy and tranquillity drew the invalid boy and orphaned girl -- plus their pal from the village, Dickon -- through the ivy-draped wooden door and into a place that was all theirs.

The lesson of this wonderful story is that secret gardens rank among the most special, the most personal places.

You can have one. The place might be carved out of native woods, a slender side yard others rarely use, even an open space you can enclose or shield. Ideally, it would be out of earshot of traffic and phones. It need not be large. It doesn't need to be a hike from the house. And it doesn't have to be furnished with 200-year-old boxwoods to be beautiful, romantic and secret.

What it needs is, of course, enclosure. Most likely, you do not have a 12-foot brick wall draped in roses and ivy like the one that shielded Mary and Colin while they and their plants began to thrive. But you could have a fence of wood or wrought iron. Or a thick hedge of evergreens such as ligustrum, hemlock, cryptomeria or holly. Even several low-limbed trees with underplantings of evergreen shrubs such as azaleas, pieris, small hollies or cleyers will create the sense of privacy that secret gardens demand.

And they need an entrance, concealed as much as possible. Mary Lennox discovered the door to her secret garden when the wind mysteriously blew back its thick ivy cover. But if your enclosure is made by plants instead of solid brick, it won't need a door. The entrance could be a gap in the hedge or shrubbery wide enough to pass through and situated away from the view of most passersby.

It's not just the destination that's important, it's the journey, too. Whether the path to the secret garden is long or short, it should create a sense of traveling somewhere. A winding path of pine needles or stepping-stones through the trees can be curved so that your mind anticipates what is around the next bend: a spring wildflower just coming into bloom, ladybugs eating aphids on a climbing rose, the first uncurling fiddleheads.

Once you reach the secret garden's concealed

Summer

entrance, you must find, as Mary Lennox told Colin, "something special." There must be a place to sit, such as a small bench or pair of chairs, but not too many places to sit. (Remember, this is for you, not the neighborhood.) And there should be a small table large enough to hold a book and a teacup or coffee mug, a tiny picnic or iced tea for two.

Putting a solid floor of brick or other pavement on portions of the secret garden will add to its year-round enjoyment. The entire area should not be paved, however, because that would reduce the possibilities for planting and make it seem more like a patio with walls. The canopy of trees should shield the people and plants in the garden from heat, yet let in filtered sunlight.

Scented plants, textured plants and plants the wind can ruffle will enhance your enjoyment of the destination garden. Pick your favorites: gardenias in bloom in early summer, potted petunias or heliotrope you bring along with you from the sunny deck, a rosemary plant you brush past en route. Consider a birdbath or a simple statue.

Early blooming bulbs such as miniature daffodils and crocuses will draw you to the garden on mild days in late winter. If the garden is sunny, it should have roses, as Mary and Colin's did. Climbers, shrub or bush roses, take your pick. Choosing flowers of restful colors, such as white or pastels, will increase the garden's serenity. Save the not-so-restful flowers of yellow, red and orange for a more public, exciting garden.

The secret garden is for you. You may not need it to restore health to your body, as Colin did, or to create an interest outside yourself, as Mary did, but a secret garden can lure you to it with its promise of peace and beauty.

A secret garden can lure you to it with its promise of peace and beauty.

HOW TO REDUCE WORK IN YOUR GARDEN

Days are hot, the evenings almost as bad. About the most gardening anyone wants to do these days is pull a ripe tomato off the vine. The term, "low maintenance," forgotten in a wave of energy and enthusiasm all spring, now has your full attention.

Low-maintenance plants don't need pruning every other day. They aren't attacked by every pest under the sun. They don't break up in ice storms or litter the landscape with messy fruits and broken limbs. Relax, there are plenty.

Two basic principles apply: Choose plants that don't bring problems with them, and set out plants where they have space to reach their mature height and width. Learn this information before you buy any plant.

But low maintenance doesn't mean no maintenance. Even a bed of ground-cover junipers or liriope will need a check for the odd weed; azaleas that are just the right size for the front border will still need fertilizer and, in dry stretches, watering; a sturdy oak will still need training and pruning.

Here are some of the trees, shrubs, perennials and ground covers that I think of as low-maintenance plants:

Trees: Ginkgo (male plants only; females produce foul-smelling fruit), Eastern redbud, magnolia, oaks, Japanese zelkova, hackberry, fruitless sweet gum, tulip poplar and American holly.

Shrubs: Barberry, deutzia, forsythia, witch hazel, beauty bush, rugosa roses, spirea, viburnum, weigela, aucuba, abelia, nandina, mahonia, osmanthus, pieris.

Perennials: Hosta, daylilies, yarrow, coreopsis, Lenten rose, crane's bill geranium, candytuft, creeping phlox, black-eyed susans, veronica, sedums, lily of the valley and lamb's ears.

Ground covers: Mondo grass, blue fescue, periwinkle, ajuga, wintercreeper and lamium.

Mahonia

CANNAS COME INTO THEIR OWN

Remember cannas, those bland bit players of the Southern garden, dependable but never dazzling?

Well, it's a new age for cannas, and the bit player is making moves toward stardom. No longer just a green screen with an oddly shaped summer bloom, cannas now make dramatic statements in huge beds along interstate highways, catch the public eye in botanical gardens and show their class in flowerbeds at malls.

The canna can thank hot summers, the increasing interest in perennials with tropical flair and an array of newer varieties dressed out in some of the boldest, fanciest leaves around.

At the same time, there is renewed respect for what cannas can do for a garden. And they can do a lot with their size, bold texture, broad foliage and wealth of color from pale green with yellow stripes to almost burgundy black.

Some varieties, such as Bengal Tiger (also called Pretoria), have been around for 30 to 40 years, awaiting broad recognition and wider commercial reach that followed rising interest in many kinds of plants with tropical allure. These include lantana, pentas, elephant ear, castor bean, hibiscus, allamanda, mandevilla and the hardier palms.

As more cannas were grown commercially, new ones emerged that were different enough to warrant introducing to world markets.

The major pest in the Piedmont is the canna leafroller, a caterpillar that gets inside the dark, damp confines of a rolled leaf, stitches it permanently closed and feeds on the leaf tissue. However, the leafroller is a tolerable problem. Spray with Bacillus thuringiensis, if needed.

Summer

Tips For Success

- If you don't want to face digging and dividing your cannas soon, give them space to develop. Space the rhizomes 12 to 18 inches apart. An array of several plants of the same variety is more effective than a single one or a mix of varieties.

- Set the rhizomes, which are fleshy, thick horizontal roots, 3 to 4 inches deep in loose, fertile soil. Set the rhizome horizontally, with the eye up, if you can see it. There is no top or bottom.

- Choose a sunny location. Cannas aren't shade plants.

- Though tolerant of dry weather, cannas benefit from regular watering and produce larger, better clumps than if subjected to extended stretches of dry weather.

- Cut off blooms as soon as they fade, to encourage more flowering shoots.

- After frost kills the tops, cut off the dead foliage at ground level, but leave the rhizomes in the ground through the winter in the Piedmont.

Canna

The striped leaves of Phasion cannas are more showy than their flowers.

SOME CANNA CHOICES

City of Portland, green leaves with rosy pink flowers on 42-inch plants.

Lucifer, a dwarf 21 to 32 inches tall with green leaves and red flowers with yellow edges.

Le Roi Humbert, bronze-red foliage and orange-red flowers; 54 inches.

Black Knight, bronze-to-brown leaves that bear dark red flowers; 6 feet.

Ingeborg, a dwarf with brown leaves and salmon-pink flowers.

Bengal Tiger (Pretoria), medium, striped green leaves with light orange flowers; 6 feet.

Dwarf cannas such as Doc (dark red blooms), Happy (primrose yellow) and Grumpy (red). they grow about 18 inches tall.

The President, scarlet flowers atop green leaves; 36 inches.

Ask Nancy
Answers to some common problems

WHAT IS THE BEST PLACE TO PLANT A JAPANESE MAPLE TREE THIS FALL?

A southwestern exposure with little protection from the harsh, hot heat of the summer afternoon sun would be a risky spot for a Japanese maple. The milder climate of an eastern exposure would be the happier choice.

If this were a cheap plant, experimentation with locations might be OK. But it would be an expensive loss (dare I say heartbreaking?) if the maple didn't survive or was so stressed by the heat that the leaves burned. A sad fate for one of the most beautiful small trees, famed for its foliage.

One variety of Japanese maple, Bloodgood, is reasonably heat tolerant. It is easy to find. I have one, but it grows in filtered shade on the cooler southeast side rather than the hot southwest.

Before making your decision -- and your investment – why not observe the front yard this summer and see whether the bigger trees provide the filtered shade a Japanese maple needs?

WHAT IS KILLING MY RED-TIPS?

Welcome to the club. Practically every owner of red-tip shrubs suffers the same problem, which has been around for years. Thanks to a fungus that mars the leaves and makes them fall off, uncounted red-tips died, and others were so severely disfigured by defoliation, the owners dug them up and planted something else.

If your plants don't look too bad and you want to try doctoring them, protect the new, uninfected foliage by spraying with the fungicide Daconil every 10 days during wet weather and every two weeks when the weather stays dry. Do this until hot weather arrives in June. And if it gets rainy between mid-October and late November, spray again. It's the combination of wet weather and cool temperatures that sends the fungus moving around the plants.

Because this has been such a widespread problem, people look for alternatives for screening and hedges. These include hardy anise, Camellia sasanqua, Burford holly, and even rabbiteye blueberries.

DISEASES ARE WRECKING MY ZINNIAS. WHAT WILL HELP?

I have two words to say about your problem: drip irrigation. Wet foliage is the incubator for powdery mildew fungus, which is most active in the milder temperatures of late spring and early summer. It ruins the plants for the rest of the season.

Your plants may also be affected by a leaf blight that causes red-brown spots with grayish-white centers. Those leaves eventually turn brown and die. Splashing water also moves this fungus from leaf to leaf and plant to plant.

You can't stop the rain, but you can reduce the amount of water you put on the leaves. An inexpensive drip irrigation system, actually a hose with tiny holes that let water seep into the soil, will help solve the wet-leaf problem. Follow up by protecting the plants with regular sprayings of Daconil at the rate and times directed on the label.

If you must spray the plants with a garden hose, do it early in the day so that the morning sun dries off the leaves as rapidly as possible. Or simply lay the hose on the ground and let the water flow gently onto the soil.

And when you're planting zinnias, don't crowd them; that keeps the sun from hitting and drying the lower leaves.

September

I'M BLOWING THE WHISTLE.

Not to stop the game, but to start the work. It's September, start of the gardener's year.

For people accustomed to launching their gardening year in April, this is a new way of

thinking. Transplanted Northerners used to sitting tight through that long, dead stretch of

time called winter may find it revolutionary to think that the gardener's new year doesn't

start with tomato-planting. Well, it doesn't. Not in the Piedmont. It starts with a rehab of

the lawn in September, continues with bulb-planting in October, advances through shrub

and tree planting in November and December and continues into January with fireside

readings of seed catalogues that came in with the holiday bills. The reason is that a

Southern winter is almost always milder and kinder to plants than a Southern

summer of scorching temperatures and spotty rainfall. The long and lovely

Southern autumn provides ample time for getting everything done.

Let's get on with it.

Autumn

A NEWCOMER'S GUIDE TO FALL LAWN CARE

Welcome to the Piedmont, all of you who just arrived in the region and all of you who just arrived at the gates of lawnkeeping.

It's a new world here, where lawns are made and remade in early autumn, where you'll learn to know aeration, get acquainted with lime and find out that, pretty often, you're still mowing grass in December.

And you'll find out that, often, a hot summer takes a huge toll on grass. Months of high temperatures leave many lawns thin and brown. So, we're all in this together, folks, whether you've been doing the September lawn drill for years – or you just arrived from Orlando, Fla., or Buffalo, N.Y.

Choose the right type of grass. Here, fescue is tops, although some bermuda, zoysia and centipede lawns show up here and there in the Piedmont. For decades, people largely planted a type of tall fescue grass seed named Kentucky 31, originally a pasture grass.

But in recent years, a number of better kinds of "turf-type" fescues – the various Rebels rank among the best known – succeeded Kentucky 31 as the cho-

PROBLEM AREAS FOR LAWNS

Slopes. Water rolls down slopes rather than into the ground to benefit grass roots. On steep slopes, mowing can be hard to handle. Many bark mulches will simply wash down a slope and away. Probably the best choices are creeping shrubs, evergreen ground covers and some perennials. Choose them based on the amount of sun or shade you have. For a sunny spot, the choices might be masses of daylilies, the shorter black-eyed susans such as Goldsturm, santolina, hypericum, creeping junipers. In the shade, consider ajuga, Lenten roses, liriope, mondo grass and vinca.

Really hot spots. Unshaded western and southern exposures rank among the hottest places in summer. Fescue, which is by nature a cool-season grass, suffers under this condition. Consider adding smaller, fast-growing trees such as crape myrtle or rose-of-Sharon with a ground cover of pine needles. Or go entirely for ground covers, and the low or creeping junipers should serve you well. Other choices for hot spots: coneflowers, globe thistle or the ground cover phlox, which many people call thrift.

Dry shade under trees. Tree roots get the water; tree leaves shade the grass. Grass struggles to grow here and often requires annual reseeding. Some choices: Thin out the tree canopy to let more light reach the ground. Give the area extra water through the year. Create a natural area of shade-loving, evergreen ground covers such as vinca, ivy, epimedium or liriope that tolerate dry soil. Work in woodland bulbs and perennials, such as epimedium, hardy cyclamen, the toad trillium and wild ginger, which also can stand a dry spot.

Autumn

sen type. These newer fescues possess thinner blades, a richer green color and better texture than Kentucky 31. Still, they require sunshine to prosper. Specially blended seed mixtures will help out people with problem areas such as shade.

Plan to sow your grass seed between Sept. 15 and Oct. 15.

Fescue lawns grow best in the cooling weather of autumn, and remain green through the brief chill of winter. Then, they start growing rapidly in the cool, yet damp weather of late February to early March.

All of that tends to surprise people from the North accustomed to storing their mowers from November to March when the native ground cover is ice and snow.

But fescues go semi-dormant when summer weather descends like a Finnish sauna. That means above 90 degrees. Not a whole lot of mowing goes on around here in July and August.

But there's mowing in your future if you kick the lawn into a fresh season of growth with aeration, seeding and fertilizer in the next month.

First, prepare the lawn by mowing it, raking up debris and digging out perennial weeds such as plantain. While you're doing this, consider whether areas of the lawn are too steep for easy mowing or too shady or too badly drained for decent grass.

Consider putting in a ground cover in those areas, a trailing one, such as ivy or vinca, or an upright one, such as monkey or mondo grass. That could save you time and effort in the long run. And you can do that work this fall.

Get acquainted with mechanical aeration as a way of loosening up clay soil. Either hire the work done, or join your neighbors and rent a machine for a weekend of aeration. Depending on the type, the aeration machine either pulls up small plugs of soil or makes tiny slits to let water, fertilizer and air penetrate the soil. (Rainfall will break down the cores.)

Finish off this initial work with a thin layer of organic matter spread across the top of the lawn after aeration. This will make the soil more drought-tolerant and help reduce compaction in the future. Aeration will also provide a loose place for new grass seeds to lodge.

If your lawn is in fairly good condition, overseed-ing will help thicken it up and restore the fresh appearance of lush grass. Calculate your area before you go shopping. The packages will tell you how many square feet the seed will cover.

A soil test will tell you just how much lime should be added to your soil to get the right pH, the acid-alkaline balance, for growing grass, as well as other details. Test information is available through county agricultural agents.

Fertilizer will push the grass into good growth during the cool days of autumn. Use a high-nitrogen lawn fertilizer at the rate directed on the package. This is a better choice than standard 10-10-10 fertilizer, because lawns benefit most from the higher level of nitrogen in specially formulated lawn fertilizers.

Some gardeners like to use "starter fertilizer" on overseeded lawns to get the seedlings growing well, then add the regular fertilizer in mid-October, after the new grass is up and growing.

Some areas may be so bare of grass, they need total renewal. Dig small bare patches by hand, at least two inches deep. Rake them smooth and sow the seeds.

After seeding, cover large areas, especially slopes, with straw to prevent the seed from washing away. Rake off the straw gently after grass begins to grow. Water gently.

And don't let the young grass dry out. It's still hot, and the seedlings could perish on a hot day.

Once the new grass is about 3 1/2 to 4 inches tall, mow it to 3 inches. Mow often enough so that no more than one-third of the blade is removed. A sharp mower blade will prevent ragged edges.

Mowing and watering will keep you busy until November, when shedding leaves must be carefully raked off the young grass. And about mid-November, you'll give the lawn a light application of fertilizer to keep it green through the winter.

Things to remember:

- Divide your work by weekends so you're not overwhelmed.

- Gather a group of neighbors to share the cost of renting an aeration machine for a weekend.

Autumn

- Dig small bare patches by hand, at least two inches deep, then rake them smooth; use a tiller that will go 6 inches or more when making a new lawn or redoing an older one. After seeding, cover large areas, especially slopes, with straw. Rake off the straw gently when grass begins growing.

Things that will set you back:

- Letting leaves pile up and smother young grass in October and November.

- Letting seeds and seedlings dry out during their fragile youth.

- Scalping your cool-season fescues with the lawn mower.

- Scattering valuable grass seed on ground that hasn't been aerated or loosened with a spade or tiller.

PLAN FOR A PERFECT LANDSCAPE

As you think about the autumn's landscape work, map out your long- and short-term plans and hopes for the property.

These things can affect your plant needs. Perhaps your family has reached the stage where a fence is necessary; or you finally will reroute the driveway. Or you will put in a swimming pool, greenhouse or play yard.

Keeping these goals in mind will help avoid the mistake of setting a shade tree in the center of your planned swimming pool or sun deck. Do you need a leafy screen for privacy? Are an irrigation system and outdoor lights on your agenda? Understanding how you will use your outdoor property is as important as decisions about what to plant.

An older home may have declining plants. Most likely, it has some real gems such as mature camellias and azaleas that you should cherish.

Mature shade trees may only need deadwood removed by a professional arborist to look beautiful. But some plants, such as red-tipped photinia, may be declining, or simply overgrown – for example, the holly you have to prune every winter to keep below the windows.

Do not be afraid to remove such problem plants and plant something that is healthy, the right size and beautiful.

Think, too, about how you feel about gardening and yard work. Are you a dedicated hobbyist who lives to grow an assortment of roses, perennials and flowering shrubs? Or would you just like your property to look neat with a small selection of spring bulbs and summer annuals at the front door?

Evaluate, too, the conditions in which your plants will grow. Sun? Shade? Wet soil? Horrible soil? All dictate the choice of plants for the area. Wet areas may require raised beds. Horrible soil demands a compost pile made from this autumn's leaves as the first order of business.

Give yourself several seasons to accomplish your plan, but start with the trees and shrubs – the structure of any landscape.

If you will be adding trees later this fall, start thinking now where you want to place them. Shade trees do the most good where they block the hot summer afternoon sun – beaming from the southwest. But ornamentals such as cherries and dogwoods may be placed where they enhance the house or create a focal point.

Shrubs, too, though smaller, go in for the long term, so plan and choose carefully. Too often, people buy a shrub with no inkling of the plant's mature size, and that leads to endless pruning. Knowing the mature height and spread of a plant is as important as knowing whether it likes sun or shade.

Today's foundation plantings are much lighter than they were a couple of decades ago. That will leave you space for flowers: the bulbs, pansies and perennials that give a garden personality and color. Make room for them as you plan your shrub beds or tuck them around the perimeter of new trees.

And don't think you have to get it all done this autumn.

MAKE IT EASY TO FIND YOUR FRONT DOOR

A favorite aunt announces plans to visit. And, although she has never visited your town, Aunt Maribelle is a sharp old lady, quite adept at following street directions and finding her way around strange places.

Alas, from the moment she rounds your corner, there is trouble.

Shrubbery and tree branches obliterate house numbers. There is no clear, dry path from street or driveway to the front door. As she finally gets to the front door, Aunt Maribelle is swatted by branches.

And so, instead of sailing grandly into the house, she arrives frustrated, her feet wet and her frock damp, wondering who's responsible for this state of disorder. If this will be soon forgotten, well, you're just not sure.

Whether it's your elderly aunt visiting once a decade or the postman and paperboy arriving every day, visitors should find an attractive and functional entry to your house – one that gives them information and is pleasant to pass through.

The most important information that the well-designed entry provides are answers to the question "Where's the front door, and how do I get there?"

A front door is not always as obvious as the nose on your face. It may be partially concealed by a grove of trees in the front lawn or even a single, spreading magnolia. Or it could be placed off to the side of the house or behind a decorative wall and not visible from the street or driveway. To prevent needless wandering, especially in wet or cold weather, the visitor clearly deserves as much help as you can give.

The path from street or driveway should be as simple, direct and as straight as possible. Do not send visitors on a curving side trip when what they need and want is a clear shot to the front door (Remember, it might be raining). Such serendipitous journeys should be on paths of less formal materials such as pine needles, gravel or even grass.

Concrete makes the classic, long-lasting front walk and should be 4 to 5 feet wide. A textured finish and soft gray color produce less glare than smooth, white concrete.

Less formal and less conspicuous (remember Aunt Maribelle's failing eyesight), but equally informative, is a path made of stepping-stones, set 24 inches from center to center and surrounded by grass.

Plants play a role in creating an inviting, informative entrance. Soften a concrete walk's hard edges with borders of monkey grass, evergreen candytuft or English ivy. Stepping-stones may be surrounded by one of the less rambunctious ground covers, such as evergreen periwinkle.

Place trees in the front yard so their vertical lines frame, instead of obliterate, the horizontal house.

The entry area may also include a stunning small tree such as a Japanese maple or a collection of fine

Low shrubbery and lines that lead toward the front door are marks of a good entrance landscape. Small ornamental trees also help set off the entrance.

Autumn

boxwood, azaleas or pieris, all evergreens that remain beautiful all year.

Their layout should naturally draw the eye toward the front door. Put the tallest plants at the corners of the house and let their height gradually move down so the eye follows this line to the front entryway.

Plants that grow into a conical or pyramid shape are not suitable to plant in front of most houses. They will grow too tall for their space, and their shape will be ruined when you prune them. Instead of enhancing the house's design, they cover it up. Plants that grow horizontally and naturally remain low make better

selections for planting at the entry and across the front of the house.

Resist the temptation to give your new landscape the appearance of a mature one. The result in a few years will most likely be a house lost in a forest of shrubbery. (There's Aunt Maribelle looking for the house number and getting hit by wet branches.)

While the shrubs remain young, make the entryway look finished by adding spring-flowering bulbs or pansies, summer-flowering annuals and autumn chrysanthemums. Such flowers will accent the entrance and show visitors they're headed in the right direction.

DARE TO PLANT FLOWERS OUT FRONT

More than once, people have asked me if they dare to plant a flower garden in their front yards.

Perhaps it is their only sunny spot. Or something is needed, they say, to enliven the mass of green lawn, green shrubbery and green trees. Or they just want it.

Any one of these three is a perfectly wonderful reason for reassigning a stretch of turf to a flowerbed. Have courage. Do it.

Perhaps the main reason that gardeners are reluctant to break the mold of the lawn-tree-shrubbery front yard is that they don't see enough good examples of it. The idea that front gardens are "public" and should be more formal and less personal is deeply ingrained in the American home landscape.

Perhaps you fear a flowerbed, blank in winter, would be dreary. I don't think this is true. If your front yard has some attention-grabbers in winter: elegant silhouettes of leafless crape myrtle, wonderful fragrances of winter daphne or winter honeysuckle or colorful holly berries, a dormant flowerbed should not be a detraction.

A front-yard flowerbed must have blooms and look good for the longest stretch possible. That means you should choose either long-blooming plants or flowers that bloom in succession.

For long bloom, hybrid tea, floribunda or miniature roses instantly come to mind, and a well-tended rose garden is beautiful from mid-spring to late fall. As

A flower garden can enhance a front yard.

Autumn

a finishing touch, give it seasonal edgings of cool-weather pansies and summer annuals.

Done correctly, this garden could be the pride of the neighborhood. But roses are a high-maintenance item, and nothing looks worse than a group of debilitated roses, plagued by disease and inattention.

Herbaceous perennials – those that die down to the roots every year – are another option, particularly if they are accompanied by pansies for winter bloom and bulbs for spring color. While most of these perennials bloom for weeks rather than months (as do marigolds), a carefully chosen mixed border – forget-me-nots, irises, daylilies, daisies, salvia, black-eyed susans; sunflowers, asters, chrysanthemums – will keep the bed in bloom, spring through late autumn.

Most perennials are quite easy to grow and very colorful. And most spend the winter dormant. Many offer a fluff of green at the soil line, which I find endearing and exciting. Their new foliage, rising in late winter or early spring, is fresh and beautiful.

Again, edgings are important because they define the bed and offer interest all year. Evergreen candytuft – long blooming and easy to grow – makes a fine alternative to pansies and summer annuals.

FOUNDATION PLANTS CAN TRAVEL

Once landscapers considered it essential to conceal the foundation of a house because it was open or unattractive; that is no longer true because most foundations today are made of nice-looking brick.

If your foundation seems overwhelmed, consider clearing it out and replanting with new plants whose size and color suit your house.

You'll want to move valuable plants such as azaleas, rhododendrons, pieris, boxwoods and camellias to roomier locations. I have seen amazing results when this is done.

Some people move plants around their gardens the way others shift chairs and sofas in the living room. An azalea growing merrily by the kitchen door one spring shows up the next year, almost magically, by the side-walk. The little tree once planted for eternity at the back of the lawn now grows out front.

Though not expensive, nandina and aucuba are worth transplanting, too. My experience is that both will recover quickly from past pruning atrocities and transplant easily. Other shrubs, such as inexpensive hollies and conifers you pruned so often the plants lost their natural shape and grace, may be cast off without guilt. That leaves you with fresh, open turf for replanting.

Keep a few rules in mind. Before you shop for foundation plants, know whether the spot where you intend to plant them is sunny or shady, very wet or very dry or somewhere in between. Know the dimensions of the place you plan to landscape. As you select plants, learn the mature height and spread of the

When azaleas grow so big that they begin to cover windows, they can be easily moved to a better location.

Autumn

What's blooming in September

❧ Asters

❧ Ageratum

❧ Chrysanthemums

❧ Sweet autumn clematis

❧ Spider lily

❧ Lablab vine

❧ Anemone

❧ Helianthus

❧ Mexican bush sage

❧ Osmanthus fragrans

❧ Joe-pye weed

❧ Toad lily

❧ Seashore mallow

candidates. That will help you judge not only how many to buy for your space but whether they will outgrow it.

Holly and azaleas, for example, are prime foundation plants in this area. But some hollies reach a mature height of 2 feet; others will soar 12 feet or higher. Some azaleas, such as the kurume and satsuki types, grow 2 to 4 feet tall; others will rise above 6 feet.

Many slow-growing dwarf conifers, such as dwarf hinoki cypress, are also good choices. Such plants lighten a landscape dominated by dark green, broad-leaf evergreens. The green and yellow of variegated plants will also help that problem.

Consider, too, the color of your house and choose plants whose flowers complement it. Gray is a popular house color, and many azaleas, whether vivid rose or red or pastel pinks and lavender, look beautiful in front of it. Brick comes in many shades of brown, yellow and red. A conservative cream looks outstanding against brown and yellow brick, but so does an outrageous orange. White flowers, safe against red brick, tend to disappear in front of gray or yellow paint.

MEET 7 LATE-BLOOMING PERENNIALS

Every autumn, chrysanthemums pop up on porch steps and deck railings to brighten the fall scene. But an array of other fall-flowering perennials can put spark and freshness into flowerbeds waning after a long, hot summer. Here are seven favorites. Plant them now or in spring in good garden soil.

❧ **Aster carolinianus**. This sprawling aster, a coastal Carolinas native that needs moist soil, tends to climb, making it well suited for a fence or trellis. In late September and October, it bears small, pinkish to purple daisy flowers, about 1 inch in diameter, with yellowish to red centers.

❧ **Aconitum uncinatum** is one of the monkshoods, and the best performer in the Piedmont. A native of the N.C. mountains, foothills and northern Piedmont counties, this monkshood requires light shade. This is one monkshood that can take our heat. The violet-blue flowers, with a distinctive hooded effect, appear in September and well into October. It's maybe my favorite.

❧ **Eupatorium fistulosum** is a Joe-pye weed that can reach 12 feet tall, usually too high for most flowerbeds. But the variety Selection is a shorter Joe-pye weed well suited for gardens, because

Aster carolinianus

Aconitum uncinatum

Eupatorium fistulosum

Autumn

it grows 5 to 6 feet tall instead of 12. Still, it will require a sunny spot at the back of the flowerbed and probably support to keep it looking stately. Let it be a structural element and a butterfly attractor. The cloudlike flowers at the top of the stems are mauvy pink.

Goldenrod

❀ **Goldenrod**, only recently thought of as a garden flower, brings its clear, sparkling yellow to flowerbeds. Newer varieties that are shorter and more compact, such as Cloth of Gold, Golden Showers, Peter Pan and Mimosa, are
excellent choices for gardens.

Salvia rutilans

❀ **Salvia rutilans** is pineapple sage, named for the scent of its crushed leaves. While often thought of as an annual, it usually survives winter in this

Tricyrtis macropoda

Kosteletskya virginica

area. The distinctive, rich red flowers that appear in autumn crown plants that are about 2 feet tall. Give it sun to keep it happy.

❀ **Tricyrtis macropoda** is a toad lily, named for the distinctive mauve spots on the creamy petals. It originated in Eastern Asia, but grows well in the Carolinas Piedmont. Despite its name, this is a beautiful flower, appearing in early autumn on plants growing in shade with moist, well-drained soil.

❀ **Kosteletskya virginica** is commonly called seashore mallow. The pink flowers resemble tropical hibiscus, which is a relative. But this is a hardy perennial, native of coastal counties from Virginia south. It blooms from late August through September and needs sun.

A TOUCH OF THE TROPICS:
ANGEL'S TRUMPETS, LABLAB VINE ADD SPICE

Part of the thrill of gardening is discovering something new. Such is the case with a vine called lablab and a tall shrub called angel's trumpets. Both aren't seen much in this area, and both have the potential to turn heads.

The lablab is a vigorous vine, bearing masses of small purple blooms resembling peas – but more dramatic. Angel's trumpets is a tall shrub bearing nodding blooms shaped like – what else? – trumpets. But no brass here; they're white, pink, peach or yellow.

In both plants, big leaves, an airy waywardness and rich color produce the flamboyant look of the tropics.

Tropical hibiscus plants practically fly out of the garden centers in May, giving the traditional potted hydrangeas and geraniums a run for star billing. The mandevilla and allamanda vines are great successes as potted plants. Pentas and lantana are diversifying the look of decks, balconies and flowerbeds.

Perhaps the lablab vine – which grows quite easily from seeds – and angel's trumpets can generate similar success and interest. Sow seeds of lablab and set out the plants of angel's trumpets in spring, and plan to really enjoy them in late summer and early fall. Each possesses a tropical flair that is appealing to many people, and they are easy to grow. Look for angel's trumpets plants in garden centers in early fall. It's not too late to plant them now.

Autumn

bloom best during full moons. The cooler evenings of early autumn also help the flowers last longer than during the hot nights of August.

Caution: Brugmansias belong to the nightshade family of plants, which means they are toxic. Look but don't taste.

Sources: Plant sales, specialty catalogs, cuttings that root easily in summer.

Meet the lablab vine

Full name: Lablab purpureus; a.k.a. Dolichos lablab, hyacinth bean and Indian bean.

Point of origin: Tropical regions of Africa. In the Piedmont, treat it like an annual vine. Freezing weather will kill roots as well as stems and leaves.

How to grow: Sow seeds, which resemble beans, in warm soil, usually early May, in a sunny place. Plants will grow 10 feet and higher and the vines will need a trellis, net or other support.

Blooming season: Mid- to late summer until late fall.

Uses: A fast-growing, warm-weather screen. A plant to cover an arbor or run up a tall post.

Sources: Seed catalogs, plant sales, saved seeds.

Meet the angel's trumpets

The genus: Brugmansia (brug-MANSE-ee-a) has five species and several descriptively named varieties such as Peaches and Cream, Ecuador Pink, Jamaican Yellow.

Point of origin: Warm regions of the Americas, including Ecuador, Chile and Colombia.

How to grow: In the Piedmont, plant in a sunny to partly shady area that is moist but well drained. Plants grow 10 feet or more tall and spread 8 to 10 feet. Roots of plants in the ground have proved hardy at the University of North Carolina at Charlotte's gardens for many years, producing new growth each spring. Store potted plants in a cool basement or garage from late fall until spring.

The flower show: Flowers may be 1 foot long and smell sweet. Experts on brugmansia say the plants

Autumn

It's time to...

- Keep an eye on the weather. September is usually dry; plants may need watering.

- Give the flowerbeds, including roses, a late summer grooming in preparation for the fall show and addition of chrysanthemums and pansies. Remove spent annuals.

- Make decisions about what shrubs and trees you want to plant in October.

- Check houseplants and repot any that are rootbound. This will give the plants time to grow new roots before they're moved indoors for the winter.

- Remain on the lookout for insects such as cutworms and other caterpillars that go after cabbage, cauliflower and other fall crops.

- Keep sowing lettuce, spinach and other leafy greens in the fall garden.

- Take a critical look at the landscape to determine what should go in advance of the tree- and shrub-planting season.

- Trim back your potted tropical hibiscus lightly to inspire new growth and bloom. This should also bring it down to a size you can bring indoors in October.

TEXTURE CAN ADD A NEW FEEL TO YOUR GARDEN

Plants have texture; but gardeners sometimes overlook it when they landscape their property or select houseplants. They go for showy flowers or bright foliage, forgetting subtle or vivid patterns on leaves and bold styles of stems as ways to make the garden even more interesting.

Textures vary, from the satiny shine of magnolia leaves to the roughness of a zelkova leaf. Most conifers, whether shrubs or trees, offer immense amounts of contrast, thanks to their soft (hemlock) to sort-of-sharp (Blue Atlas cedar) needles. Consider these other characteristics for adding texture to your indoor or outdoor garden:

- **Smooth and shiny.** This offers background and contrast to more highly textured foliage. Examples: magnolia, philodendron, vinca, sweet woodruff, ficus, jade plant.

- **Velvety.** The soft texture of the leaves – usually caused by minute hairs – demand you touch. Some examples: streptocarpus, peppermint geranium, African violets and various kinds of stachys, notably the lamb's ear.

- **Ruffles and ridges.** Some plants have wavy edges; others have seersucker-type effects that may be deep enough to form ridges. Many types of hostas have wavy margins and seersucker texture; the peperomia has very ridged leaves loaded with texture. Many hollies have wavy edges to add interest to their leaves, which may be glossy to dull green.

- **Thorny.** Though often a choice for barriers, plants with thorns or spines possess a distinctive look. There's barberry, Russian olive, many shrub roses, cactus, thistles, bougainvillea.

- **Feathery.** Leaves are dissected to the nth degree to create the feathery effect. Consider the mimosa tree, many types of hardy and tropical ferns, false aralia, sago palm and powder puff plant.

Autumn

Thick and fleshy gray-green foliage tipped in red and arranged in rosettes is the distinctive characteristic of this **sempervivum**. This plant is best known by its common name, hen and chickens.

The **cypress vine** is a summer annual with red flowers and foliage so finely textured it resembles pieces of thread. The twining vine climbs up to 20 feet outdoors in the sunshine.

This **plectranthus** is one of the Swedish ivies, and brings to the house plant gardener a rich texture in the deep veining and downy softness of the grayish-green leaves.

This ornamental asparagus named **Asparagus officinalis pseudoscaber** is an upright mass of feathery foliage. The deep green leaves turn golden yellow in the fall.

The **peppermint geranium** is a choice patio plant for its wonderful scent, but the baby-soft texture of its foliage is another major asset. Bring it indoors in winter.

An **ornamental yam**, this plant bears leaves that possess distinctive veining both horizontally and vertically and a contrasting blush of red on the younger foliage. Bring it indoors in winter.

A false cypress, **Chamaecyparis pisifera Boulevard**, bears layers of soft blue-green needles with a silvery cast at the tips. This small tree grows 8 to 10 feet tall.

Autumn

MUM'S THE WORD FOR FALL

The geraniums are in a major sulk these hot days, bearing only flashes of pink bloom. Gardens and gardeners alike are suffering in the wake of weeks of summer heat and humidity.

There is, of course, no way to turn back the calendar to May. But there is a way to look toward cooler days of fall.

It's the chrysanthemum cure.

It's painless, not too costly, and the side effects are quite fantastic. The quick fix that chrysanthemums promise is sold in garden centers in late summer. These are plants loaded with buds that are ready to pop.

You can take them out of the pots and plant them in flowerbeds or at the front of shrub borders. Or you can do it even more simply (meaning lazily) and leave them in the pots, grouping them in threes or sixes or nines (The triple multiples make for more artistic and pleasing designs).

The pots, which are usually black, won't be too noticeable while the buds and flowers open. Set them around the deck or patio, front steps or the porch. If the marigold or zinnia beds look puny, dig them up and put in chrysanthemums.

This is contrary to my usual view that annuals should carry on until wiped out by frost, but if you are bored with these long-lasting plants, by all means dig them up and put in something that looks more like fall than summer. It is good for the gardener's psyche.

Even if you decide to leave them in the pots, don't worry about whether this gives the garden a tempo-rary look. After they fade, you'll probably want to pitch the whole thing anyway because fall-planted chrysanthemums don't survive cold winters very well. They do, however, survive mild winters.

The color range of garden mums is among the best in flowerdom: yellow, gold, bronze, red, cream, purple, lavender and pink. The shapes of flowers include perky little button types, daisies and doubles.

And that raises the question that faces the gardener surveying this delightful array: Do you choose a favorite and stick with that, or do you choose two of this type, another of a different color, one more button and yet another red double?

Choosing a range of varieties will give you a longer show of flowers but will reduce the visual impact that comes when everything blooms at one time in stunning harmony.

With chrysanthemums, I prefer one color and one variety, especially a clear yellow that looks so cheerful and complements the grass, which is still nice and green in October. Yellow also accents the trees as they slowly change to gold, red, orange and bronze later in the fall.

About the only thing you have to do for these plants is water them regularly, perhaps several times a week to ensure that the pots don't dry out and the plants wither before their time.

But that's not a difficult thing to do for them. It's what they are doing for you that counts. They will help you forget the heat of July and August.

Autumn

Ask Nancy

Answers to some common problems

IS ANYTHING FIT TO GROW IN A DAMP, SOMETIME SOGGY PLACE?

If any place needs a plant tailor-made, it is a wet one. Such soil is the ideal breeding ground for root rot, a malady that leads to a quick death for plants. Some things, however, possess the ability – developed in their native homes in bogs, swamps and riverbanks – to resist this plague. The trees are red maple, the Yaupon hollies, sweet gum, sweet bay magnolia, wax myrtle, willows and bald cypress. The shrubs are calycanthus, clethra, hypericum, the deciduous hollies and leucothoe. Cardinal flower, marsh marigold, Siberian irises and lily of the valley also perform well.

WHAT CAN I USE BESIDES GRASS ON A STEEP SLOPE?

Grass is difficult to grow on a bank because water rolls down the slope instead of sinking into the soil. But some vines and low shrubs can find happy homes on the slope of a bank. These include barberry, cotoneaster, euonymus, English ivy, low, spreading junipers, Lady Banks rose and periwinkle.

Another way to deal with this is to create flat flowerbeds by terracing the slope with landscape timbers. The beds can be planted with spring-flowering bulbs and summer annuals or shrubbery selected to suit the amount of sun that the terrace receives.

WHAT CAN I DO WITH GROUND BETWEEN BUILDINGS THAT LOOKS LIKE A MUDDY PATH?

Such bare, uneven ground leads to puddles, muddy shoes and erosion. Pounding feet stomp grass seedlings before they get a chance to grow strong.

Small stepping-stones provide instant solutions where space is needed to walk. Grass will have a better chance of growing when stepping-stones get the impact of foot traffic.

If the area isn't needed as a pathway, consider small shrubs. Some good ones will grow to a maximum spread of 2 or 3 feet. Gumpo azaleas, which bloom in early summer, are perfect if the spot isn't too hot and dry. If it is, various low evergreen junipers or Japanese hollies should fill the bill.

Don't select something like Chinese holly, barberry or roses with thorns because you will bump into them. Ground covers are a possibility, but most of the better evergreen ones, such as ivy or periwinkle, tend to sprawl, and you will find them sneaking into the pavement, which creates more work. Complete the job with a mulch of pine needles. It looks good and will keep your shoes clean if a foot slips off the pavement.

October

FINALLY, IT IS HERE.

The golden month of October. When trees transform themselves into canopies of red,

gold, burgundy and purple. When gardeners are down on their knees planting tulips

and daffodils and crocus. And thinking how pretty spring will look. When well-worn

jeans and favorite cardigans – left in a dark corner of the closet since

April – get rediscovered and put on again. The golden month of October brings

tasks, but they often don't seem like work, so pleasant it is to

be outdoors these days. Even for those with nothing big to do,

it's a time to savor the crisp air, behold the clear blue sky

and marvel at a landscape, burnished in some places,

fiery bright in others. It's October.

Finally, it is here.

Autumn

CHOOSE TREES FOR THEIR AUTUMN COLORS

Splashes of scarlet, dollops of bronze, globs of gold combine to make the Piedmont forest a colorful delight through the autumn.

In the home landscape, you can enjoy fall color, too, with careful selection of shade and ornamental trees. Fall color is indeed one of the main factors, along with such qualities as the height, flowers, bark texture and shady canopy, to consider when selecting an ornamental or shade tree.

Fortunately, leaf season arrives in tandem with the tree-shopping, tree-planting season. Selecting trees now gives a buyer the chance to judge a tree's fall color, then plant it in prime time.

There is much to choose from.

The palette includes vibrant reds, rich purples, mellow golds, bright bronzes and sunny yellows. And all these colors complement each other and their surroundings. There is none of the disharmony that sometimes occurs in spring when, for example, a red or pink azalea has the misfortune to stand before an orange-brick house. Fall colors, quite simply, go together easily with style and harmony. For example, pair a burgundy-leaved Bradford pear with a golden yellow oak, and the effect is dynamite (even though the Bradford is falling out of favor and planted less).

Some of your best choices are also great year-round trees. These include the flowering dogwood beloved for its lovely spring flowers, the crape myrtle famed for long-lasting summer blooms and the less well-known sourwood, a great, medium-size native.

Sourwood, botanically named Oxydendron arboreum, shows up often in woods where its scarlet foliage stands out, and would make a nice addition to a landscape already well populated by dogwoods, crape myrtles, cherries and Japanese maples. The latter also contribute mightily to the fall color scheme; most varieties turn scarlet, crimson or reddish purple in the fall.

Perhaps the stars of the fall show are the maples, with October Glory and Red Sunset red maples among the most popular red maples for both summer shade and fall color in this area. Other possibilities are the sweet gum, zelkova, Chinese elm, Oriental and native persimmons, ginkgo (buy only male plants and avoid the horrible-smelling fruit of the female ginkgo), green ash, hickory and Heritage river birch.

Many of the oaks, including scarlet, black, northern red and white oaks, produce good fall color. The willow oak, the dominant street tree in Charlotte, produces yellow-gold to brownish fall color. Even though it is less dramatic than the vibrant maples, sourwood, ginkgoes and sweet gums, it still contributes to the golden haze than is autumn's glory.

Other trees that produce good fall colors include

• **Sassafras**, orange to scarlet.

• **Sumac**, brilliant red.

• **Black gum**, burgundy.

• **Sugar maple,** orange and scarlet.

• **Ash, poplar, birch, tulip poplar and redbud**, light to medium yellow.

• **Beech**, golden bronze.

Autumn

STARS OF THE FALL FOLIAGE SCENE

A GUIDE TO FALL COLOR

Japanese maples usually grow slowly to 15 to 25 feet tall and spread, often gracefully, about the same. A few named varieties mature at less than 10 feet. A specimen Japanese maple, with distinctive, finely cut foliage and vivid fall color, can make a landscape's focal point. Plant it in part shade.

Sourwoods, also called sorrel trees, sport shiny green leaves, unusual lacy white summer flowers and scarlet autumn color. They grow slowly to 20 to 30 feet. Give this low-maintenance, native tree part shade.

The **sassafras**, a native tree, grows slowly to about 40 feet and possesses outstanding yellow, orange and red autumn color and a horizontal branching silhouette that is interesting in winter. Give it sun or part shade and well-drained soil.

A **ginkgo** tree makes a dramatic sight, growing slowly to 70 feet in full sun. Give it a prime space on a large lawn. The summer leaves are bright green, turning to a clear yellow in autumn. Male and female flowers are on separate plants. Get only male plants propagated by cuttings to avoid the foul-smelling fruit of the female tree.

Scarlet oaks grow rapidly, eventually reaching about 75 feet in three to four decades. The fall foliage, usually bright scarlet or brownish-red, ranks among the better for oak trees. Give this shade tree full sun and good drainage on the lawn or in the background.

Red maples grow easily and rapidly in a landscape, usually reaching about 60 feet in sun or part shade. Many named varieties exist, and some have an uninteresting yellow fall color. Others, such as October Glory and Red Sunset, produce a better, more interesting orange-to-red autumn color. This shade tree grows fastest with soil on the moist (but not wet) side.

Sweet gums have a distinctive, star-shaped leaf and, usually, dramatic, wine-red fall color. The trees grow at a moderate pace in moist soil to about 75 feet, more slowly in dry soil, and require full sun. Many named varieties are on the market. When you buy, check out their autum color, which varies. Burgundy, Moraine and Rotundiloba have vivid fall color. The latter does not bear fruit, so there are no sticky gumballs to contend with.

Autumn

WHY LEAVES CHANGE COLOR

One day they're green, the next, there's a hint of new color. Call it magic or call it nature at work, but every fall, the trees change color. But what causes the transformation?

As the days shorten in early autumn, trees begin to store moisture to keep cells and tissues alive during winter. Shedding leaves is one way the tree preserves water.

To do this, a layer of corky cells develops at the base of each leaf stalk, which cuts off the flow of water to the leaves and the flow of sugars to the tree trunk. This decreases production of chlorophyll, which causes the tree's green to fade.

As the green fades, yellow appears, thanks to two pigments, pale yellow xanthophyll and rich yellow carotene. These are the same pigments that make carrots orange and daffodils yellow.

Reds, purples and their blends develop from another set of pigments called anthocyanins, which develop in autumn when the days are sunny and the nights are cool. Anthocyanins often mix with yellow pigments to give the deep oranges, fiery reds and rich bronzes that create outstanding displays of color.

The most vivid colors appear after a warm, dry summer and early autumn rains, which prevent early leaf fall. Drab colors usually result from drab, damp fall days.

SELECT BULB COLORS FOR MAXIMUM BEAUTY

Dogwood leaves are showing crimson, the first chill of fall is in the air, and I am thinking of spring. Not because I wish autumn away, but because spring starts in autumn – with the selection of bulbs that will make it colorful, bright and beautiful.

Walk through a garden center these days and prepare to be dazzled by the array of colors, shapes and sizes of spring-flowering bulbs. You could choose one of each. But don't. You are making a garden, not a horticultural zoo. A gardener should be selective, choosing colors that appeal to personal tastes as well as the garden environment. Love yellow? You can pick a pale yellow daffodil, an apricot tulip or golden yellow crocus. Crave pink? Shades abound from palest to brightest.

The first rule is this: Aim for simplicity. Simplicity is beautiful. It is sophisticated. Simplicity means shades of the same color, patches of the same color or a combination of complementary colors – yellow and purple, for example.

It means planting bulbs of a single color in enough numbers to make an impact -- at least seven to 15 before adding another group of a different color.

If you garden in pots, choose one color of tulip and add an array of pansies in a harmonizing color or a neutral such as white. I love red tulips rising above white pansies, yellow daffodils rising above apricot pansies and blue hyacinths over pale pink pansies. These are simple, effective color combinations. When you choose colors, keep in mind that some bulbs, such as early daffodils and hyacinths, will be bloomed out before tulip season.

A second goal in selecting bulbs is to make the flowering season last as long as possible. Make it start early with very small bulbs such as winter aconites or species crocus, both of which launch the flowering year in January. Keep it going with the larger, Dutch crocuses, a variety of early, midseason and late daffodils and at least two kinds of tulips. Dutch irises, which come in a variety of beautiful yellows and blues, will finish the bulb season in early May.

Most bulb boxes tell you whether the bulbs are early, midseason or late. That will help you make selections to stretch the season.

It is unlikely that you will be able to accomplish this variety your first season. Don't worry. Daffodils and crocuses are long-lived bulbs and will be with you for years. Both multiply fairly rapidly.

Tulips and hyacinths have a much shorter life span in the South, usually just two or three years. Do not let that discourage you from planting them, however.

MINOR BULBS OFFER MAJOR REWARDS

Some hug the ground; others rise a bold 6 inches or more. Some bloom in the snowy whites and pale blues of late winter; others bear flowers of spring's clearest yellow and boldest violets. Plant these offbeat bulbs, often called minor bulbs, this fall, and they'll reward you with something different next year.

Their shape – an allium's round purple globe atop a slender stem – is often different, an exciting contrast to the trumpet-shaped yellow daffodil.

Their style – tufts, bells and stars – makes them a charming alternative of solid-color tulips and crocuses.

Their colors – icy white, bright yellows and purples, make dramatic or secondary accents in flower beds.

Or scatter the smaller types – particularly the earliest bloomers, such as snowdrops, winter crocuses or winter aconites informally around trees or shrubs. Then let them surprise you with winter bloom as you're dashing off to work in the chill of February.

❀ **Snowdrops.** Little bulbs that never fail to charm in January, snowdrops bear glistening white flowers. The blooms rise about 6 inches atop sturdy green stems. Snowdrops, botanically named Galanthus nivalis, require a sunny to partly sunny spot in moist but well-drained soil. Plant about 3 inches deep.

❀ **Crocuses**. Early crocuses bloom in January and February, usually in clusters of white, violet, lilac or yellow flowers. Dutch hybrid crocuses usually bloom in March and bear larger flowers of bright yellow, vivid purples or golden yellows. Some hybrids are striped. Plant crocuses 3 to 4 inches deep in well-drained soil in a sunny spot.

❀ **The leucojum** most commonly planted here is popularly called snowflake, but it blooms in early April with the tulips. The bulbs, robust and long-lived, produce stems 18 to 24 inches tall, with nodding, white flowers tipped with dots of green. This snowflake needs moist, rich soil and bright light. Plant bulbs 3 to 4 inches deep. Leucojum is often confused with a shorter bulb commonly called snowdrop that blooms in winter and grows just a few inches tall.

❀ **Ornamental onions**. Just don't call it onion. This is an ornamental onion grown for the dramatic shape and color of its blooms, not for culinary use. Depending on the variety, ornamental onions (botanically allium) may be as short as 6 inches or as tall as 4 feet. Most bloom from late spring to early summer. While alliums made their debut as garden flowers a century or more ago, they became popular recently, as a wider range of colors and heights came onto the market. Look for them in pure white, cream, yellow, pink, red, blue and an eye-popping purple named Purple Sensation. The blooms make dramatic cut flowers

Crocus

Leucojum

Ornamental onion

Autumn

What's blooming in October

- ❀ Chrysanthemums
- ❀ Japanese anemones
- ❀ Late asters
- ❀ Camellia sasanqua

- ❀ Colchicum
- ❀ Autumn and saffron crocuses

- ❀ Sedums
- ❀ Elaeagnus pungens

Winter aconite

for indoors; and don't worry – the garlic scent disappears once the stem is put into water. Grow alliums in sun or light shade. Plant them twice as deep as the bulb's diameter in well-drained soil that's on the sandy side.

❀ **Winter aconite**. A tiny plant that grows about 2 inches tall, eranthis, also called winter aconite, bears golden-yellow, cup-shaped flowers atop green tufts in the dead of winter. Grow eranthis in dampish, shady spots. Summer drought shortens the life of the plants, which grow from brown tubers. Set the tubers about 2 inches deep; don't delay planting after you buy them, as dried-up tubers may be hard to jostle into growth.

SPRINGIN' THE BLUES: SOOTHE YOUR SOUL WITH BULBS THAT BLOOM IN TRANQUIL HUES

Think spring, and I'll bet you see pink azaleas and yellow daffodils. Maybe red tulips, too.

You probably don't think of blue. But for those who love blue, choices await for the landscape – although you will need to stretch your definition of blue to include blues with a dose of violet. True blue tulips don't exist, but purple tulips with a bluish cast, such as The Bishop, are on the market.

For delightful blues, look instead to hyacinths, crocuses, scillas, spring starflower, camassia, irises, grape hyacinths and chionodoxa. Within these bulbs you'll find enough blue and violet-blue. Like all spring bulbs, they require planting in fall.

Hyacinths you probably know almost as well as tulips and daffodils. Some superb blue varieties are widely available, including Delft Blue, a medium shade of clear, porcelain blue; Blue Ice, which is powder blue; and Blue Jacket, which is bright blue with a hint of violet. Blue Magic has more than a hint; it's violet-blue.

Less well known are these six spring-flowering bulbs, suited for beds and containers. You could have great sweeps of bluebells that will make you want to write a poem, or little niches filled with Iris reticulata

Autumn

that will have you reaching for a close-up lens. All these plants will grow in part shade to full sun.

Muscari, or grape hyacinth, is a long-lasting, nearly foolproof little bulb that grows 5 to 8 inches tall, depending on the variety, and comes in blues ranging from pale violet-blue to true violet. The variety of grape hyacinth, Blue Spike, is a bright blue. Plant in full sun. Bulbs will multiply into clumps, so pay attention to spacing: about 3 inches apart, 6 inches deep from the base of the bulb. When coupled in a bed or pot with bright yellow pansies, the effect is cheerful.

Scilla siberica is commonly called Siberian squill, and has been grown in gardens since the late 18th century. The plants grow about 6 inches tall and bear blue, star-shaped flowers. Spring Beauty, which is a brilliant deep blue, is the best-known and most widely available named variety. They even grow in the difficult environment under evergreen trees. Set bulbs about 4 inches deep and 4 inches apart.

Hyacinthoides (aka Scilla campanulata) is the Spanish bluebell , a robust bulb that produces stalks of bright blue (as well as pink or white) bell-like blooms atop strap-shaped leaves. The flower stem rises about 15 inches. These are easy, long-lived bulbs. Set bulbs 4 inches deep and 4 inches apart.

Iris reticulata is a miniature iris that bears elegant deep blue, pale blue or cornflower blue blooms on single stalks about 6 inches tall. The effect is like a blue butterfly sitting just over the ground. Though the bloom season is short – mine have come and gone in

Hyacinthoides

a week when the weather got warm in April – they are still rewarding and picturesque. Give them a space of their own at the front of the garden, so they'll be seen closely and not be swamped by pansies or daffodil foliage. Set bulbs 4 inches apart and 4 inches deep.

Camassia is commonly called Indian hyacinth. A member of the lily family and a North American native, it bears violet-blue flowers on stems about 18 inches tall and is suited for an area that is damp. Set bulbs 8 inches apart and 6 inches deep.

Chionodoxa, commonly called glory-of-the-snow, even in areas such as the Piedmont, where snow is rare, ranks among the earliest flowers to bloom, usually in February. The little plants grow 4 to 6 inches tall with blue blooms that are light to dark, depending on the variety. Set them 3 inches apart, 4 inches deep.

Iris reticulata

Muscari

Chionodoxa

Autumn

INTRODUCE SOME OFFBEAT COUSINS TO YOUR FAMILY OF BULBS

Say ornithogalum. Sounds like a bird. Say fritillaria. A bit of drapery?

Behind those crazy names are some plants worth knowing. Take erythronium (e ri THROW ni um), for example. Those five syllables name a wonderful native plant with yellow flowers; ornithogalum (orni-thuh-GAY-lum) produces clusters of glistening white blooms.

These perennials are interesting and different enough (note, I didn't say weird) to add variety and spice to a spring garden already packed with azaleas, tulips, daffodils and hyacinths. Now is the time to plant them.

Fritillaria. This belongs to the lily family. The most dramatic type is an old one named Crown Imperial. This is one of the older cultivated plants, and illustrations date to 1610. Fritillaria (fri-til-LAIR-ree-uh) plants bear musk-scented flowers that are red, orange or yellow on stalks 40 inches tall. It has nodding clusters of blooms that look like open coffee cups. Fritillaria persica, another tall grower, can hit 3 feet. It bears deep purple-violet flowers that are shaped like bells. Plant the big bulbs, which have a decidedly unpleasant scent, as early as possible in the fall, in well-drained soil. Bulbs rot in wet soil. The bottom of the bulb should be 8 inches deep. Plant the bulbs in a partly shaded area. They bloom in mid- to late spring.

Erythronium. Known as the trout lily, this is another spring bloomer. It grows about 12 inches tall and bears flowers, usually yellow or white, that look like small lilies. Set the small tubers 4 inches deep in full or partial shade. The trout lily is suited for planting under trees and shrubs, as well as in rock gardens and flowerbeds. Put mulch on the beds, particularly during summer, when the weather is hot and dry. Plants bloom in mid-spring.

Eremurus. Commonly called foxtail lily, this is probably the least known of this quartet of unusual characters. All of the species of eremurus (ehr-uh-MUR-us) arose in the dry grasslands and semidesert of Western and Central Asia, which means they can really stand winter and dry weather. Plants grow from thick, fleshy roots, set 6 inches deep on very well-drained soil in full sun. The flowers, which appear in late spring to early summer, are dramatic spikes of pink, white or yellow. Foxtail lilies can grow quite high, 6 feet and up, so put them in the back of the flowerbed.

Fritillaria persica

Fritillaria imperialis

Erythronium

Autumn

It's time to...

- Keep looking for and prune away dead stems in deciduous shrubs and trees; they're easier to spot before the leaves fall.

- Shop for shrubs to replace worn-out, dried-up and overgrown ones in your landscape.

- Divide and replant tropical ferns that must come indoors for the winter if they grew too large during their summer outdoors.

- As trees shed their leaves, notice which windows get the most sun. Put your tropicals that spend the winter indoors there, once night temperatures drop below 50 degrees.

- Pay close attention to the falling leaves and rake them gently off your new grass.

- Shop for seeds of hardy annuals such as poppies, bachelor's buttons and larkspur. Sow them late in the month as the soil cools.

- Clear out all vegetable crops that have finished producing.

- Start planting pansies in beds and containers.

- Look for nuts, seedpods and other bits of nature you can use for autumn and Thanksgiving decorations indoors.

- Continue to clear away spent annuals. Let the good-looking ones stay until frost gets them.

Ornithogalum. This name translates as "bird's milk" (ornis plus gala). That probably stems from the milky-white color of the flowers. The best-known species is Ornithogalum umbellatum, which grows about 8 inches tall and blooms in mid-spring. The star-shaped flowers, often called stars-of-Bethlehem, close up on dark days. The flowers have a green stripe on the outside. Plant the bulbs 4 inches deep and 4 inches apart in partial shade.

Eremurus

Ornithogalum

Autumn

SPRING BULBS CAN SHARE A POT

Even if your garden is a balcony, a porch, a deck or just steps, you can plant bulbs for spring beauty. The same containers that held impatiens, begonias, geraniums or petunias all summer can make a home for tulips, daffodils and hyacinths that will bloom next year.

Perhaps you think a pot isn't big enough to grow an impressive array of daffodils, but think again. When you put bulbs in the ground, you set them several inches apart. In pots, you stuff them, not quite touching each other.

The equipment you need is simple: containers with drainage holes, bulbs and packaged lightweight growing mixes.

Your container may be as small as a 6-inch pot, into which you can stuff about five tulip bulbs. Set a group of small pots together and you'll have a garden. Or pack a half-barrel or window box with a couple of dozen bulbs.

Consider your color mix. Bulbs in a single color, such as yellow, are very effective. but so is a merry mixture of color. If you have a large pot, you can mix the bulbs: perhaps crocus around the edges, tulips, daffodils or hyacinths in the middle. You could even top off the containers with pansies, which will bloom in a sunny spot. Plant them over the taller bulbs, and tuck the smaller bulbs, such as crocuses, between them.

Perfect drainage is required to avoid the soggy soil that will rot bulbs. Containers must have holes in the bottom to let the excess water drain. It helps to cover these holes with a small shard of broken pottery to keep soil from washing out. Garden soil dug out of the ground is not light enough for containers. Get yourself a bag of potting mix.

Once you assemble the ingredients, follow these steps.

- Set the container on newspaper, place the shard of clay over the hole and fill the container about half full with soil.

- Nestle bulbs into the container so that they are not quite touching. With tulips, place the flatter side of the bulb toward the outside of the pot.

- Fill the pot with soil, shaking the pot gently to make sure it settles around all the bulbs. Be sure the tops of the bulbs are covered. Leave an inch or so of space between the top of the soil and the top of the pot's rim.

- Water the container thoroughly but gently, so the bulbs don't move. Water will stimulate fresh root growth.

- Set the containers in a place where they will get rain but not stand in any water during wet weather this winter. I've had no luck trying to grow potted bulbs on a covered screened porch. I just didn't water them enough. The steps are better, but the outdoors brings the problem of wildlife. Squirrels dig around bulbs, and rabbits eat winter crocuses. To solve the problem, cover the pot with a wire mesh to protect the bulbs until the flowers are ready to bring indoors to enjoy.

PUT LEAVES TO USE FOR COMPOST

When the leaves fall this autumn, put them to work. Their job is composting; the result is a rich-looking, good-smelling, dark-brown organic material called humus. Humus, which most people simply call compost, will keep working when you dig it into our ever-present, loudly criticized red clay.

For those of you who don't know compost from cake batter, there are some remarkable similarities. Both require measured ingredients, a good stir and

heat to cook the mixture to just the right texture.

Once finished, cake batter provides a temporary pleasure; the virtues of compost last far longer.

I call it a red-clay cure-all. Delectable dirt.

Compost provides the easiest and most direct path to better soil, which means a better garden, regardless of whether yours contains flowers, vegetables or shrubs.

Instead of casting off leaves, grass clippings, twigs

and other debris, you transform them into dark brown, crumbly compost that will lighten and enrich your garden's soil. It's not hard.

A compost bin can be sophisticated or simple. Buy a compost bin or make yours of cement blocks, snow fencing, boards, bricks or even just chicken wire formed into a circle.

Then, assemble your ingredients. They're easy to find. The bulk will be showering off the trees for the next couple of months. But leaves alone will take a long time to cook into compost.

Here's how to speed up the process.

Put a layer of rough debris such as twigs, stems and small branches on the bottom of your bin. Then follow up with 10 inches or so of leaves; a sprinkling of fertilizer (it helps disintegration), and then an inch or two of soil (which is teeming with useful bacteria and fungi that do the work of compost-making). Next, add more layers of leaves, fertilizer and soil. Make the pile about 4 feet high, or fill the bin.

Such kitchen scraps as potato and banana peels (bury them deeply to avoid attracting flies), earthworm-attracting coffee grounds and eggshells also may be used in the compost heap.

Experts in organic gardening don't recommend composting grass treated with herbicides and pesticides or meats, bones, fat and grease. The meats could attract rodents, create odors and slow the process. Put grass in your compost if you can mix it well with the other ingredients. Grass alone tends to pack down instead of break down.

Keep your compost heap damp -- about the same as a wrung-out sponge. Turn or stir the pile every couple of weeks or so and it should produce finished compost in three to six months. Unturned compost takes longer because less oxygen gets down to the fungi and bacteria, which are doing the work. Brush and limbs make useful additions to the compost torte, but require breaking up first. Small amounts will help create the air spaces necessary for faster decomposition.

The compost is finished when it is dark and crumbly, although the texture may still be uneven. You can till it into the garden and use it to top dress an aerated lawn or as mulch.

Plant Profile

CAMELLIA SASANQUA

NAME:
Camellia sasanqua (sa-SAN-kwa) is a close relative of the better-known Camellia japonica, which blooms in winter and spring. The sasanqua blooms in autumn, and the plant is usually smaller.

VITAL STATS:
The sasanqua grows about 12 feet tall, but may be kept shorter by artful pruning after the flowers fade. The flowers, usually pink, rose or white, are 2 to 3 inches in diameter, appearing from October into December.

FAVORITE SPOT:
A semishady spot with slightly acid soil and excellent drainage.

PLANTING TIP:
Look for named varieties that bloom in early to mid-autumn. Flowers of December bloomers can get zapped by freezing weather.

LANDSCAPE USE:
Though attractive as a solitary specimen, the sasanqua serves even better as a low-maintenance hedge. To encourage dense growth, set plants 4 to 5 feet apart and prune the tips of branches for the first few years. Prune solitary sasanquas that need rejuvenation by removing lower limbs and creating a small tree with one or several trunks.

Autumn

FALL IS A PERFECT TIME TO MOVE PLANTS

So you're ready to move plants. **Your timing is great.** That's because most shrubs, perennials and ground covers go dormant in early autumn. While some gardeners believe you can move almost anything at any time, the dormant season is best.

By transplanting things during the Piedmont's mellow autumn, you give plants time to grow new roots. By spring, they'll be settled down and ready to put out fresh stems and leaves.

Think of moving plants in three different ways:

Individually. If you want to move a single shrub, such as a small azalea, holly or abelia, use your shovel to dig a circle around the perimeter of the root ball. Loosen the root ball gradually with a slight rocking motion of the shovel as you make the circle.

That done, tuck the shovel deep under the root ball from a couple of different points on the circle. This should loosen the bottom of the root ball so that you can lift it.

Always move a plant by lifting or holding the root ball, not the trunk or stems. Put the plant in a pot, which will make it easier to carry. If the trip is just across the lawn or street, roll the plant onto a sheet of plastic, fold the plastic diaper-style and pull it to the new spot.

Digging and dividing. Plants that grow in thick clumps, such as daylilies, most irises and monkey grass, rank among the easiest plants to move. Sink a sharp-edged shovel into the clump and rock it gently to separate plants. It's easiest if you do this along the sides of the clump, pulling out plants from the perimeter rather than the center.

Either replant a clump or divide it further into smaller plants. Cut back leaves of deciduous perennials such as most daylilies and irises (they send up new leaves each spring), but keep the leaves of evergreen ones such as monkey grass or Lenten roses.

Dig spring-flowering bulbs such as daffodils, Dutch irises and crocus during summer or fall, separate the clumps and replant.

Collecting seeds. Nonhybrid flowers will reproduce true, meaning the flowers of the new plants will look like the parent plant. So the seeds are worth collecting and replanting. Sweet peas, hollyhocks, poppies and other old-fashioned favorites are also well worth collecting, particularly if they have a sentimental family connection.

Look for seed pods that appear dried and ready to pop open. Cut them off the plant and open the pod into an envelope. Sow the seeds at the appropriate time for the plant, such as early November for the poppies, late winter to early spring for the sweet peas and hollyhocks. If that's months away, keep the seeds in an envelope in a cool, dry place.

Replant shrubs and perennials at the same depth as they were growing. If in doubt, check the difference in the color of the bark near the base of the plant. Be sure the location is right. For example, pick sunny spots for daylilies, semishady spots for azaleas and shady spots for hostas.

With all three methods of replanting, watering is critical. Keep seedlings moist, and water shrubs and perennials regularly while they settle down in their new homes. A thin layer of organic mulch will also keep soil moist while the plants grow new roots.

PREPARE TROPICALS FOR LIFE AFTER SUMMER

With shortening days and cooler weather in store, now is a good time to take stock of the tropical plants that grace your porches, decks and patios.

Most likely, they grew robustly over the summer, and many have grown out of their pots. Baby plants may spill over the sides of baskets filled with spider plant. A fluffy fern that was once no larger than your hand now is as big as a shrub. The hibiscus on the

deck, once table-top size, looks too big to bring inside once cold weather hits.

While there is plenty of growing weather ahead for these plants, there's also an opportunity: You can propagate new plants and bring the bigger ones down to a more manageable size before they come indoors in mid- to late October.

Many common houseplants that spent the summer

outdoors are prime candidates for division that will create new plants. Tiny plantlets at the tips of leaves of the spider plant or strawberry geranium may be removed and replanted in small pots to develop roots and grow.

Plantlets of ferns and other tropicals that rose at the perimeter of pots may be dug out gently with a trowel and replanted in a small pot. But take care to bring up roots as well.

Pushed to grow and develop through the fall, these young plants should be large enough by December that, wrapped in festive paper and ribbon, they can become holiday gifts for friends and neighbors.

Tropical houseplants must come indoors when night temperatures sink to 50 degrees, which is usually in late October or early November, long before the first killing frost.

Large plants, such as hibiscus and mandevilla, present a different set of challenges.

These valuable deck and patio plants don't make the transition indoors in the same easy way as a fern, prayer plant or Swedish ivy because they require a higher level of light than is found in most houses.

A second problem is that both hibiscus and man-

devilla grow quite large through the summer, raising the problem of where to put them indoors.

Tropical mandevilla may go into cool dormancy through the winter. Before temperatures drop below 40 degrees, cut it back to about 1 foot and withhold water. Then store it in a cool but not freezing corner of the garage, storage shed or crawl space under your house.

Water the plant once or twice during the winter, especially during warm stretches of weather, say 60 degrees or higher. Then wake it up next April by placing it in the shady outdoors during warm days and giving it water-soluble fertilizer. Don't cut back the plant yet; it has plenty of bloom time ahead.

The tropical hibiscus needs a different treatment, and now is a good time to prepare the plant to come indoors, particularly if it has grown too big to fit near a sunny window.

If you have a suitable place, figure out how large the hibiscus needs to be and trim it down now, so that it will have time to put out new growth before it comes indoors, where you can treat it like a houseplant. Given a sunny spot, it may even bloom indoors.

PLANT PANSIES IN FALL FOR MONTHS OF BLOOM

One of the dilemmas of October is that some summer flowers – notably impatiens and begonias – are still pretty, yet garden centers are filled with pansies in all manner of colors. Yes, it's pansy-planting time.

So, if you can stand it, rip out the summer flowers and put in the stars of fall, winter and spring. If you can't stand to do it now, wait until late October. But plant those pansies by Nov. 1 for optimum root development before winter.

Garden centers offer pansies in a wide range of colors: sparkling yellows, rich blues and purples, gentle whites and glorious reds.

Some pansies have the classic dark blotch at the center, while others are solid yellow, white, orange and silver blue. Planted in the fall and given fertilizer and sunshine (gray winters are not conducive to a good show), pansies will bloom until heat broils them next summer (or you rip them out in May to make room for the impatiens and begonias).

It's one of the best shows for the money, and just one more reason the Piedmont is one of the best places for a gardener to call home.

If you wait until spring to set out your pansies, as they do in the cold North, you'll miss a large part of the show. By coupling pansies with a spring array of crocuses, daffodils and tulips, you can make the show even better.

The flower beds that were shady enough for impatiens and begonias all summer may turn out to be bright enough for pansies. And the sunny spots where

Autumn

zinnias and marigolds stood up to hot weather should be cool enough now to make a perfect home for your pansies. Large pots are also well-suited.

Cold isn't a problem. The plants may look icy during cold stretches but they will perk up when weather warms. Winter weather, Piedmont-style, is far less hard on pansies than summer heat. That's a chief reason pansies tend to burn out in May or June, but that's not so bad: Summer flowers are ready to move in.

In the South, given sun and a regular boost of fertilizer, pansies will bloom most of the winter. Flower development may fall off during a stretch of gray and gloomy weather, but will pick up when the sun breaks out, particularly if the soil is laced liberally with manure and the plants are given occasional doses of liquid fertilizer.

At planting, work a slow-release, balanced fertilizer into the soil at the rate directed on the package. Or work in liberal amounts of packaged cow manure: 5 pounds or more per flat of 36 or 48 plants. Set the plants about 8 inches apart, even closer in pots. Set each plant in an individual hole, then bring soil in to cover the root ball. Water after planting.

If you want to add bulbs underneath, plant the larger ones first. After planting the pansies, add the smaller bulbs -- the snowdrops and crocuses.

Through the winter, remove seed pods and spent flowers. A pine-needle mulch helps keep the soil at an even temperature. In early winter, particularly for potted plants, a boost of liquid fertilizer applied with warm water will also help. Do this again in early spring.

If you pinch off the spent flowers, it will encourage plants to keep blooming.

CELEBRATE FALL WITH FLOWERS AS FRESH AS SPRING

As days shorten and leaves turn, a flower garden needs a fresh look to stay in sync with the shifting of seasons. Chrysanthemums help. Their bold colors always say fall.

But so do a host of other beauties – autumn-blooming bulbs and perennials – that you might have missed in the rush for begonias and impatiens. Asters and anemones, late sunflowers and salvias, even the goldenrods of roadsides, will do for your flowerbeds in fall what tulips do for spring and what daylilies do for summer. They signal the season.

Sometimes I wonder why these distinctly autumn flowers aren't at the top of everyone's plant list. Their colors looked clear and fresh as springtime; the plants seem scarcely bothered by the harsh heat that plagued the Piedmont all summer. Best of all, in September and October, they just look new.

Look for them in garden centers, at plant sales and in catalogs, and put them out in the fall or spring.

They attract migrating hummingbirds and butterflies en route south for the winter. And just when you thought an Aster tataricus was just another really pretty lilac daisy, an orange and black Monarch butterfly, heading to Mexico for the winter, might land on it. The pleasure grows.

Many kinds of fall-flowering plants – including goldenrods, the various daisies such as asters and sunflowers, Joe-pye weed, buddleia, spider lilies and sedums – attract hummingbirds and butterflies. Lingering summer flowers such as lantana, zinnias and verbena also help signal that nectar is waiting for the taking.

And they'll steal the show from the impatiens and begonias that refuse to go away. Until it freezes.

• This **Japanese anemone**, named Honorine Jobert, is an old variety that grows about 3 feet tall. These fall-flowering anemones, which also come in pinks and roses, prosper in moist soil and some shade at midday.

Autumn

- A butterfly lands on **Aster tataricus**, commonly called Tartarian aster, at the Daniel Stowe Botanical Garden. An easy-to-grow aster that originated in Siberia, it can soar well above 6 feet in sunshine.

- This perennial has style – despite its common name of swamp sunflower. **Helianthus angustifolius** will hit 6 feet, topped by billows of golden-yellow daisies with dark centers. Happy in dampish ground, it will tolerate dry soil. It requires sunshine.

- The descriptively named **spider lily** (Lycoris radiata) grows from a bulb and produces strap-shaped leaves and clusters of early autumn flowers at the tip-top of a stalk. Plants grow about 16 inches tall. It requires full sun and well-drained good soil.

- **Mexican bush sage**, Salvia leucantha, is a tender perennial that normally doesn't survive the hard freezes of late autumn. Its rapid growth and dramatic flowers make it worth planting each spring in a sunny spot. Plants will grow 5 feet tall and start blooming in late summer to early autumn.

- The yellow beauty of a **Seaside goldenrod** makes a dramatic background for purple asters. Goldenrods come in many named varieties, such as Seaside, most growing 2 to 3 feet tall in a sunny location.

Autumn

Ask Nancy

Answers to some common problems

HOW CAN I ATTRACT WILDLIFE, ESPECIALLY BIRDS?

Put out water and food, including seed and suet, and plant a variety of plants that bear seeds, berries, nuts, pollen and nectar. Install birdhouses, and plant such trees as the eastern red cedar with dense evergreen foliage for shelter. A diversity of settings, including brush piles, will give birds places to raise their young. Use organic gardening methods. Look to beneficial insects to control insect pests.

Other good plants include trumpet creeper vine, which draws hummingbirds, bee balm, butterfly weed and columbine for attracting butterflies and shagbark hickory, which provides nesting cavities.

WHAT CAN I DO ABOUT YELLOW JACKETS AROUND MY HOUSE?

The yellow jacket is potentially harmful to people because of its aggressive nature. Nests are usually found in the loose soil of gardenbeds, raised beds or ground cover. Treat the nest at night with Sevin while the insects are there. Take care not to disturb the nest with a light while you are doing this.

CAN WE USE GRAPEVINE TO COVER AN ARBOR SHADED BY A SHADE TREE?

You probably don't have enough light for a grapevine to bear flowers and fruit (full sun required), but you could have luck with the vines atop your arbor. So why not go for it? Give them a season or two for the roots to get established before you expect vigorous growth in the spring to cover your arbor. If you want a year-round green look, be aware that grapes aren't evergreen, even in our moderate climate.

Keep in mind that when the shade tree is bare of leaves, the spot will get more sunshine, and that could make it right for Carolina jessamine (Gelsemium sempervirens). This vine bears the state flower of South Carolina and good-looking, glossy green foliage.

The flowers emerge in early spring and show up for a month or so on a plant with some age to it. You will probably have enough spring sun to bring out the flowers.

To attract birds to your yard, provide food, water and shelter.

November

AND THE DAYS GET SHORTER

November defines the meaning of crisp and cool.

Crisp enough that you want to breathe deeply the fresh autumn air.

Cool enough that you take a sweater outside with you. Just in case

you need it. Yet the days get shorter and shorter in November, slicing

precious daylight off the evening, just when the gardener is keen to do

more and more. The leaves are still with us, shedding more each

day, yet many trees won't be bare for weeks yet. Fresh plantings of

pansies give the garden a perky feel. More bulbs await planting.

There is much to do. You could go into a frenzy of activity,

because November – even with its short days – is one of the

perfect months to garden in the Piedmont. Or you could

take it more slowly, and savor the moment.

Crisp and cool.

Autumn

BRANCHING OUT:
IT'S TIME TO PLANT A TREE

Now is the time to buy and plant a tree. Though leaves are flying off deciduous trees in the Piedmont, roots will continue to grow through much of the winter. That will get the tree well established in its new location before it leafs out again in the spring.

Planting a tree is not hard, particularly if you start with a young tree under 6 feet tall.

1. Evergreen and deciduous trees are sold most often with their roots in plastic or metal pots or encased in burlap. When moving a tree, carry it by the pot or root ball to prevent breakage.

2. Before you plant a tree with roots wrapped in burlap, remove the twine from around the top of the root ball. If the burlap is a synthetic material, cut away as much as possible. Natural burlap will disintegrate once it is planted in soil.

3. Prepare a large hole to receive the roots. Turn over and loosen an area at least twice the width of the root ball, even more if the soil is compact. It isn't absolutely necessary, but you could add small amounts of fertilizer and lime, about 1 1/2 pounds of lime and a half pound of 5-10-10 fertilizer per 25 square feet.

4. Dig out a hole a little bigger than the root ball. In the Piedmont, where soil tends to be heavy, set the tree in the soil so that the top of the root ball is a couple of inches above ground level. That keeps the roots from sinking too deep.

5. After establishing the tree's correct depth and placing it, fill about one half of the hole with soil and pack

it gently. Water, then fill the hole until the top of the root ball is covered. Don't pack the soil again. You risk pushing the root ball too low into the ground. And don't add more soil on top of the root ball because it could suffocate the roots.

6. Make a raised collar of soil above the perimeter of the root ball to collect and direct water to the roots. Add a thin layer of mulch, such as pine bark, pine needles, hardwood chips or leaves. This will keep the soil cooler, conserve water and reduce weeds. Make the circle of mulch at least 5 feet in diameter, wider if possible. Keep the mulch several inches away from the tree trunk to discourage insects and diseases, especially borers that invade cherry, plum and peach trees.

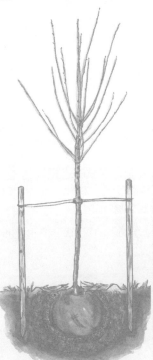

7. Once the tree is planted, add support stakes if it is taller than 6 feet or begins to blow over. Place a pair of wooden stakes into the ground just outside the root ball on opposite sides. Fasten the trunk to each stake with flexible, heavy-gauge wire threaded through short lengths of old garden hose to protect the trunk. Take out the stakes after six months.

ONE, TWO, TREE:
YOUR STEP-BY-STEP GUIDE TO LEAFY BEAUTY

Trees represent an important investment in your landscape's beauty. But they require careful selection, correct planting and proper maintenance to pay you back. That's why it's important to plan carefully before you plant.

• Know where you will put the tree, and learn how tall and wide the tree will grow at maturity. Be sure it suits the space.

• Find out whether the type of tree is suited for the growing conditions in the planned location. Many types of trees will suit stressful sites, such as along urban streets (the willow oak) or areas that get soggy in wet weather (the river birch).

• Look for branches 6 to 8 inches apart, spiraling around the tree. Avoid buying trees that are topped with stub cuts on branches.

• Look for improved, modern varieties that offer better disease resistance and brighter fall color. Newer varieties of crape myrtles, such as Natchez and Cherokee, for example, are more resistant to powdery mildew; red maples such as October Glory and Red Sunset offer better fall color. There's even a sweet gum that doesn't produce the spiky fruits that many people object to.

• Consider a small tree. It's usually a very good buy, will settle down in its new place quickly, suffer less transplant shock and grow rapidly. It is also much easier to move and handle.

Remove stakes from trees after six months to avoid girdling damage shown here.

Tips For Success

• Water regularly, especially for the first two years after planting. During the first year, plants should be watered one to two times a week if it hasn't rained. An easy test to see if the roots are dry: Poke your finger under the mulch and into the soil. If it's dry, saturate the area with a hose or buckets of water.

• Keep tree wrap on the trunk during the winter for the first two years after planting. Take it off in the spring. Since boring insects can develop behind the tree wrap, use it only on trees with smooth bark, such as maples and magnolias – not trees with rough bark.

• Be careful with fertilizer. A small amount at planting time should help the tree get established. By the second year, in late February, use a granular or wettable fertilizer. Then, every three to five years, fertilize again. A soil test, available through state extension services, will determine the precise needs for fertilizer and lime.

WHAT WILL SURVIVE IN THE DESERT BENEATH A TREE?

Under the spreading oak tree not much grows. For Piedmont gardeners, dry shade ranks among the most vexing problems. Right up there with hull tallow soil and unrelenting attacks by kudzu. But all is not hopeless.

First, do you have dry shade? The test comes in summer, with the tree in full leaf and the roots absorbing lots of water from the ground every day. Particularly under shallow-rooted willow oaks, one of the dominant shade trees of this area, the soil will feel very dry, and the light filtering through the dense canopy will be very low.

You can attack the problem now, creating raised beds and planting ground covers and perennials. If your choice is annuals, you can do that in the spring. You have three weapons in the arsenal: evergreen ground covers, raised beds and a set of perennials and annuals that prosper even in dry shade.

Ground covers. This is the first and easiest choice. Some evergreen and semi-evergreen ground covers perform remarkably well in dry shade. The best known is liriope, which is dependable but boring, except when the spikes of purple or white flowers rise in late summer. Other good ground covers for dry shade are vinca, ajuga, pachysandra and mondo grass. All are worthy for their foliage, texture and more or less trouble-free lifestyle.

Raised beds. There's nothing complicated here, and I don't mean a high bed – just one that will allow you to add a couple of inches of soil to make a new root zone for plants. Do not put more than 4 inches of soil on top of tree roots; more than that risks smothering them. But a simple enclosure of landscape timbers, the wider side flat on the ground, should help you add enough good soil and compost to make a place for the annuals and perennials. Additions of compost, peat and leaf mold will help clay soil absorb more water.

Annuals and perennials. You won't find an encyclopedia of ones that will prosper in dry shade, but some good choices exist.

Hostas are the ultimate perennials for shade gardens and will grow faster in moist, well-drained soil. But they grow and bloom reasonably well in dry shade, and there is usually less damage from slugs than in damper areas. Although these plants are amenable to dry shade, they will still appreciate watering during long stretches of dry weather in the summer.

Fibrous-rooted begonias – the bedding begonias seen in garden centers in spring – are probably the best choice among annuals for dry shade because they can store water in their leaves. A cousin, the hardy begonia, Begonia grandis, is another possibility. It doesn't bloom until late summer, but it is perennial in the South.

Epimedium, a wildflower, thrives in dry shade.

Other choices include the hardy, autumn-flowering cyclamen; bleeding hearts; a lovely wildflower named green and gold (Chrysogonum virginianum) that blooms in spring; bergenia; and a nearly evergreen perennial called epimedium that comes in many varieties. Consider tucking in some crocuses, not because they love shade, but because they are up and bloomed out before the leaves come out.

The epimediums are definitely worth a closer look from Piedmont gardeners. The flowers come in a range of colors, from white and yellow to red and purple. Blooms rise on little stems and are saucer or cup shaped. They look like colorful flying insects that have spread their wings.

Autumn

THESE EASYGOING PLANTS WON'T TAKE YOU ON A GUILT TRIP

While no tree or shrub ranks as trouble-free, some possess a remarkable ability to get along with their owners when planted in the right environment and given enough space to reach mature size. They resist pests and diseases, prove reasonably sturdy and look good. Among a wealth of choices, here are just 10 to get you thinking about building a harmonious relationship with plants in your landscape.

Trees

- **Sourwood,** Oxydendrum arboreum. A native of the eastern United States, sourwood ranks among the outstanding small trees, growing slowly in sun to part shade to about 25 feet. You see it frequently in the woods – the drooping clusters of white flowers in late summer and the distinctive, brilliant red to purplish foliage are dead giveaways. Plant this tree instead of a second dogwood or your first Bradford pear.

- **Eastern redbud,** Cercis canadensis. The familiar pink to purplish flowers signal spring. White varieties also exist. This easy tree, which grows rapidly to about 30 feet, likes sun or a bit of dappled shade and moist but well-drained soil. While redbuds tend to blend into the landscape during the summer, they stand out when their foliage turns a pretty yellow in autumn.

- **Ginkgo biloba.** Give it space and make sure you buy a male tree (that's one propagated in plant nurseries by cuttings from a male tree) because female ginkgos produce the most foul-smelling fruit this side of a skunk harem.

  A ginkgo tree will soar 90 feet or higher, so look up to check for power lines or other obstacles before you plant one. Choose a sunny spot in practically any well-drained soil. The fan-shaped foliage turns an exquisite clear yellow in autumn. Leaves fall within a couple of days, so you get your raking done quickly.

- **Dwarf Alberta spruce,** Picea glauca. This slow-growing dwarf of a conifer makes a cone-shaped tree. Mine grows about an inch a year in full sun. Eventually, maybe while I am still alive, it will get 8 feet or so tall. These conifers require moist, well-drained soil. Perfect for a little spot.

- **Flowering dogwood,** Cornus florida. I can't omit practically everyone's favorite ornamental, a native that grows slowly to about 25 feet tall in cool, moist, but well-drained soil. Borers will invade, so don't bump the trunk with the lawn mower or weed trimmer. An alternative is the Kousa dogwood from Asia, which blooms after the flowering dogwood. For a long dogwood season, aim to have both.

Flowering dogwood

Shrubs

- **Glossy abelia,** Abelia grandiflora. A semi-evergreen shrub, abelia blooms all summer, bearing dainty pink to white flowers shaped like funnels. Left to grow into a bush plant, abelia usually reaches 4 to 5 feet. Abelias require sun or a tad of shade and do best in good soil. If a very cold winter hits, don't panic; just cut off the deadwood, shape up the plant and wait for it to grow. Abelia makes an attractive, short hedge.

- **Japanese andromeda,** Pieris japonica. Certainly one of the outstanding evergreens of the landscape,

Autumn

What's blooming in November

❀ Chrysanthemums   ❀ Asters   ❀ Pansies

❀ Confederate rose   ❀ Camellia sasanqua

pieris comes in many varieties, usually growing slowly to 3 to 6 feet tall. The late-winter to early-spring flowers appear as clusters of white, cream or pink, which some people believe resemble an oversized lily of the valley. Pieris requires light shade, moist, but well-drained soil and a place to stand out all year. Truly, its shape, foliage and flowers make it a shrub for all seasons.

• **Heavenly bamboo,** Nandina domestica. Too ordinary, you say? Hardly. Nandina serves a variety of uses, from evergreen hedge to Christmas decorations. Once established, it bounces back after a hard December pruning. The lacy foliage and clusters of red berries are major attributes for this much-used shrub. While amenable to light shade, most nandinas produce brighter foliage in sunshine. Dwarf varieties such as Nana will stay low, but the ordinary nandina will top out about 5 to 6 feet.

• **Burford holly**, Ilex burfordii. Growing reasonably fast, this evergreen makes an excellent screen or dense informal hedge. Homeowners will probably want the dwarf form that tops out about 8 feet. Grow it in full sun or part shade in ordinary soil. You can also turn this plant into a tree by pruning off the lower branches. The berries are dark red; the leaves are glossy green.

• **Doublefile viburnum,** Viburnum plicatum, variety tomentosum. More great viburnums exist, but this one, particularly the type named Maries, ranks as one of the outstanding shrubs for the home landscape. It grows about 8 to 10 feet tall in sun or part shade. The branches grow in a horizontal, layered pattern and bear flat, white blooms in mid-spring.

HOW TO SOLVE TREE TROUBLES

Healthy, well-maintained trees live longer, look better and cause less trouble, particularly in stormy weather. Although a tree in excellent condition could blow over or break up in a storm, it's more likely that weak or diseased ones will be the victims. When you can't solve your tree problems, hire an arborist certified by the International Society of Arboriculture, a professional organization.

Here are seven common tree problems and their solutions.

Problem:
The trunk flares at the base of the trunk, where the roots extend, sometimes get buried. The tree is planted too deeply.

Action:
If a flare is buried at planting time or an existing tree is buried due to construction work, the trunk will rot. You'll see leaves dying. Remove soil, if possible, to reveal the trunk flare. If the tree is small and newly planted, dig it up and reset at the correct level.

Problem:
The trees are victims of a bad practice called topping. That means the crown of the tree was cut back severely, usually the same distance all around.

Action:
Hire a certified arborist to evaluate the tree and see if its shape, health and beauty can be restored by corrective pruning.

Autumn

Problem:
Leaves or needles on Leyland cypresses, azaleas, rhododendrons and cherries turn brown. The cause is probably root rot. Abundant spring rainfall causes root loss. When followed by summer drought and excess water loss, needles and leaves turn brown.

Action:
Prune out the brown areas. Soak the root zone of newly planted and established plants once a week if it doesn't rain. Do not overwater.

Problem:
Mushrooms appear at the base of the tree. Mushrooms, along with carpenter ants, termites and peeling bark, are symptoms, but not the cause, of decaying wood.

Action:
A certified arborist should assess the decay. If the decay is severe, the tree should be removed. If not, keep watch on it and reassess every three to five years.

Problem:
Lightning struck the tree and blew off bark.

Action:
Monitor the tree. If more than one-third of the leaves die, remove the tree. Don't use tree paint and don't fertilize. Watering a large area around the tree may help. For majestic, valuable trees, consider lightning protection such as a framework of aerial rods and wires connected to a grounding rod placed near the tree.

Problem:
Leaf-eating caterpillars, such as bagworms, that emerge from cocoons and defoliate trees.

Action:
Identify the caterpillar. This is essential to determining what should be done about it. Spring and summer caterpillars are usually more detrimental to trees than ones hatching in late summer.

Problem:
Branches break off because of poor branch structure and weak angles.

Action:
Select trees in the nursery or garden center that have branches about 1 foot apart on the trunk. Or thin out branches to that distance. Remove branches attached to the trunk at less than a 15-degree angle; those are weakly attached branches subject to breakage. Wider angles make stronger branches.

Topping

Buried trunk flares

Poor branch structure

Autumn

It's time to...

- Fertilize houseplants with liquid fertilizer diluted to half strength. Foliage plants grow at a slower rate in the winter.

- Observe which of your windows get the most sunlight during the shortening, dim days of fall, and park your houseplants there and rotate them every couple of weeks.

- Finish planting bulbs. Life gets even busier and days even shorter in December.

- Keep those showers of leaves off your new grass by diligent but gentle raking.

- Sow seeds of poppies, larkspur and other hardy wildflowers for bloom next spring.

- Start to watch diligently for chickweed, the bright green cool-weather weed that sprouts about mid-autumn. Pull it up before it goes to seed and produces a new crop.

- Cover summer flowers such as begonias on nights that frost threatens; this will keep them alive longer.

- Spray houseplants, particularly ferns, with a gentle mist twice a week to keep up humidity once the furnace is running.

- Cut back chrysanthemums to the ground as they finish flowering. (Tuck in pansies to brighten the vacant space.)

- Give the fescue a light application of lawn fertilizer around Thanksgiving for a pre-winter boost.

CANKERWORMS: A MENACE TO CHARLOTTE LEAVES

If you live in parts of Charlotte, N.C., you live in an area where cankerworm caterpillars have been so prevalent, they destroy tree foliage in early spring, weakening and even killing some trees.

Late autumn is the time to take steps against them. The insects begin to stir, usually in late November, and shake off the blanket of soil in which they have rested since late spring.

Once awake, they will choose their trees. There, the wingless female moths will roam the bark in search of winged males.

Once mated, they'll make their long climb to the treetops. And up there on the twigs, each female will lay a hundred or so eggs that, come spring, will hatch into little green caterpillars destined to drive you crazy.

The weapon of choice for fall and winter is tar-paper bands stapled to tree trunks and coated with a sticky substance that doesn't freeze and doesn't slide down. The dense goo called Tanglefoot traps the female as it climbs the tree.

HOW TO FIGHT CANKERWORMS

1. Sticky band traps are an effective way to reduce the number of cankerworms in the spring. Between Nov. 29 and Dec. 7, locate the trap on the tree trunk between the ground and the lowest limb.

2. Wrap 2-inch-wide cotton or fiberglass batting around the tree. This will prevent the moths from crawling under the tar paper and bypassing the sticky bands.

3. Fasten tar paper, cut 8 to 12 inches wide, over the batting to the trunk with staples or duct tape.

4. Use a putty knife to apply Tanglefoot Tree Pest Barrier in a 6-inch-wide band on top of the tar paper. Spread it about 1/8-inch thick. It should look tan. Wear gloves.

5. If the sticky band gets full of bugs or clogged with leaves, install a second band above the first band. Remove the bands in February.

Autumn

HOUSEPLANTS 201:
TRY SOMETHING UNUSUAL

You've made philodendron prosper and ficus flourish. Now you're ready – at least tempted – to try a flashier houseplant. Something that will reward you with unusual foliage, maybe even some pretty, possibly weird, blooms. It could be a begonia that reminds you of stained glass or a blooming bromeliad. The reward for meeting the challenge will be something special.

Samuri bromeliad. Bromeliads are a large family of plants. The pineapple is the most famous member. This is the Samuri bromeliad. Its long, upright leaves form a stiff vase where you pour in the water. The plant needs bright light, a warm environment and medium humidity. Plant in a very well-drained soil with coarse bark added to reduce any chance of sogginess. After flowering, the vase, as with all bromeliads, will die, but this could take months, maybe a year. Propagate the plant by removing and planting the newer side shoots after they form roots.

Stained glass begonias. An array of rex begonias are popularly called "Stained Glass" because of their dramatic leaves colored red, silver and vivid greens. This one is San Diego Sunset. Leaf colors tend to brighten with good light, but direct sunshine can burn. Too much water will be fatal. Water the plant sparingly and fertilize spring through early fall. The plant may slink into dormancy and drop leaves during the winter. Don't assume it's dead.

Streptocarpus. Relative of the popular African violet, streptocarpus deserves a higher profile. It bears white, pink, purple, red or blue flowers in fall and winter that are shaped like funnels. Its elegant look – clusters of nodding flowers, thin stems and a rosette of leaves – translates to some people as temperamental. Have no fear. The hybrid streptocarpus is reasonably easy to handle if you give it high humidity, bright light, even watering and African violet fertilizer. It's also called cape primrose.

Shrimp plant. Shrimp plant is another old-fashioned favorite suitable for a pot or hanging basket. In the tropics and subtropics, it's a shrub. The botanical name, Justicia brandegeana, is rarely applied because "shrimp plant" is so descriptive of the pink, golden or yellow-green bracts from which the white flowers emerge. This plant requires bright light and evenly moist soil to bloom through the year. Fertilize every couple of weeks in spring and summer. Cut back the plant in spring.

Cryptanthus. Its starlike spread and distinct leaf color makes cryptanthus a conversation piece in a pot or hanging basket. Easy to grow, it needs only well-drained soil and bright, indirect light or sunlight

Samuri bromeliad

Stained glass begonia

Streptocarpus

Autumn

Shrimp plant

Cryptanthus

Abutilon

filtered through a sheer curtain. Good light makes the colors intensify. Let the soil dry out slightly between waterings. Don't expect cryptanthus, also called earth star, to grow like gangbusters. It's slow. Fertilize the plant spring through fall; then give it a rest for the winter.

Abutilon. Abutilon's common name, dictated by the shape of its leaves, is flowering maple. Popular in the 19th century, abutilon is enjoying a renaissance of interest thanks to its flower power. The bell-shaped flowers come in red, orange, white, yellow or pink. This is the variety Pink Supreme. The more sunlight the plant gets, the more flowers it produces. Fertilize it weekly and keep it watered evenly. The plant usually grows about 1 to 2 feet tall.

DESKTOP DELIGHTS:
PUT PLANTS TO WORK IN YOUR OFFICE

Within the walls of your office cubicle, between the mouse and the keyboard, below the out basket and above the pencil cup, have you planted your garden yet?

It's perfect for desktop-size foliage and flowers that are suited to life under the fluorescents. Some, such as flowering poinsettias, chrysanthemums and kalanchoe, will be transients, offering a bright spot for several weeks. Others may prove such a lasting success, they'll be with you until retirement.

Yet, like workers, not every indoor plant is suited for every job. Here's how I'd write their job descriptions.

Seasonal workers. They arrive at your desk, make a big splash, impress everybody, then leave. Of course, these are small, potted plants such as cyclamens, chrysanthemums, kalanchoes, cinerarias, streptocarpuses and poinsettias. These are seasonal plants, often available for $5 or so in small, 4-inch pots suitable for even the most crowded desktop. Look upon these blooms as a temporary breath of fresh air

Cyclamen

Autumn

Bird's nest fern

Grape ivy

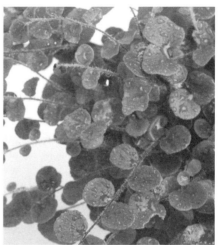

Button fern

inside your cubicle. Keep the plants evenly watered; enjoy them while the flowers last; then recognize you've gotten your money's worth and send them on their way. (You could plant the chrysanthemum outdoors.)

May stay until retirement. Despite their origin in tropical jungles, some potted plants seem tailor-made for office life. Leave the lights on day and night. Go off on vacation and leave them untended. Get involved in a major project and forget to water them for days. No matter. Like employees who prosper despite repeated changes of management and reassignment, these plants hang tough. Of course, that means philodendron – it's like the dullest yet most dependable member of the staff; Chinese evergreen, heaven-sent from Southeast Asia for cubicles planted far from natural sunlight; grape ivy, a vigorous vine you might choose to climb the walls for you, and dieffenbachia, also called dumbcane. Other choices include the golden pothos, cast-iron plant, peace lily and prayer plant.

Need close supervision and time away. Here we have choice indoor plants that, after a time, will need a summer vacation out of the office and in the warm, shady, moist environment outdoors. These include the Norfolk Island pine (which could serve as your cubicle Christmas tree), most ferns, schefflera and most begonias.

Chrysanthemum

Arrowhead vine

Chinese evergreen

Autumn

Cozy in cubicles (if you're within sight of a window). Some valuable indoor plants prosper with rays of sunlight from a window nearby. These include asparagus ferns, spider plants, crotons, zebrinas, tradescantias, arrowhead vine, piggyback plant and peperomias.

Never take a vacation, but will make you dream of faraway places: Hawaiian ti, which requires bright light without direct sunshine; Dutch crocuses, available in bloom through the winter; Chinese jade plant (also suited for those who routinely forget to water plants).

Finally, there's English ivy, which prefers to work in a much cooler clime (below 70 degrees) than found in most American offices. Consider it an immigrant holding a green card.

Kalanchoe

Fittonia

Dieffenbachia

Tips For Success

- **Misting the plants a couple of times a week** will raise the humidity level temporarily. That's a benefit to tropical plants, whose native turf is the humid jungle. Yellowing leaf tips on many plants are usually a sign the humidity level is too low. Use a nozzle with a fine mist to spray the leaves. Occasionally, wash office dust off the leaves by setting the plant outdoors during a shower when the temperature is above 60.

- **Regular watering is essential.** Desktop plants come in small pots that dry out fast because they are packed with roots. Flowering plants last far longer if the soil is kept watered. Use warmish water, neither hot nor cold. Drooping leaves signal that the plant needs watering more often, and possibly replanting in a larger pot. Schedule waterings on Fridays, so the plants aren't left to wilt over the weekends. On Mondays, check the soil. If it feels dry to the touch, water then. You'll soon learn the plant's schedule. Combine the water with a water-soluble fertilizer labeled for foliage plants diluted to half strength.

- **Make sure the pot sits in a saucer.** That will keep moisture from seeping onto your desk, papers and books. But don't let water stand in the saucer. That could lead to root rot. Drain the saucer shortly after you've watered the plant.

- **Repot the plant as it grows.** As your plant prospers, signaled by strong growth, you'll eventually move it up to a slightly larger pot. Look for attractive, plastic ones in colors that suit most offices, such as gray, green, brown, black or burgundy. Some have concealed watering wells you fill with water. The water rises by capillary action to the soil, making it easy to keep the soil moisture right.

Autumn

CONFEDERATE ROSES ARE PERFECT FOR SWAPPING

The rose isn't really a rose, and its roots are Chinese, not Confederate. No matter. The name is Confederate rose.

Botanically named Hibiscus mutabilis, the Confederate rose is a large shrub. (Some might call it a multi stemmed small tree.) It puts up new growth from ground level each spring, sends out fresh foliage that resembles oversize maple leaves, and in autumn bears big, fluffy blossoms. The word *mutabilis* means "changeable," a reference to the changing color of the blooms, from palest pink to deepest rose.

One relative is the tropical hibiscus with its bright red, yellow, melon and pink blossoms that is so widely enjoyed as a potted plant. Another is the well-known, hardy rose of Sharon, which blooms in summer.

That the Confederate rose originated in China is undisputed; plant historians report it was brought to European gardens by 1690. Knowledge of its use in Southern gardens is fuzzier, but the history passed down is that the Confederate rose was planted widely in the 19th century. The common name probably stems from the plant's use in the South and the close resemblance of its flowers to old-fashioned garden roses.

Although not widely available at retail garden centers, Confederate rose plants are available from wholesale growers.

A vertical, multistemmed large shrub or small tree, it grows, usually rapidly, to about 12 to 15 feet tall. Full sun produces the best growth and bloom. The plant needs moist, well-drained soil.

The plant's roots are hardy in the Piedmont, but freezing weather normally kills the plant above ground. Cut it back to about ground level after frost.

The roots will generate new stems and leaves in the spring.

After frost, when you cut down the plant, take stem cuttings, about 10 inches long. Root them in water through the winter. Keep the cuttings in a frost-free place with good daylight. Then, after the last threat of frost in spring, plant the rooted cuttings in the ground.

The plant's easy propagation makes it perfect for passing around among friends and families.

DO SOME FALL CLEANUP IN THE GARDEN

Really cold weather is still beyond our horizon, and clear, bright days encourage the gardener to plant and tend. (But why must it get dark sooooo early?)

Pushed to plant trees and shrubs, bulbs and perennials, and get the leaves raked and into the compost bin, gardeners may be tempted to overlook two important tasks for mid-autumn. These are cleaning up the garden and dealing with problems that proved

vexing though the spring and summer.

The cleanup, however, consists of more than raking leaves and collecting twigs and branches blown down in an autumn breeze. It is the first step toward the health and well-being of your vegetable garden and flowerbeds.

Getting rid of old annual flower and vegetable plants, dried flower blossoms and stray fruit makes a

Autumn

garden tidier and removes a harbor for dormant pests through the winter. Slugs, always a nuisance, will also hide out in this low forest of stems and leaves, even after the vegetation is killed by hard frost, whenever it arrives.

Your perennial bed also needs attention. If you look closely, you'll see old flower stems that should be removed by cutting, not pulling.

Once frost kills the tops of such perennials as chrysanthemums and peonies, you can cut them off near the ground and throw them away. Chrysanthemum stems left to blow and sway in the winter wind could dislodge roots and shorten the life of the plant; peony leaves are especially prone to a leaf fungus that spends the winter on old leaves.

However, cut the foliage of tall bearded irises about 6 inches high. Certain annuals, such as snapdragons, that live through the winter should be left; let alone, too, the evergreen foliage of dianthus and daylilies (The brown stems of daylilies are easily removed with a gentle pull).

A second thing to deal with are any problems that continue to plague the garden. The most common are the red tip photinia shrubs affected by a leaf-spot fungus that causes defoliation and eventual death. Many of these plants have already died and been removed from the landscape, but others continue to decline.

Rather than continue to fight the battle, why not surrender? Remove the diseased plants, once and for all. Put in something good, healthy and better looking. There's still plenty of time to do it this fall, and the plants will settle in nicely before hot weather hits next year.

Other problems you may want to deal with are the final removal of a tree or shrubs you consider unsightly. It's much easier to get rid of a plant when it's leafless and its beauty lies dormant for the winter.

If only we had a few more hours of daylight to deal with all this work.

BLUEBONNETS CAN THRIVE FAR FROM HOME

If you've arrived from Texas – or if you simply love the color blue, there are bluebonnets in your future and your garden.

Wildflower books written for gardeners in the eastern United States rarely, if ever, mention this lovely flower, native of grasslands rather than forest. Yet it can be grown here, but you must think about it in November.

To improve germination, spread the seeds on a cookie sheet, then cut a small incision in each seed – like a paper cut. Put the seeds in a cup of room-temperature water for about 24 hours. When they have puffed up and become a bit swollen, plant them in the garden. They can go in beds or containers.

The seeds come up in about 10 days, and the little green plants will live through the winter. Put on a thin mulch of dried leaves, if you wish.

Autumn

SCULPTURAL PLANTS OFFER WINTER BEAUTY

As gardeners shop this autumn, some will look for trees with breathtaking spring flowers; others will want a dense canopy of leafy summer shade, while still more will go for bright fall color.

That leaves winter uncovered and overlooked, a gap in the four seasons of beauty that is the goal of all Piedmont gardeners. For winter, the descriptive word for interesting plants is sculptural.

Once the leaves come down and the trunks and branches are revealed, most trees have this sculptural effect. But some do it better than others. The mature willow oak, for example, displays a round, twiggy canopy that is dramatic against a sparkling blue winter sky. The crape myrtle, one of the Piedmont's most widely planted ornamentals, has a graceful trunk with peeling bark in shades of gray, beige and cinnamon.

But there are more and even better selections for this special type of winter beauty. I have three in mind that are reasonably easy to find and will grow well in our climate. They also serve as dramatic focal points in a garden because of their year-round beauty. These are not plants to stuff among other trees and shrubbery, hiding their beauty. They should stand alone and stand out.

Weeping Higan cherry. Gorgeous in spring, this magnificent tree also looks graceful when it is leafless in winter. A mature specimen can reach 30 feet, with its drooping branches cascading toward the ground. The spread is about 15 feet, so give this tree space to develop and show its beauty. The growth rate is quite rapid for such a spectacular plant.

The flowers are pink and appear in early spring. Varieties to look for include Pendula, Autumnalis, Pink Cloud and Yae-shidare-higan. Plants tend to be quite expensive. Just think of it as investment gardening.

Japanese maple. This small, but superb, ornamental comes in a large number of varieties with dark red, purple or green foliage, and excellent shape. The branches tend to be layered, which adds to its artistic value. The overall shape is low and round. Japanese maples are short, growing perhaps 15 to 20 feet tall after many years.

They are prime candidates to use as small accent plants, particularly if you've already met your quota of flowering dogwoods.

Bloodgood is one of the better-known red-leaf varieties. Burgundy Lace has reddish-purple leaves. There are lots of others to choose from.

Transplant with special care to reduce shock and choose a spot protected from direct summer sun; dappled shade is excellent.

Harry Lauder's Walking Stick. A truly weird plant, but one to consider. Consider the variety Contorta of the European hazel, Corylus avellana. Actually a large shrub, it grows about 10 feet tall, its vertical limbs and twigs twisting and curling in a bizarre fashion. The effect is quite conspicuous. Some might say this is a plant having a bad-hair day, but I think it is fascinating to look at.

Plant it where the summer sun will be least harsh. Hot, dry summers – often found in the Piedmont area – are hard on this plant of northern climes.

Japanese maple

Autumn

GRACE YOUR TABLE:
AN EASY THANKSGIVING CENTERPIECE

You're cool with the turkey, the cranberry sauce and the pumpkin pie. You are not cool about the centerpiece.

Relax. Making a centerpiece is not difficult. You can make a simple, round or oval centerpiece with a mixture of colorful, cut flowers and greenery, even greenery from your backyard.

By combining standard arranging techniques with individual taste in flowers, you can create something unique.

While flower arranging is an established art, it offers much creative freedom. Today's designs are looser, more natural and less formal; exacting styles in which each flower is placed in precise order are less popular today.

Leaves in autumn tones, sweet-gum balls, wheat and cuttings of greenery all will enhance the cut flowers and add to the natural look. Once you develop an eye for this, you will see your landscape as a treasure trove of things to enhance your arrangements.

While many people opt for the traditional Thanksgiving color scheme of russet reds, soft oranges, golden yellows and burnished golds, it isn't mandatory. Pick colors you like and that suit your home. And plan to use a favorite glass or silver bowl, or even a basket, for your arrangement. That's what holidays are for.

A design based on such long-lasting flowers as chrysanthemums and carnations can be made a couple of days ahead of Thanksgiving. Just keep it cool and make sure there's water in the container.

What You'll Need

• Container.

• Floral foam.

• Waterproof floral tape.

• Scissors.

• Three stems of primary flowers such as chrysanthemums, lilies or carnations.

• Two stems of secondary flowers such as smaller carnations, daisies or alstroemeria.

• Three stems of frothy filler flowers such as statice, goldenrod or baby's breath.

• Foliage such as purchased leatherleaf or tree fern or evergreen cuttings from the garden. Accents of bittersweet, wheat stems and candles may also be added.

Autumn

How To Do It

- **First, design the foliage framework.** Insert the foam snugly in the container and anchor with waterproof floral tape. Cut two stems of fern foliage across the middle, partway down, to reduce the height. Insert the two bottom pieces back-to-back to form a V-shape in the center of the foam. Insert about six pieces of foliage, all cut the same length, into the sides of the foam around the rim of the container. Place them an equal distance apart, at right angles to the V-shaped cone. Add some short pieces of accent foliage if desired.

- **Finish with flowers.** Make the height and width of the design 1 to 1 1/2 times the container's height. To establish the height and width of the primary flowers, place one in the center, then one on each side of the bottom part of the foam. Then insert the secondary flowers to further define the round shape. Distribute the flowers evenly, making sure all radiate from the center of the design. Finally, add the filler flowers and a little greenery to fill in bare spots and help shape the design. Place flowers at varying depths for variety and interest.

Relax. Making a centerpiece is not difficult. You can make a simple, round or oval centerpiece with a mixture of colorful, cut flowers and greenery, even greenery from your backyard.

Ask Nancy

Answers to some common problems

WHEN CAN I PRUNE MY ROSES?

You can do some slight pruning now. Cut your established hybrid tea roses back to 3 to 4 feet tall. This makes a neat appearance through the winter and helps avoid root damage that may occur when winds whip long canes around during storms.

You'll do the major pruning of hybrid tea plants in early March. Shrub roses and climbers that will bloom on this year's growth should not be pruned until after their major bloom ends next summer.

Be sure to take off or pick up leaves affected by diseases. You'll reduce the population of fungi that will spring to life and damage your plants when the weather warms.

HOW DO I RIPEN TOMATOES INSIDE?

Pick light green to medium green tomatoes that are in good condition and approaching maturity. Wrap them individually in newspaper and store in single layers in a cool but frost-free place, such as an unheated garage. The tomatoes will ripen slowly.

Put nearly mature, reddening tomatoes on a shelf or countertop at room temperature. They should ripen in a couple of weeks.

HOW DO I PLANT RHODODENDRONS?

Plant high. Sinking the root ball of a rhododendron into the ground is asking for root rot, a common cause of death for them in clay soil. Azaleas and camellias also benefit from high planting, with all or part of the root ball above ground level.

Rhododendrons should be planted with the root-ball on top of the loosened soil in a sheltered spot under a canopy of large trees. That will protect them from harsh sun and forceful winds.

Most shrubs are sold in plastic pots or metal cans. When you remove the plant, roots may appear tightly bound around the root ball. With a knife or trowel, gently loosen the roots on the bottom and sides of the root ball to encourage them to spread into the soil after planting. Take care not to break any branches.

Dig a hole that is 1 1/2 times as deep and as wide as the root ball. Work copious amounts of organic material such as compost into the soil taken from the hole, then use that improved soil to fill the hole about halfway for most shrubs. When planting rhododendrons, fill the holes almost completely before placing the new plants.

Finally, add more soil peat to fill the hole and cover the root ball with a thin layer of soil.

Finish the job by putting on a mulch of pine needles, which will protect the shallow roots, preserve moisture in the soil and contribute to the soil acidity that plants such as azaleas, camellias, rhododendrons and gardenias require.

WHAT ARE THOSE BUGS COLLECTING ON MY WALLS?

It's a quirky half-inch-long insect called the box elder bug; they're a nuisance, but not harmful because they don't bite, sting or carry disease. The oval-shape bugs are usually dark blue, red or bluish red. During cool weather, they congregate on the warm side of a house and sometimes get indoors. People bothered by the bug can spray the door sill outdoors with an insecticide suitable for use against ants and other indoor insects.

Azaleas and camellias also benefit from high planting, with all or part of the root ball above ground level.

December

BERRIES OUTDOORS; BLOOMS INSIDE

Glistening evergreens spark the Piedmont winter.

Colorful blooms and berries decorate it. Soft fragrances

scent it. Defined more by spurts of chill and the rare snowfall

than by days on the calendar, winter may arrive this month. Or maybe

not. In December, the landscape, so recently colored by autumn's

mellow hues and flashes of brightness, lets the greens stand

out. Cream, gray and beige play their part, often giving a

lively spark in the soft sunlight of the year's shortest

days. Sometimes, those days draw you outdoors to clear

away the last of the leaf litter. Or, more often, just to

discover the gentle beauty all around.

Don't take your coat.

A sweater will probably do.

Winter

THREE EASY HOLIDAY CENTERPIECES

You can make your own centerpiece. Use fresh flowers, small potted poinsettias, your own treasured Christmas candles, figurines or music box. Put it together, easily and inexpensively. Here are step-by-step directions for three projects.

PROJECT 1

Make an inexpensive floral gift. Or keep it yourself for the coffee table.

1. Gather the materials. You need a glass bowl, a small bag of uncooked cranberries or red glass marbles, a bunch of flowers such as small carnations or chrysanthemums, six to eight stems of foliage from your garden such as nandina, narrow ribbon in a color that suits the flowers and cranberries.

2. Fill the bowl with cranberries and add water.

3. Cut flower stems in lengths of 7 to 9 inches. Cut garden foliage 6 to 8 inches long.

4. Position the tallest stems at the top so the highest flower is about 10 inches above the bottom of the 4-inch bowl. Arrange the other stems to create a roundish effect.

5. Fill in the bouquet with the foliage, positioning most of it to create a frill around the top of the bowl. Shorten the stems of the foliage if necessary. Add a simple bow.

1, 2, 3

4, 5

Winter

PROJECT 2

Build a poinsettia pyramid that's small enough for your dining room table or buffet.

You need a glass cake stand with a rim, a margarita glass big enough to hold a 4-inch pot, florist's sticky clay, four small poinsettias (4-inch pots), three small pots of trailing ivy and ribbon for a bow.

1. Secure the bottom of the margarita glass to the center of the cake stand with sticky clay. Put a bow around the bottom of the cake stand just above the base.

2. Place a poinsettia in the glass and secure it with sticky clay.

3. Set three poinsettias vertically in the cake stand and nestle the ivy pots horizontally between each one for stability.

1, 2,

3

Winter

PROJECT 3

Show off your treasures.

Turn a figurine, special candle, music box or other Christmas treasure into a centerpiece. You need a round 12-inch tray, an evergreen wreath to cover it, your "treasure," a short glass or round box, florist sticky clay for the center of the wreath and assorted decorations such as battery-powered lights and ornaments.

1. Set the wreath on the tray and secure the glass or box with sticky clay.

2. Add the lights (tuck the batteries under the foliage) and arrange the ornaments.

3. Place the treasure on the glass or box and secure with sticky clay.

4. Fluff up the foliage on the wreath to conceal the glass if necessary.

FOR PAPERWHITES, KEEP COOL

It's getting close to paperwhite season, and I have two words for you: cool temperatures.

That's what these popular bulbs need after you set them in a bowl or jar of pebbles to "force" them into bloom in December. Keep them too warm, and the leaves rise mightily, then flop over. The flower stems get so tall, you wonder if this is Jack's beanstalk you're

growing instead of pretty flowers.

But first – and I realize I've gone beyond the promised two words – back to the beginning. Paperwhite narcissus are seen by many as almost magical. Pop the bulbs into a bowl or pot, and within a few weeks, you have flowers. They don't require the long stretches underground in cool soil that daffodils and tulips demand.

Plant the bulbs either of two ways: in a pot of lightweight soil or other potting mixture, the tips of the bulbs rising just above the soil line, or in glass bowls with pebbles or small decorative rocks to anchor the bulbs. It's easier to keep watch on the water level if you use a clear container.

Plant the bulbs as closely together as possible for maximum effect.

Now, once they're planted, think about the temperature. It's best to keep the planted containers in a cool spot, between 45 and 50 degrees, in low light or even complete darkness (the crawl space of your house, for example).

This should last for about three weeks or until the roots are well formed. You'll see them through the glass bowl. Then they are ready for warmer weather –

Winter

in the 60s – and a bright location such as a windowsill or sun porch to stimulate growth of the leaf and flower stems.

Turn the bowl or pot every couple of days to keep the stems from bending toward the light. The flowers should appear in about two to three weeks, depending on the variety.

If the bulbs are in a leak-proof container, keep water just up to the bottom of the bulbs. In pots, excess water will run out the drainage holes, so set the pot on a saucer.

The flowers will last longer (Is there a party in three days?) if you set the containers in the refrigerator or out on the cool, but not freezing, porch overnight.

And one last thought: Don't plant all your paperwhites at once. Plant a pot or bowl every two weeks for a steady parade of blooms in December and January.

ENJOY THE AMAZING AMARYLLIS

The dramatic amaryllis is a defining flower that says winter. While amaryllis will bloom outdoors in late spring in the Piedmont, most people embrace them for the drama they produce indoors in December and January. Even before the straplike leaves get much out of the bulb, a stalk or two rises above the bulb and produces trumpet-shaped blooms that are red, pink, orange or white.

It's an easy plant to grow indoors; success is more certain if you heed the bulb's temperature requirements, which fortunately are close to human preference.

If you won't plant the bulb right away, store it in a dry, dark place that's about 50 degrees.

To plant, use a pot only slightly bigger than the bulb. Put good soil in the bottom of the pot, then set the bulb so its top will rise just above the rim of the pot. Add soil to fill the pot, tamping it down so that it doesn't leave air pockets. Leave an inch or so of space between the soil and the rim so that watering will be eas-

ier. Once you water, check the soil and add more, as necessary.

Now for the fun of watching the amaryllis unfold.

The potted bulbs grow best at about 68 degrees and in a well-lighted spot. Water sparingly at first; as the stems develop, water more often and generously; excess water should drain out the holes in the bottom of the pot, which means you must set the pot on a saucer.

It usually takes 4 to 8 weeks from planting to bloom in the winter, which means you can stagger plantings for a succession of bloom.

Once you've enjoyed the blooms, cut the faded flowers from the stalk, leaving the stalk to wither on its own. The leaves will develop and keep the bulb growing through the winter, spring and summer. Water the plant and give it balanced liquid fertilizer regularly.

You can plant the bulb outdoors in the spring, where it should bloom again. Or keep it in the pot; fertilize it regularly or it won't bloom again.

Winter

What's blooming in December:

❀ Poinsettia   ❀ Amaryllis   ❀ Witch hazel

❀ Paperwhite narcissus   ❀ Christmas cactus   ❀ Camellias

❀ Cyclamen

KEEP THE PLANTS OF CHRISTMAS PRESENT FROM BECOMING GHOSTS OF CHRISTMAS PAST

If you take care of your holiday plants, they'll look good for a long time. Some, like the poinsettia, you'd like to look their best for many weeks, and then you just might discard the plant. Others, such as the Christmas cactus and Norfolk Island pine, you'd like to grow for years and years.

While they vary in the details of care, their need for a well-drained pot is universal. Often these gift plants arrive wrapped in colorful foil and ribbon. Take the pot out of its foil wrapping to water and drain. If the ribbon is too complex to allow this, cut a hole in the bottom of the foil to let the water drain out in the sink or the saucer holding the plant.

Now for the details.

Norfolk Island pine

Environment: This native of the South Pacific is often used as a tabletop Christmas tree, but should be enjoyed at other times as an attractive houseplant. It needs bright indoor light or curtain-filtered sunlight and a room temperature that is cool (mid- to high 60s, even lower at night.)

Life outdoors: In warm weather, put it outdoors in light shade. Direct, broiling summer sun is too much for a potted Norfolk Island pine.

Water: Soil should remain just moist. Water when the soil surface feels dry. Limp needles often signal overwatering.

Fertilizer: In spring and summer, fertilize the plant lightly with acid fertilizer every two weeks.

Special tasks: Repot the plant every few years in highly organic potting soil. Don't worry; it may soar to 200 feet in the South Pacific, but not in a pot.

Winter

Poinsettia

Environment: Give it the brightest spot indoors that you've got, and a location in the 60s or low 70s far from the heat registers and fireplace. Keep it away from drafts.

Water: Water when the soil surface begins to feel dry, but don't let the root ball dry out; leaves will turn yellow and drop off.

Fertilizer: Give the plant a dose of liquid fertilizer every month.

Reflowering: In spring, trim back the plant to encourage fresh, branching growth. (You don't have to trim, but the plant will be huge by summer's end.) Keep it in a sunny, but not too hot location, watering regularly, through the summer. To rebloom, the poinsettia requires 14 hours of frost-free, uninterrupted darkness every night for about two months starting Oct. 1.

Cover the plant with a box each evening or put it in a closet.

The easiest way: Pitch the poinsettia when you're tired of it, it looks weary and you want to make space for the Valentine roses.

Christmas cactus

Environment: It requires a sunny, cool spot indoors until spring, then a lightly shady spot outdoors in the summer. Do not plant outdoors. Regular misting will help preserve the blooms and buds.

Water: Water when the top of the soil starts to feel dry. Don't let the soil stay soggy.

Remember this: A warm room, especially at night, can make the flower buds drop off. So will underwatering and overwatering.

Reflowering: The plant rests and prepares to bloom in the cooling days of autumn. About mid-September, reduce the amount of watering and set the plant to rest in a cool spot (the 50s at night and a daytime temperature under 65 are excellent). In a month or so, set the plant in a warmer place, water more often and begin to fertilize every two weeks with balanced liquid fertilizer once the buds start to emerge.

Winter

GIVE CYCLAMEN A CHILLY RECEPTION

Cyclamen, the winterpot plant with its lovely white, pink, purple or red flowers, likes it cool. Really cool. When it shows up at your house, turn down the thermostat to 60, put on a sweater and let your cyclamen enjoy life, even if you shiver. Actually, 55 degrees is better.

Failing that, keep the cyclamen in an unheated room or enclosed porch with sunlight and bring it out to star at dinnertime or on special occasions. Just don't let it freeze.

And keep it moist but not soggy. The cyclamen goes into a deep slump in dry soil. Also – is this starting to sound like more trouble than one plant is worth? – don't let water linger around the base of the plant where the stems rise. That may encourage the dreaded rot.

With all that, the semi-Arctic temperature, the tedious watering, the chance of rot, this is still a great plant to have in the house in winter.

GARDEN GREENERY GIVES A NATURAL LOOK

The pioneers had it right. Come Christmas, they marched outdoors to cut fresh and fragrant greenery in the woods and gather nuts, seed pods, berries and pine cones. Inside, they arranged their finds on mantels, tables and windowsills, in doorways and stairwells.

No glitz and no glitter.

Two centuries or so later, the all-natural look still works, especially for the well-stocked gardener.

Many of the Piedmont's most popular evergreens – boxwood, aucuba, pine, ivy, magnolia, yew and cedar – provide an excellent foundation for such decorations. Finish them with bright berries of holly, pyracantha and nandina; pine cones from the garden; and lemons, limes and apples from the grocery.

The simplest decorations are evergreen wreaths for the door, a mantel laden with pine boughs and brightened with fresh fruit, a few sprigs of fragrant cedar tied with a ribbon, a vase of holly, a piece of mistletoe hung above a doorway.

Or, go all out in the 18th-century manner with ropes of pine winding up the staircase and draping a doorway or with elegant pyramids of yellow, green or red fruits.

The beauty of such arrangements is in their luster, texture and color and their simple design.

Select the foliage carefully because flaws will really stand out when the greenery is displayed indoors. Look over the leaves and branches for insects and dirt and, if necessary, wash them off with the hose to get them sparkling clean. Wash carefully to avoid knocking off the berries.

To keep the foliage fresh as long as possible, put the cut end of the branches in a bucket of water (bath temperature) for several hours or overnight. The leaves will soak up the water. Cuttings arranged in water should last several weeks. If not put in water, greenery will last about 10 days, depending on the temperature in the house.

Two centuries or so later, the all-natural look still works, especially for the well-stocked gardener.

START WITH GREENERY, END WITH FESTIVE BOW

Next to the Christmas tree, a wreath is the essential Christmastime decoration. Placed above the mantel, on the front door or in the windows, evergreen wreaths are festive reminders of the season.

Please notice I said evergreen. That means real greenery, fresh and fragrant, not plastic and permanent. That means a plain and simple wreath with a basic bow, or perhaps adorned with berries, cones, nuts, twigs and other natural materials. I use the same wire frame every year. It came with a finished wreath I bought at a Christmas tree lot many years ago. The frame is still perfectly good and showing no signs of becoming obsolete, overworn or out of date. It will probably outlast me. Wire and straw frames are available in craft, hobby and garden shops, along with bows and equipment you'll need to attach the greenery. If the frame is wire, you'll need flexible, lightweight wire; if the frame is straw, get some florist's picks. A pick is a strange thing that looks like a toothpick made for gorillas and has a small wire attached to one end.

You'll need small pruning shears to cut up the greenery to the proper lengths. The best sources of greenery are the Christmas tree sales lots, where you will likely find cut branches of Fraser fir and white pine sold in bunches for a couple of dollars. I think the fir makes a more elegant wreath than the pine, but that's a matter of taste. The fir is easier to handle, doesn't seem as fragile and works on either wire or straw frames. Use a straw frame for the pine wreath. Cedar also makes a wonderful Christmas wreath; boxwood makes the best Christmas wreath of all.

Mixing types of greenery – pine with boxwood, for example – is OK, too. How much do you need? One little armload should be more than enough to make the wreath. Assembling this masterpiece is a job best done outdoors. If it's raining, spread some newspapers on the kitchen or den floor and get on with it.

When you finish, you'll have a simple evergreen wreath that only needs a red bow to be finished. But you may want to add a touch of individuality through sprigs of holly berries, variegated English holly leaves, small pine cones attached with wire or florist picks or other natural things.

Okra pods, pomegranates and Fraser fir make an unusual, natural wreath.

Winter

AN EVERGREEN WREATH, STEP-BY-STEP

Use evergreen foliage such as Fraser fir, white pine or boxwood and a purchased wreath frame. Assembling this masterpiece is a job best done outdoors or in the garage.

1. Cut the greenery into sprigs about 5 inches long. Gather two or three sprigs and place them with the stem ends together.

2. Tie the ends together with wire and secure them to the inner perimeter of the frame with either the wire or the florist pick.

3. Continue around the circle, counterclockwise, covering the end of each sprig with the next one you're placing.

4. As you go, judge whether the greenery is too full, too sparse or just right and adjust accordingly. It's important that the wreath keep a circular form and that the greenery is evenly distributed.

5. Work in a spare sprig here and there to fill in any gaps. That's easy with short lengths of lightweight wire you can tie into the wreath. Add a bow for the finishing touch.

Sweet gum balls sprayed gold make an attractive alternative to a traditional green wreath.

Tips For Success

- Make a wreath or other natural decoration last longer with a clear aerosol spray that will slow down evaporation of water from the needles and help keep them from falling. Products are made just for that job, but you could use hair spray. An acrylic spray will put shine on fruit, pine cones and leaves.

- Enhance ready-made natural wreaths and even artificial wreaths and garlands by tucking in contrasting evergreen cuttings, as well as ornaments, berries and pine cones, before adding the bow. Use the flexible wires of the artificial garland to tie on small bundles of cuttings and make it look very natural.

- To give an all-green wreath color, contrast and texture, include several kinds of evergreens in small bunches. Attach mixed bundles as you go around the wire or straw wreath. Once put together, the greens show remarkable variation – from light to deep green.

- When making a wreath for a glass door, finish the back with greenery, too. The wreath will look good from inside the house as well as outside.

Winter

It's time to...

- Finish cleaning up the flower and vegetable beds.

- Check your gutters and downspouts to make sure leaves aren't clogging them.

- Keep your poinsettia, Christmas cactus and other holiday plants in a bright but cool spot away from furnace vents, fireplaces and other heat sources.

- Dust thick layers of fallen tree leaves from evergreens with a broom.

- Cut short lengths of pretty evergreens such as Burford and Nellie Stevens hollies, nandina and mahonia to use in vases indoors.

- Finish planting your spring bulbs, either in the ground or in pots you can leave outdoors for the winter.

- Finish planting the potted shrubs and other plants you bought this fall.

- Pay attention to birds by offering food and water.

HOLLY'S A STAR IN DECEMBER

They grow without fanfare all year, usually upstaged by their plant cousins with bolder flowers and a flashier style. But come December, nothing competes with the hollies for sheer brilliance. You can leave them alone outdoors in the garden, fashion them into a wreath for the front door, or decorate your tables and mantles with them; in December, the Christmas holly is a plant for the moment.

Unlike other December plants, such as poinsettias and the white pine or Fraser fir Christmas tree, which are of temporary interest, the holly possesses virtues that make it worthy all year.

Need a barrier hedge? Burford Chinese holly is your plant. Looking for low-maintenance shrubbery by the front steps? Japanese holly or dwarf yaupon could be the answer. Want a loose, billowy screen? Try lusterleaf.

In short, holly isn't just a Christmas plant. And it doesn't always have shiny green leaves and bright red berries. Some hollies have black, dull red, orange, yellow and even blue berries.

Each species has many varieties, named and selected for such characteristics as variegation of leaf color, shape of the plant or the unusual shade or color of the berries.

They are often so different, you'd hardly guess they are hollies. That's because the holly genus, ilex, contains hundreds of species, but only a couple dozen are considered garden worthy.

Some drop their leaves in the fall. Some hug the ground; still others grow 20 feet or taller. Some have leaves as small as a fingernail; leaves of others are bigger than your hand.

Uniting this diverse group of plants is the similarity of flowers and fruit. People scarcely notice the small flowers in early spring, but the red-berried hollies grab lots of notice from late autumn through the winter.

The fruit is, botanically, named a drupe, but you'll rarely hear anyone outside a classroom call it that. Something about "red holly drupe" doesn't sound quite right. A drupe is a hard seed covered by a fleshy layer and a thin skin. A peach and a cherry are also drupes. End of botany lesson.

The red-berried hollies that interest us so much in December are not at all like the small hollies such as Japanese or dwarf yaupon used widely along walks and among azaleas.

Hollies that show up as a Christmas motif on cards and as decorations usually belong to three red-berried kinds that are easiest to remember geographically: American, Chinese and English.

• The **American holly**, Ilex opaca, makes a large evergreen tree. And it's one of such grace and style

Winter

that it will stand out among a forest of oaks and pines. Most varieties of American holly will slowly reach 20 feet, and you'll need male and female plants to get berries.

• The **Chinese holly**, Ilex cornuta, is a vigorous, large shrub or dense hedge. It is commonly used as a hedge plant. Once established, it is virtually impenetrable and will grow to about 10 feet tall or higher. The edges are prickly and the leaves glossy green. A variety of Chinese holly that is most popular is the Burford holly, whose leaves have fewer sharp spines.

• The **English holly**, Ilex aquifolium, is a slow-growing, medium-size tree that looks like the very model for Christmas card art. It possesses glossy leaves with wavy margins and lots of prickly edges. The fruit is the truest Christmas red of all. This plant grows slowly into a medium-size tree. Male and female plants are needed for pollination and fruit.

ENJOY A BLAST OF BRIGHT BERRIES

Of course you know hollies with their classy red berries. But do you know ruscus? How about cotoneaster, callicarpa, sarcococca and cocculus? And don't forget the rugosa rose and winterberry. Now is the time to check them out for planting. Your reward will be a dramatic fall show of berries, hips and other colorful fruits. Plus you get to impress your friends and neighbors by saying their weird names right.

Ruscus (RUS-kus) is commonly called butcher's broom, the legacy of olden days, when its stiff stems and prickly leaves were used as a sweep. Ruscus is a rare bird of an evergreen plant that actually thrives in deep, deep shade. Darkest olive green plants grow into mounds about 1 1/2 to 3 feet tall and bear bright red, oblong berries in the fall. It's very useful in Christmas decorations. Caution: Both male and female plants are needed to ensure pollination and produce the berries.

Callicarpa (kal-li-KAR-pa) is an easy-to-grow shrub whose arching branches rise like a forsythia 4 to 6 feet. It gets the common name "beautyberry" from the clusters of bright purple, violet or white berries that appear along the stems. Plant in a perennial flowerbed or a sunny to lightly shaded corner. Tip: The flowers that produce the berries appear on new growth. Prune the plant to about 6 inches tall in late winter or early spring.

Cocculus (KOK-yu-lus) is a vine commonly called Carolina moonseed. Often planted to attract and feed birds, cocculus produces clusters of red drupes in the fall. Plant this vine among shrubs or let it twine up a small tree. But don't worry; though vigorous, it's not a kudzu that will take over the landscape. Home turf: Cocculus grows wild throughout the Piedmont.

Rosa rugosa (ru-GO-sa) is popular at the beach because it tolerates salt spray, and in cold climates because it can stand subzero weather. But in the Piedmont, it proves useful for difficult spots such as banks. The flowers – rosy, pinkish lavender or white – appear in summer, and an interesting brick-red fruit called a hip follows in the fall. It grows 5 feet tall and loves sun. Hint: The hips are loaded with vitamin C and make a nice jelly or tea, but only if you didn't spray the plants with a pesticide.

Winterberry

Winter

Sarcococca (sar-co-COCK-a), best known as sweet box because it belongs to the boxwood family, is more often grown as ground cover than solitary shrub. Slowly growing 1 to 2 feet tall in part shade, it produces lustrous dark green leaves and a small, shiny, blue-black fruit called a drupe (like a cherry). Bonus: White flowers that appear below the foliage in spring are sweetly fragrant.

Winterberry. The scarlet berries of Ilex verticillata are nothing short of sensational, starting in early winter. Usually growing 5 to 15 feet tall, winterberry is a deciduous, arching shrub. To ensure pollination of flowers and development of berries on female plants, get a plant with male flowers as a mate.

Clockwise, from top center:

1. Ruscus	2. Callicarpa	3. Rosa rugosa
4. Cocculus	5. Sarcococca	6. Cotoneaster
7. Nandina		

Your reward will be a dramatic fall show of berries, hips and other colorful fruits.

Winter

Ask Nancy

Answers to some common problems

WHAT CAN I DO WITH MY OLD CHRISTMAS TREE?

Two words: bird feeder. After you take off the decorations, cut off the top 2 feet or so and put it back in the holder. Set the tree on a table on your deck or patio. Then make a bird treat by mixing 1 cup of smooth peanut butter, 1 cup of solid shortening, 4 cups of cornmeal (not a mix with additives) and 1 cup of white flour. Store the mixture in a closed container in the refrigerator. Smear it on the tree limbs like thick frosting through the winter. Put the tree in a quiet spot outdoors. Just lay it flat on the ground or stand it against a pole.

WHAT ARE SOME USEFUL LANDSCAPE PLANTS FOR DECEMBER?

That's easy: Southern magnolia, but it requires a really big lawn to look right; Nellie Stevens and Foster's No. 2 hollies, which bear oodles of red berries; nandina, whose graceful fernlike leaves and branches work beautifully in all flower arrangements; boxwood, which adds elegance to any arrangement or decoration; Japanese aucuba, with its deep-green foliage that looks good in a big vase on the mantel or in the fireplace; and eastern red cedar, which makes beautiful, fragrant old-fashioned wreaths.

HOW DO I CARE FOR MY DWARF ALBERTA SPRUCE?

If you're using a dwarf Alberta spruce, a little cone-shaped evergreen, as a tabletop Christmas tree indoors, take good care of this valuable plant. Give it as much sunlight as possible; make sure the roots don't dry out, but don't keep the pot in standing water. You can plant it outdoors in mild weather this winter. Have patience; the dwarf Alberta spruce grows very slowly.

Red cedar makes attractive wreaths.

Author and Editor

❧

Credits

Nancy

Nancy Brachey, garden editor of *The Charlotte Observer,* has written about gardens and gardeners of the Piedmont Carolinas since 1976. She has worked for *The Charlotte Observer,* since 1969 and lives in Charlotte, N.C. She is a journalism graduate of the University of Florida and studied horticulture at North Carolina State University.

Sandy

Sandy Hill is an editor at *The Charlotte Observer* and has worked with *Observer* garden editor Nancy Brachey for 14 years. During that time, she's gone from someone who kills cactus to knowing how to propagate pothos. She is a graduate of Pfeiffer College in Misenheimer, N.C.

Credits

All-America Selections: 88

Layne Bailey: 61

Dr. Donald Booth: 50

Nancy Brachey: 11, 27, 35, 69, 97, 98, 159, 160, 173, 174, 178

George Breisacher: 31, 119

Sherry Chisenhall: 146

David Cupp: 63

Hank Daniel: 20

Jim Denk: 34

Phil Drake: 4

David T. Foster III: 91, 104, 170

Ginger Sigmon Fox: 161

Tommy Franklin: 107

T. Ortega Gaines: 64, 103

Susan Gilbert: 123, 151

Goldsmith Seeds, Inc.: 65

Clyde Gorsuch: 78

Meredith Hebden: 57, 120, 130

Sandy Hill: 153

Davie Hinshaw: 77, 128, 166, 167, 168

Kent D. Johnson: 155, 156

Keith Kenney: 84

Lou Kinard: 118

Francisco Kjolseth: 32

Susan Brubaker Knapp: 40, 132, 133

Ray Kriner: 76, 77

Robert Lahser: 12, 68, 87, 110

Diedra Laird: 59, 79, 171

Stephanie Grace Lim: 5, 36, 37, 128, 150

Kirk Lyttle: 44, 45, 111

Lisa Massey: 111

Larry Mellichamp: 9, 124, 125, 126, 176

Philip Morgan: 21

Laura Mueller: 41, 54, 59, 162, 163, 168, 169

Tom Murray: 92, 93

N.C. Cooperative Extension Service: 96

Dean Neitman: 71, 72, 90

Netherlands Flower Bulb Information Center: 59, 135, 136, 137, 138, 139

Gary O'Brien: 50, 148

Erik Perel: 86, 87

Al Phillips: 16, 17, 42, 43

Jacob Piercy: 49

Brenda Pinnell: 23, 25, 149

Charles Punch: 143

Christopher Record: 69, 70

Jamie Rector: 74

Nell Redmond: 38, 41

Patrick Schneider: 55

Gayle Shomer: 25, 113, 144, 145, 153

John D. Simmons: 59, 115, 129

Jeff Siner: Cover, 6, 114, 156, 157, 158

Mark Sluder: 3, 26, 50, 62, 181

Ken Sorensen: 76, 77

Walter Stanford: 2

Todd Sumlin: 69, 80, 102, 122, 171, 177

Harry Whitesides: 121

Jeff Wilhelm: 77, 153

Don Williamson: 105, 106